Jihadist Peace

Islamist civil wars pose a major challenge to peace and security around the world. Written by two leading scholars of conflict resolution, *Jihadist Peace: Ending Islamist Civil Wars* offers a groundbreaking analysis of why these conflicts are among the most difficult to end, and what can be done about it. The book makes a theoretical contribution by explaining their intractability, arguing that the transnational ideological framing of Islamist civil wars increases uncertainty about the capabilities and resolve of the warring parties. Drawing on conflict resolution theory, rigorous statistical analysis, and detailed case studies of Afghanistan, Mauritania, Mali, and Syria, the authors explore the conditions under which these wars can both come to an end and be resolved. They argue that the local dimension is key: *Jihadist Peace* emphasizes the need to disentangle armed actors from broader jihadist networks and charts a path toward resolving some of the world's most intractable civil wars.

DESIRÉE NILSSON is a professor in peace and conflict research at Uppsala University. With over 20 years of experience in studying civil war dynamics and resolution, particularly inclusive peace processes and multiparty dynamics, her work has been featured prominently in leading academic journals, including *International Organization* and *International Studies Quarterly*.

ISAK SVENSSON holds the Dag Hammarskjöld Chair at Uppsala University. His extensive publication record includes acclaimed books such as *Confronting the Caliphate* (Oxford University Press, 2022) and *The Peacemaking Mandate* (Cambridge University Press, 2025). He is internationally recognized for research on religion and conflict, international mediation, and civil resistance.

Jihadist Peace

Ending Islamist Civil Wars

DESIRÉE NILSSON
Uppsala University

ISAK SVENSSON
Uppsala University

Shaftesbury Road, Cambridge CB2 8EA, United Kingdom

One Liberty Plaza, 20th Floor, New York, NY 10006, USA

477 Williamstown Road, Port Melbourne, VIC 3207, Australia

314–321, 3rd Floor, Plot 3, Splendor Forum, Jasola District Centre, New Delhi – 110025, India

Cambridge University Press is part of Cambridge University Press & Assessment, a department of the University of Cambridge.

We share the University's mission to contribute to society through the pursuit of education, learning and research at the highest international levels of excellence.

www.cambridge.org
Information on this title: www.cambridge.org/9781009688079
DOI: 10.1017/9781009688093

When citing this work, please include a reference to the DOI 10.1017/9781009688093

First published 2026

Cover image: Cover photograph: destroyed building interior overlooking Damascus by Mohamad Daboul.

A catalogue record for this publication is available from the British Library

A Cataloging-in-Publication data record for this book is available from the Library of Congress

ISBN 978-1-009-68811-6 Hardback
ISBN 978-1-009-68807-9 Paperback

To our families

Contents

Figures

Tables

Acknowledgments

Not long after the Islamic State (IS) rolled into Raqqa and declared the city its capital in 2014, a few peace researchers in Uppsala gathered in the kitchen of the Department of Peace and Conflict Research. Were we now, we asked ourselves, facing armed conflicts in which the ordinary methods of conflict resolution, such as dialogue, negotiations, mediation, and peace agreements, were simply inapplicable? Was the focus of our scholarly attention – conflict resolution – still relevant for understanding this challenge of Islamist civil wars? This marked the beginning of a large-scale research project devoted to this key problem, funded by one of Sweden's major research funders, the Riksbankens Jubileumsfond, entitled *Resolving Jihadist Conflicts? Religion, Civil Wars and the Prospect for Peace*. The project was interdisciplinary at its core, bringing together international scholars from various perspectives during a six-year period to focus on this challenge. This book arose from those discussions.

Mimmi Söderberg Kovacs was part of the initial discussions and the core group, and we have worked jointly with her on this important research problem over the years; she has thus significantly shaped our thinking on this topic. Mimmi, a great colleague and friend, also provided extremely valuable feedback on the various iterations of this book throughout the years, for which we are very grateful. Insights from discussions with the other members of the project's core group, including Mark Juergensmeyer, Mona Kanwal Sheikh, and Ebrahim Moosa, and the members of the advisory board have also been tremendously valuable to us. While we followed different theoretical and methodological trajectories, we all shared a common interest in the quest for understanding the conditions for the resolution of Islamist civil wars.

Many people have offered their input and support in various ways. We are grateful to those who participated in discussions during international research workshops, seminars, and panels within the project – some co-organized by the Folke Bernadotte Academy (FBA) and the Danish Institute for International Studies – held in Uppsala, Krusenberg, Schwarzenberg (Switzerland), and Copenhagen, and more recently during an international workshop in 2025 in Krusenberg, outside Uppsala. This includes Harmonie Toros, Emy Matesan, Ron Hassner, Matthias Basedau, Andreas Hasenclever, Johannes Vüllers, Regine Schwab, Jason Klocek, Peter Henne, Jeroen Gunning, Morten Valbjørn, Jonah Schulhofer-Wohl, Raphaël Lefèvre, Jerome Drevon, Matthew Bamber, Emin Poljarevic, Göran Larsson, Julia Palmiano Federer, Magnus Lundgren, Kristen Kao, Saer El-Jaichi, Kristian Berg Harpviken, Mia Bloom, Monica Toft, William Zartmann, Cecilia Albin, Henrik Angerbrandt, Jan Hjärpe, Jannie Lilja, Marco Nilsson, Tomas Lindgren, Teije Donker, Mélida Jimenez, Lisa Hoffman, Matthew Zelina, Mara Revkin, Ken Menkhaus, Karin Göldner-Ebenthal, Sophie Haspeslagh, Dino Krause, Linnea Gelot, John Gledhill, Andrea Ruggeri, and Morten Boås. The discussions at these events, both in the meetings and at more informal get-togethers afterward, have been intense yet always constructive, providing a great combination of inspiration and challenge.

Earlier versions and iterations of this research have been presented at various conferences, including the annual meetings of the International Studies Association (2016, 2018), Conflict Research Society (2017), Peace Science Society (International) (2016, 2017), and the Network of European Peace Scientists (2016, 2017), as well as the Nordic conference on research on violent extremism (2017), research-policy workshops arranged by the FBA, and research seminars at the universities of Uppsala, Lund, and Gothenburg. We would like to thank the participants in these research workshops, seminars, conferences, and policy events for their valuable comments and feedback. Our thinking on this subject has also benefited from the collaboration around the special issue of *International Negotiations* on "Negotiating Islamist Civil Wars" (edited by Mimmi Söderberg Kovacs).

Moreover, our understanding has been enriched through discussions in meetings on related themes. As members of the FBA's International Working Groups, we have had the opportunity to present earlier versions of this project at multiple seminars and workshops, gaining valuable feedback from other attendees, including Govinda Clayton, Marie-Jöelle Zahar, and Arthur Boutellis, who all brought to bear both academic and policy insights on the subject. Additionally, we have benefited from discussions within the European Union's Horizon 2020 Framework Programme-funded PAVE (Preventing and Addressing Violent Extremism through Community Resilience in the Western Balkans and the MENA) project on preventing violent extremism, led by Véronique Dudouet, as well as from dialogues within the research project on how to create entry points and de-escalation in conflicts involving Islamist armed groups, led by the Berghof Institute in Germany. Moreover, we gained insights from discussions within the project on how to engage Islamic jurists in constructive engagement in Islamist-framed violent conflicts, led by the Cordoba Foundation in Geneva, especially through interactions with Lakhdar Ghettas, Emanuel Schaeublin, Ferdaous Bouhlel, Eric Mornier-Genoud, Toby Matthiesen, Mahjoob Zweiri, Jean-Nicolas Bitter, Megann Lenoble, Simon Mason, Abdulkader Maan, Marion Hischier, and Cora Alder. In the final stages of this book project, we also received excellent input from Mikael Hiberg Naghizadeh.

We are grateful for financial support from the Riksbankens Jubileumsfond for the original research grant (NHS 14-1701:1), as well as support from the Swedish Research Council (2020-01796 and 2021-03247). We also extend our thanks to the FBA for research support and collaboration in organizing a workshop and policy-research dialogue on the theme of conflict resolution in Islamist armed conflicts, and to the Templeton Religion Fund (TRT-2022-30419), which co-organized the international workshop held in 2025. We are also grateful to the Politics Programme at the University of Otago, and to funding from Uppsala University, which supported a Matariki Visiting Fellowship there and enabled more intensive work on the book.

We received brilliant support from several research assistants during this process, and we would like to express our sincere gratitude to Daniel Finnbogason, Dino Krause, Tom Renvall, Anton Stjernmira Ruus, Alanna Smart, Tim Gåsste, Tami Sandyarani, Jakob Faller, Luís Martínez Lorenzo, Sara Razavi, Puck van der Donselaar, and Selma Mustafic. This collaboration has been a true privilege for us.

We are very grateful for the constructive and helpful review comments from the two anonymous reviewers on this book, as well as our editor at Cambridge University Press, John Haslam. We also wish to express our gratitude to the anonymous reviewers and editors of our *International Studies Quarterly* article, which helped shape the argument and was where we first presented the global analysis on termination and recurrence (Desirée Nilsson and Isak Svensson, 2021. "The Intractability of Islamist Insurgencies: Islamist Rebels and the Recurrence of Civil War." *International Studies Quarterly* 65 (3): 620–632). We also wish to thank Oxford University Press for making it possible for us to include parts of the material from that article in this book.

We feel fortunate to have such supportive colleagues at the department whose invaluable feedback and support – whether through commenting on papers, giving advice, or providing a second opinion when meeting up by the coffee machine – have greatly enriched our work. This includes but is not limited to Lisa Hultman, Hanne Fjelde, Kristine Höglund, Karen Brounéus, Nanar Hawach, and Peter Wallensteen, as well as the team at the Uppsala Conflict Data Program. This book would not have been the same without the generous support of all our friends and colleagues. We are thankful to be part of such an environment, surrounded by so many supportive and inspiring individuals.

Finally, we also thank our families: Your patience and loving support throughout the years made this book possible. We dedicate the results of our efforts to you.

Abbreviations

AQIM	Al-Qaeda in the Lands of the Islamic Maghreb
ASG	Abu Sayyaf Group
BRN	Barisan Revolusi Nasional
CMA	Coordination des Mouvements de l'Azawad
ECOWAS	Economic Community of West African States
FARF	Forces armées pour la République fédérale/Armed Forces of the Federal Republic
FIS	Front Islamique du Salut/Islamic Salvation Front
FLM	Front de Libération du Macina
FSA	Free Syrian Army
GAM	Gerakan Aceh Merdeka/Free Aceh Movement
GDP	gross domestic product
GIA	Groupe Islamique Armé/Armed Islamic Group
GSIM	Group for Support of Islam and Muslims (also known as JNIM)
GSPC	Groupe Salafiste pour la Prédication et le Combat/ Salafist Group for Preaching and Combat
HCUA	High Council for the Unity of Azawad
HTS	Hayat Tahrir al-Sham/Organization for the Liberation of the Levant
ICG	International Crisis Group
IG	Islamic Group/Al-Gama'a al-Islamiyya
IJ	Islamic Jihad
IR	International Relations
IRP	Islamic Renaissance Party of Tajikistan
IS	Islamic State
ISI	Islamic State in Iraq
IS-K	Islamic State – the Khorasan province

JNIM	Jamaat Nusrat al-Islam wal-Muslimin/Group for the Support of Islam and Muslims
MENA	Middle East and North Africa
MILF	Moro Islamic Liberation Front
MINUSMA	United Nations Multidimensional Integrated Stabilization Mission in Mali
MNLA	Mouvement National de Libération de l'Azawad/ National Movement for the Liberation of Azawad
MNLF	Moro National Liberation Front
MUJAO	Mouvement pour le Tawhîd et du Jihad en Afrique de l'Ouest/Group Committed to Propagating the Prophet's Teachings and Jihad, Movement for Oneness and Jihad in West Africa
NoWA	Non-Warring Actors in Peacemaking (Uppsala University)
PRIO	Peace Research Institute Oslo
RELAC	Religion and Armed Conflict (Uppsala University)
SCIRI	Islamic Supreme Council of Iraq
UCDP	Uppsala Conflict Data Program (Uppsala University)
UK	United Kingdom
UN	United Nations
US	United States
USD	US dollar
USSR	Union of Soviet Socialist Republics (Soviet Union)
V-Dem	Varieties of Democracy (University of Gothenburg)

1 Introduction

Why Study the Ending of Islamist Civil Wars?

Islamist civil wars present a key challenge to peace and security in the world. Islamist armed conflicts – where at least one of the actors makes self-proclaimed Islamist demands – have emerged as one of the most common forms of civil war in the world.[1] Islamist armed conflicts have become more frequent over time, whereas other conflicts around the world have become less common. It is essential that we understand whether and how these conflicts can be brought to a successful end and how these conflicts can be resolved. Therefore, in this book, we seek to understand if and why Islamist civil wars are more difficult to end than other conflicts and to what extent Islamist civil wars can be resolved. We present an explanation for why Islamist armed conflicts are so intractable – and what can be done about them.[2]

THE PROBLEM

When comparing Islamist civil wars to other types of intrastate armed conflicts over time, the difference in frequency is striking (see Figure 1.1).[3] At the start of our time period in 1975, there was not a single active Islamist armed conflict. Since then, there has been a steady increase in the number of conflicts fought over Islamist claims,

1 This is based on data on armed conflicts from the Uppsala Conflict Data Program (UCDP), version 25.1 (Davies et al. 2025) and updated data on Islamist claims from the Religion and Armed Conflict (RELAC) dataset (Svensson and Nilsson 2018).

2 In this book we use the terms Islamist civil war and Islamist armed conflict interchangeably.

3 Figure 1.1 refers to armed conflicts where either the government or the rebel group makes an Islamist claim at the outset of the struggle. Since there are only a handful of Islamist conflicts where it is the government that is making the claim, and as we expect the dynamic to be different in those cases, we focus on Islamist claims on the rebel side for the remainder of this book.

FIGURE I.1 Islamist and non-Islamist conflicts, 1975–2024. Number of conflict dyads per year.

and in 2024 there were 30 conflicts of this nature. This stands in stark contrast to the trajectory of armed conflicts that are *not* fought over an Islamist claim. In 1975, more than 30 non-Islamist armed conflicts were active. While this category increased until the early 1990s, peaking at 55 conflicts, the trend has since reversed, stabilizing at around 30 armed conflicts in recent years. Hence, in terms of frequency, the pattern is clear: The share and number of Islamist armed conflicts have increased over time. Other conflicts have generally decreased since the end of the Cold War period, yet we observe a slight increase in non-Islamist conflicts in recent years. In 2015, for the first time, Islamist armed conflicts represented the majority of armed conflicts, and as of 2024, roughly half (47%) were fought over Islamist claims. Thus, armed conflicts where one actor makes explicit Islamist claims have become more common. Some of the most intense and complex civil wars that have raged over the last decade, and that have taken an enormous toll on the civilian population, have seen one or more armed actors fighting over Islamist aspirations. Cases in point include Syria, Iraq, Yemen, Nigeria, Somalia, Israel–Palestine, and Mali.

Yet some Islamist civil wars have indeed been brought to an end. In 2014, the Moro Islamic Liberation Front (MILF) reached a peace settlement with the government of the Philippines, ending a decades-old armed conflict through negotiations and power-sharing arrangements. In 1997, a coalition led by Islamist groups agreed to a peace settlement in Tajikistan's civil war. We have also seen peace attempts and negotiations occurring in Islamist civil wars in Mali, Syria, southern Thailand, Indonesia, and Egypt. Thus, while most Islamist civil wars tend to eschew negotiations and attempts at resolution and are difficult to end, some conflicts display a different dynamic.

WAYS OUT OF INTRACTABILITY

This book explains why Islamist civil wars are generally so difficult to end and identifies the conditions under which parties engulfed in them can avoid the trap of intractability. Islamism comes in many different forms. While recognizing that there are important variations across Islamist groups, Kalyvas and Naghizadeh (2025, 394) point out that the term Islamism can be used to "describe groups drawing on Islamic ideas to justify their political actions." Simply put, Islamism can be seen as a political ideology that has a religious anchoring, where Islamic principles are applied not only in the private sphere but also across all facets of public life. As such, it transgresses national borders and appeals to a larger community beyond individuals confined to a single nation-state. Islamism is not necessarily transnational, but it has an inbuilt capability to appeal across borders and create networks and identities not confined to the border of a specific nation-state.

We develop an argument based on a bargaining perspective (e.g., Fearon 1995) when explaining the intractability of Islamist conflicts, which we refer to as the strategic embeddedness of Islamist civil wars. The thrust of our argument is that Islamist civil wars are embedded in a particular strategic environment – engulfed in a transnational network of groups and actors supporting the rebels and, in parallel, entangled in a web of intergovernmental commitments and support structures backing the government side. Such international support tends to create a high degree of uncertainty in terms of the extent and nature of support, making it harder to assess one another's resolve and capabilities, which in turn makes these conflicts more difficult to end. This support structure in the forms of a potential influx of foreign fighters, monetary support from a web of sponsors on the rebel side, as well as a plethora of institutional intergovernmental support structures on the government side makes many Islamist conflicts different from other types of conflicts around the world, which tend either to be more localized on both the side of the government and the side of the rebels or to have support structures that are less dispersed and diverse. This is not to say that international involvement in civil wars is not a relatively common feature also in conflicts not fought over Islamist claims. However, the internationalization of Islamist conflicts follows specific routes, and understanding these dynamics is essential to ending Islamist armed conflicts. The particular strategic environment in which Islamist civil wars are embedded can explain why it is so difficult to end Islamist civil wars, why conflict resolution efforts tend to be so challenging in Islamist civil wars, and what needs to be done to pave the way for conflict resolution.

Our argument can thus explain why Islamist conflicts have a worse track record than other conflicts when it comes to resolution. It can also help us better understand why a few Islamist conflicts still venture along the conflict resolution path. Islamist civil wars that are insulated from the globalized fight for and against radical Islamism should have a better chance for resolution and termination. Islamist civil wars can also change over time. Once governments distance themselves from the international military alliance against transnational Islamist actors, they are more likely to be able to seek solutions. Likewise, once rebel groups distance themselves from the international web of transnational Islamist groups and individuals, they are more likely to be able to pursue solutions. Turning to local grievances instead of transnational aims, actors should be more open to finding negotiated solutions. This insight provides an important policy implication: Measures to disconnect Islamist civil wars from their (potential) connections to the global battle between transnational Islamist networks and intergovernmental alliances fighting them will pave the way for the mechanisms of conflict resolution.

THE EVIDENCE

In this book, we find support for our argument based on a global analysis of all intrastate armed conflicts, where we focus on the trajectories of termination, recurrence, and conflict resolution. We demonstrate that Islamist civil wars are less likely than others to be terminated and more likely to recur once ended. Conflicts framed in Islamist terms are thus systematically more intractable compared with other types of conflicts. Exploring the conditions leading to termination in all intrastate armed conflicts between 1975 and 2013, we show that Islamist conflicts stand out from other conflicts, even after considering different factors that potentially influence their chance of termination. Islamist conflicts are also at a higher risk of relapsing into armed conflict, involving either the same group or new insurgency manifestations. We find that Islamist armed conflicts are 73% more likely to recur compared with intrastate armed conflicts fought over non-Islamist claims. We show that this finding holds when we account for the mainstream explanatory factors identified in previous research.

Our theory emphasizes the transnational dimension of Islamist civil wars. One manifestation of this is the increased uncertainty relating to the potential influx of foreign fighters; another is the uncertainty arising from the plethora of institutional intergovernmental support structures on the government side. In our global analysis of termination and recurrence, we find that Islamist conflicts differ from other conflicts on this dimension. Islamist rebels and governments fighting them have attracted more foreign support than other types of conflicts. The statistical analysis lends further support for the expectation that transnational assistance in the form of government support, as well as foreign fighters, is a pathway through which Islamist conflicts become particularly intractable.

In addition to the global analysis on intractability, we provide two case illustrations – Afghanistan and Mauritania – to show how our argument plays out in depth. Afghanistan represents one of the most intractable Islamist armed conflicts, and the ambivalence about resolve and capabilities created by the extensive American-led military intervention (from the year 2001) and the interconnections between the Taliban movement and al-Qaeda help to explain why this is so. The termination of the conflict – through military victory – was preceded by disengagement regarding the external dimensions: the US decision to withdraw in exchange for the Taliban's decision to distance itself from the al-Qaeda network and make a commitment not to allow a foreign group to launch attacks from Afghanistan. A very different case of an Islamist civil war is Mauritania, an outlier in the sense that it experienced a short-lived Islamist armed conflict. The fact that the conflict was insulated from the broader interregional battle between interconnected transnational Islamist groups on one side and aligned governments on the other is an essential explanation behind the country's ability to escape the intractability commonly associated with Islamist armed conflicts.

In addition, we explore conflict resolution efforts – negotiations and peace accords – and find a similar pattern: Negotiations are less likely to occur in Islamist civil wars. Exploring new global data on the occurrence of negotiations between 1989 and 2018, we show that Islamist civil wars are notable for their underutilization of this form of conflict resolution. We find that, generally, conflict resolution efforts in the form of peace negotiations are rare in Islamist civil wars, whereas we do not find any robust evidence that peace accords are less likely. However, in line with our argument, we find that the transnational dimension is central here: Both these conflict resolution efforts are less likely in those Islamist conflicts where the claims are transnational, extending beyond state borders. Nonetheless, as we show in this book, conflict resolution efforts in the form of negotiations and peace agreements between Islamist radicals and more secular-leaning governments do exist. Of key importance for such conflict resolution efforts to occur is that the conflict actors are able to avoid or overcome the obstacles relating to external support and transnationalization of the armed struggle.

In addition to the global analysis of conflict resolution patterns, we provide two case illustrations to analyze the implications of our argument for conflict resolution in Islamist civil wars. We focus on *variations between groups* by comparing the Mali-based groups Ansar Dine, Katiba Macina, and Al-Qaeda in the Lands of the Islamic Maghreb (AQIM), as well as *changes over time* by studying the Syrian-based Hayat Tahrir al-Sham (HTS). We show how variations in openness to engagement in conflict resolution processes between groups in the Malian insurgency were largely dependent on the degree to which they were of a local nature and orientation. Groups with stronger transnational ties were less willing to engage in dialogue and were not perceived by the Malian government as potential partners for meaningful negotiations. We also show that one of the critical obstacles to deeper engagement in conflict resolution was found on the government side: their main external supporter, France, which opposed any negotiation attempts. The Malian case thus demonstrates how our explanation for intractability – the external support structures for rebels and governments engaged in Islamist armed conflicts – works in more detail. Adding to this analysis, we bring in the case of HTS in Syria. While we categorize conflicts in our quantitative analysis based on rebel groups' original demands, we can more closely follow developments over time through the Syrian case. HTS has transformed from a transnational outlook to a more local orientation in terms of their demands. While HTS in late 2024 came to overthrow the Bashar al-Assad regime, we center our analysis on earlier periods and how HTS's openness to dialogue changed over time. We demonstrate how these opportunities for conflict resolution are preceded and driven by detachment from the transnational dimension.

Islamist armed conflicts vary along a spectrum from localized to globalized, and many transnationalize beyond local grievances. Reversing that trend, decoupling Islamist armed conflicts from global support patterns, is, as we demonstrate in this book, essential to paving the way for conflict resolution efforts in Islamist armed conflicts. Insulating Islamist civil wars from the transnational agenda is an important condition for creating the necessary space for conflict resolution efforts to succeed. We find that Islamist civil wars that have seen conflict resolution efforts are those that were either locally anchored or disconnected from the global Islamist agenda and instead focused on addressing local grievances. As long as Islamist conflicts are locked into the strategic environment of foreign fighters, government support, and transnationalized global aspirations, these civil wars are unlikely to end. If an Islamist conflict does reach an end, it is likely to be temporary, with the prospects of a more sustainable resolution remaining dim.

SITUATING THE BOOK

We have written this book because Islamist civil wars present a unique challenge in terms of conflict resolution. For a long time, Islamist conflicts were not singled out in the field of civil war conflict resolution (e.g., Kriesberg 1998; Wallensteen 2015; Zartman 1995), including different subfields such as the study of mediation (Bercovitch, Anagnoson, and Wille 1991; Clayton and Dorussen 2022; Greig and Diehl 2012; Wallensteen and Svensson 2014), negotiated settlement (Stedman 2002; Walter 2002), conflict termination (Licklider 1995; Quinn, Mason, and Gurses 2007; Toft 2010), civil society and women inclusion (Krause, Krause, and Bränfors 2018; Nilsson 2012), power sharing (Hartzell and Hoddie 2007; Mattes and Savun 2009; Mukherjee 2006), the transformation of rebel groups (Dudouet 2014; Söderberg Kovacs 2008), and peacekeeping (Duursma et al. 2023; Fortna 2004; Hultman, Kathman, and Shannon 2016; Kroeker and Ruggeri 2022). Therefore, although these studies included Islamist conflicts in their analyses, the literature generally did not specifically focus on Islamist civil wars or compare them with other types of conflicts.

Previous research has explored Islamist conflicts more broadly (Hamid 2016; Kalyvas 2018; Kepel 2006; Maher 2016; Roy 2017), including the globalization of radical Islamist movements (Gerges 2009; Hegghammer 2010, 2020; Moghadam 2008; Sheikh 2017), mobilization processes (Fox et al. 2024; Hafez 2003; Naghizadeh 2025), intra-insurgency relations (Bunzel 2021; Byman 2014; Hamming 2023), intra-party dynamics (Haenni and Drevon 2025), fighting between groups (Gade, Hafez, and Gabbay 2019), the tactical choices and changes of Islamist groups (Bloom 2005; Drevon 2022b; Matesan 2020b; Schwab 2023), the networks of jihadist groups (Stollenwerk, Dörfler, and Schibberges 2015), various aspects of governance under jihadist groups (Bamber-Zryd 2022; Drevon and Haenni 2021; Furlan 2025; Kao and Revkin 2023; Lefèvre 2021; Lia 2015), and how terrorist groups generally, or armed Islamist groups in particular, end, transform, or deradicalize (Ashour 2009; Crenshaw 1991; Cronin 2012; Hwang 2018).[4] Thus, research on Islamist conflicts has been frequent in the academic fields of political science, sociology, religious studies, strategic studies, and connected subfields, such as terrorism studies. However, the focus has predominantly been on why these conflicts occur and spread, and how counterinsurgency efforts and other types of interventions can be made effective, without seeking to understand the conditions for conflict resolution.

The result is a gap between different fields, where insights from one field are not integrated into others. However, this has started to change, and a thriving research agenda is now more broadly exploring the conditions for conflict resolution in religiously framed conflicts (Deitch 2022; Hassner 2009; Keels and Wiegand 2020; Pearce 2005; Svensson 2007, 2012, 2021; Toft 2006), and more recently, in Islamist civil wars, studying this more generally (Lundgren and Svensson 2020; Nilsson and Svensson 2021; Söderberg Kovacs 2020b; Toft 2021) or in relation to specific cases (Cantey 2018; Engvall and Svensson 2020; Göldner-Ebenthal and Dudouet 2019; Jones 2015; Matesan

[4] There is also an extensive literature on religious conflicts, which includes Islamist armed conflicts (Basedau, Fox, and Zellman 2023; Basedau, Pfeiffer, and Vüllers 2016; Isaacs 2016; Klocek and Hassner 2019; Toft 2021).

2020a, 2020b; Sheikh 2020; Söderberg Kovacs 2020a; Thurston 2018; Toros and Harley 2018; Zenn and Fox 2020), or focusing on their intractability more specifically (Matesan 2020a; Toft and Zhukov 2015).[5] In this book, we contribute to the growing scholarly discourse on ending Islamist civil wars by connecting it with what we already know from a bargaining perspective about the conditions for ending wars more generally.[6] In particular, while much of the debate in this emerging field has focused on domestic internal explanations for intractability (e.g., Matesan 2020a) or has concentrated on either the government (e.g., Klocek 2017) or the rebel side (e.g., Toft and Zhukov 2015), we contribute to this ongoing debate on the intractability of Islamist civil wars by examining the external dimension and how it relates to the *strategic relationship* between rebels and governments.

WHAT IS AN ISLAMIST CIVIL WAR?

We define *intrastate armed conflict* according to the criteria established by the Uppsala Conflict Data Program (UCDP). According to the UCDP, an intrastate armed conflict is a conflict that takes place between the government and one or more rebel groups over a stated incompatibility, either over government power or a specific territory (or both), and which results in at least 25 battle-related deaths in a year (Davies et al. 2024). The conflict issue, based on the stated aspirations of the parties that have taken up arms, is thus at the very core of the definition of armed conflict. We use the term intrastate armed conflict interchangeably with *civil war*.

Islamism, as we define it here, is an ideological framework that views Islam as a complete system encompassing the political sphere, advocating for the implementation of its religious principles across

5 For an overview of the emerging literature on negotiations in Islamist civil wars, see Krause (2025).

6 On the problem that much of the previous research on religion and conflict has developed its own theoretical arguments that are not necessarily anchored in mainstream explanations for war, see Bormann, Cederman, and Vogt (2017).

all facets of public life. Islamism thus builds on the fundamental idea that the teaching of Islam applies not only to the private sphere but to the public as well, and therefore it is an inherent political ideology, grounded in theology. The ultimate authority in making political decisions, and the basis for political institutions, is thus anchored in the teaching of the Prophet Mohammed and the tradition following him.[7] The core idea of applying Islamic principles to governance and society is a defining characteristic shared by all Islamist movements. In the next chapter, we will develop the difference between *jihadist* and *Islamist*, as well as other intra-Islamist variations; for now, we use the term Islamist as a generic term.[8]

Regarding Islamist armed conflicts, we focus on the conflict issue and refer to armed conflicts in which a rebel group has made self-proclaimed Islamist goals, such as demands for Sharia law in society. Thus, we define *Islamist civil wars* as armed conflicts involving a government and a rebel group, where the rebel group, at the start of the struggle, frames the conflict in Islamist terms.[9] It is imperative to clarify that religious issues here are understood in terms of the parties'

[7] It should be noted that Islamist groups disagree widely on how this should be implemented.

[8] The title of our book, *Jihadist Peace: Ending Islamist Civil Wars*, is intended to resonate not only with scholars of Islamist civil wars but also with those who focus on, and employ, the concept of jihadist violence. Throughout the book, we primarily use the term *Islamist armed conflicts* to describe the broader phenomenon under examination. When we do use the term *jihadist*, we apply it more narrowly – referring specifically to conflicts driven by militant Salafi ideology within the Sunni Islamic tradition (see Chapter 2 for further elaboration), or to describe the act of taking up jihad as an armed struggle.

[9] Since some civil wars involve multiple rebel groups – some of which may have Islamist aspirations while others do not – we apply a dyadic perspective that focuses on the armed conflict between the government and each rebel group. For example, in the Israel–Palestine conflict, some groups such as Fatah have not made any Islamist claims, while others such as Hamas frame their struggle in Islamist terms. Similarly, in the Philippine conflict in Mindanao, MNLF (Moro National Liberation Front) has not expressed Islamist aspirations, but MILF (Moro Islamic Liberation Front) and ASG (the Abu Sayyaf Group) have made such claims. To capture such variations, a dyadic perspective is essential. It should also be noted that our large-N analyses rely on data that focus on the claims made at the beginning of the struggle, but in our case studies, we also explore how the transnational dimension of those claims evolves over time.

own explicit references. We focus on what the conflict parties claim the issue is about, without making assumptions about its causes. This definition enables us to distinguish conflicts in which the warring parties explicitly frame their struggle in Islamist terms from other conflicts.[10] These demands can be more or less salient in nature, and there is also likely variation in the extent to which the warring parties make other claims that concern issues that may be political, economic, or social in nature. To classify a conflict as "Islamist" is to say something about how the parties have chosen to frame their demands and aspirations, but it does not rule out the possibility that there are other factors beyond religious ones that are important. Moreover, it is essential to note that we focus on ideology and the claims made (Islamist) rather than identity (Muslims). In some of the previous debates on Muslim exceptionalism (e.g., Karakaya 2015), the focus has been on the identities in conflicts, which may overlap with the ideology of those taking up arms, but not necessarily so. This is an important distinction. Our primary focus here is on whether civil wars are fought over Islamist claims or not, and the strategic dilemmas that arise once a conflict is framed in Islamist terms. Thus, contrary to the arguments made about "Muslim exceptionalism" and conflict, we do not expect any effect from either of the warring actors having a Muslim identity.

There is a broader scholarly debate on understanding and defining religious dimensions in conflicts (e.g., Brubaker 2015; Klocek and Hassner 2019; Sheikh 2012; Svensson 2016, 2019). By using explicit statements regarding what the warring actors aspire to achieve in the conflict as the basis for measuring whether a conflict is Islamist, we focus on how the parties frame their own conflict. No assumption is made here about whether the groups making Islamist claims are authentic representatives of the Muslim faith or sincere in their

[10] This approach is in line with the UCDP's coding criteria for assessing the incompatibility at stake, focusing on the warring actors' stated positions: https://bit.ly/3ZY7d8o (accessed June 24, 2024).

expressed beliefs. Instead, we show how framing a conflict in Islamist terms can affect the dynamics and prospects for its resolution.

It is important to emphasize that although it is useful to contrast Islamist armed conflicts with other types of armed conflicts, there are also crucial variations within this particular category. There are many ways in which Islamist armed conflicts can be subcategorized. Our scope here is broad, and in the wider category of Islamist civil wars, we thus include a diverse set of conflicts involving actors such as the Islamic State (IS) and its affiliates, MILF in the Philippines, Ansarallah (known as Houthis) in Yemen, and the Patani insurgents in Thailand. Hence, Islamist civil wars encompass armed conflicts involving both Shia and Sunni groups, as well as warring actors fighting for self-determination, change in government, or transnational aspirations. As we will show in this book, from a conflict resolution perspective, the critical distinction lies along the global–local continuum: Resolving Islamist armed conflicts is more challenging compared with other conflicts but still feasible as long as the conflicts are local and not globally framed.

A few words about the scope of our study are needed. First, our focus here is on a particular type of organized violence – state-based armed conflicts between a government and one or more rebel groups – and we are not exploring Islamist-framed violence between civilians or against other rebel groups. While one-sided violence is a significant security issue globally, the majority of such violence occurs within the context of civil wars (Fjelde, Hultman, and Sollenberg 2016). Second, we are not studying violent Islamism in general. For example, many attacks in Western countries have been carried out by "lone wolves" who are either not associated with or only weakly associated with organized groups, which may be driven by other dynamics (on lone wolves, see, for example, Phillips 2017). However, although we do not focus on isolated terrorist attacks, many of our findings are relevant to the broader literature on terrorism (on the distinction and relationship between terrorism and civil war, see, for example, Findley and Young 2012; Fortna 2015; Polo and Gleditsch

2016; Stanton 2013). Third, we analyze Islamist *conflict dyads*, not Islamist *groups*. Conflicts consist of at least two actors, but previous research tends to overwhelmingly focus on the non-state actors in Islamist civil wars. While some studies recognize government incentives (e.g., Klocek 2017; Matesan 2020a; Söderberg Kovacs 2020a), the bulk of the literature focuses on the insurgents. From our perspective, the intractability and resolution of Islamist armed conflicts cannot be fully comprehended without taking into account both sides.

A key feature of our approach is that we do not exclusively focus on Islamist civil wars but apply a comparative perspective. If we want to understand the extent to which Islamist civil wars are different from other conflicts, we cannot study Islamist civil wars in isolation. Much of the scholarly work examining the prospects for conflict resolution in Islamist civil wars focuses solely on Islamist civil wars (e.g., Drevon 2022b, 2024; Haenni and Drevon 2025; Matesan 2020a; Sheikh 2020). While these studies have provided important insights into the dynamics within Islamist civil wars, we cannot draw any inferences about whether and how Islamist civil wars are different – from a conflict resolution perspective – unless we systematically compare them with other types of conflicts. Therefore, we apply a broad comparative approach by studying the general trends and trajectories of armed conflicts, including but not limited to Islamist conflicts. In this book, we rely on the Religion and Armed Conflict (RELAC) dataset, which contains information on religious dimensions of all armed conflicts worldwide from 1975 onward (Svensson and Nilsson 2018). We are thereby able to provide insights into the trajectories of Islamist civil wars over time in ways that have not been previously possible. We also use new data from the Non-Warring Actors in Peacemaking (NoWA) dataset to study negotiations (Nilsson et al. 2024).

CHALLENGES TO OUR ARGUMENT

This book can be situated within several ongoing scholarly debates. While we engage with alternative explanations throughout the book, we focus on specific alternative explanations in different chapters, depending on the particular research design used. On a more general level, there is a more extensive debate on religion and conflict, with two contrasting perspectives on the role of religion in civil war. On the one hand, there is the *instrumentalist* perspective, which has been prevalent in the field of International Relations (IR) in general and in research on peace and conflict in particular. According to this perspective, religious conflicts are not different from other disputes, and framing a conflict in religious terms plays a minor and insignificant role compared with the underlying material drivers of conflict dynamics. Thus, there is no need to study religious conflicts, or Islamist conflicts, as standalone categories since this perspective rejects "the idea that religious conflict or violence is sui generis" (Brubaker 2015, 2), as "it perceives Islamists like any other actor situated in a similar context" (Sheikh, Valbjørn, and Krause 2023, 215) and "tend[s] to consider ideational developments epiphenomena broadly susceptible to material changes" (Drevon 2022b, 195).[11] On the other hand, as discussed by Drevon (2022b, 195), there is the *essentialist* perspective that focuses on the ideologies of armed groups and, as described by Sheikh, Valbjørn, and Krause (2023, 215), builds on the assumption that "Islamists are like no other actors, and they must accordingly be approached on their own distinct Islamic terms." In this book, we take issue with both approaches. In contrast to the instrumentalist perspective, we suggest that even if the root causes of conflicts may be similar, once conflicts have been framed in Islamist terms, they stand out from others from a conflict resolution perspective: They are more difficult to end and tend to become more intractable. In contrast to the essentialist perspective, we propose that this is not driven by religious ideologies or identities per se but rather by the specific strategic environment created when groups raise the banner of Islam and governments confront them.

[11] There is no consensus on the terms used to describe these ideal types. Drevon uses the term "rationalist," and Brubaker uses "generalizing stance" to describe this particular ideal type.

There are a few potential challenges to the argument we are presenting here. First, it could be questioned whether Islamist civil wars are so different after all, a critique derived from the instrumentalist perspective. The premise of our argument is that Islamism is a transnational ideology that transcends the borders of nation-states, and this creates conditions for a particular strategic environment that makes Islamist civil wars challenging to end. However, Islamism is not the only global fault line. Left-wing ideologies, similarly, possess a transnational character and may appeal to actors beyond the confines of specific nation-states to garner support for conflict actors. Indeed, it has been argued that Islamist civil wars are not exceptional but bear striking similarities to other revolutionary movements, such as the Marxist insurgencies during the Cold War (Kalyvas 2018). We demonstrate that Islamist civil wars indeed resemble and share similarities with leftist movements – another transnational ideological movement usually associated with larger external support structures – yet we also show that Islamist civil wars follow a particular trajectory as to how they are internationalized. That is, while both leftist conflicts and Islamist civil wars tend to be more intractable compared with other types of conflicts, and this can be partly tied to the prevalence of external supporters engaging in these conflicts, the kind of transnationalization of Islamist conflicts is strikingly different from that of earlier leftist revolutionary conflicts. Historically, leftist conflicts tended to include state sponsors on both the rebel and the government sides, for instance, as Marxist rebels were drawn into the global systemic struggle between the US and the USSR. However, in Islamist armed conflicts, rebel-affiliated state sponsors who intervene with troops on the ground are uncommon, and the support structure, driven by individuals and non-state actors rather than major countries, is much more diverse and dispersed, making the strategic setting even more unpredictable and uncertain. While state support in the form of troops on the ground is rare on the rebel side, states do provide other forms of support to rebels in Islamist armed conflicts, such as military aid, arms transfers, or economic support. It is well recognized that countries such as Iran, Saudi Arabia, Türkiye, the United Arab Emirates, and Qatar, as part of regional power struggles, have provided various forms of support in different configurations. For example, Türkiye and Qatar backed the Muslim Brotherhood, whereas Saudi Arabia and the United Arab Emirates supported the other side (Lynch and Schwedler 2020; Matthiesen 2022). Having said this, intervention with troops on the ground on the rebel side is overall a rare phenomenon. It is only in recent years that we have seen a slight increase in state interventions in the form of troops on the ground, for example, from Türkiye to the Syrian insurgents.[12] Yet the support on the rebel side commonly takes a more decentralized and dispersed form than troop support on the ground. Thus, we show that while there are indeed similarities between leftist conflicts and Islamist civil wars in terms of the transnationalization of ideologies and support that creates obstacles to ending them, this problem is particularly acute for Islamist civil wars.

Secondly, partly related to the essentialist perspective, it could also be questioned whether we take the *religious* nature of Islamist conflicts into account when explaining their intractability. In both the quantitative analysis and the case studies, we demonstrate that ideology in civil wars can serve an instrumental role in shaping external support structures, thereby increasing the uncertainty of conflicts.[13] Therefore, our argument takes the religious nature of these conflicts seriously by demonstrating how the religious ideology of these conflicts shapes the strategic context of Islamist civil wars, thereby making the bargaining process of this particular type of armed conflict particularly challenging. The key religious aspect explaining the intractability of Islamist conflicts lies in their international dimension. While previous research has focused on other religious aspects of religiously framed conflicts, including the absolutistic worldviews

[12] See the UCDP/PRIO Armed Conflict Dataset version 24.1 (Davies et al. 2024).

[13] On the instrumental use of ideology, see Sanín and Wood (2014) and Walter (2017).

of cosmic proportions and scales (Aslan 2013; Juergensmeyer 2018, 2022), religious emotions and imaginaries (Sheikh 2016), religious dogma and theology (El-Jaichi and Sheikh 2020), issue indivisibility (Hassner 2009; Svensson 2007), the time dimension (Hassner 2011; Toft 2006), and religious leadership (Bock 2001; Little 1996), we instead provide a strategic information failure perspective on religion and conflict. In line with the essentialist perspective, another counterargument to the one we propose concerns the extremist nature of the religious movements. According to this line of thought, Islamist armed conflicts are more intractable and more difficult to resolve since the actors are so radicalized that they resist any attempt at conflict resolution. As we will later return to and discuss, we do not find any support for this counterargument. The intractability of Islamist conflicts is not primarily driven by the rebel side's religious intransigence and ideological absolutism.

WHY DO WE NEED THIS BOOK?

There are three overall rationales for this book. Firstly, our book can serve to bridge insights from different fields of study, in particular by creating synergy between the separate research fields on strategic studies of Islamist armed conflicts, on the one hand, and conflict resolution on the other, synergies that are also important for the field of religion and conflict – and these fields have to a large extent been siloed in previous research.

Secondly, our book provides a way to shed new light on whether Islamist armed conflicts differ from other conflicts. As argued earlier, if we want to understand what, if anything, distinguishes Islamist armed conflict, we cannot study it in isolation; we must compare it with other types of conflicts. We apply a broad comparative approach by analyzing the general trends and trajectories of armed conflicts, including, but not limited to, Islamist conflicts. This book shows that Islamist conflicts represent a unique challenge to conflict resolution practice and theory, and it explains why Islamist armed conflicts are so difficult to resolve and end.

Understanding the conditions under which these conflicts can be resolved requires us to study the particular strategic environment in which they occur.

Thirdly, there is also a policy ambition that motivated us to write this book. Previous efforts to tackle the security challenge of Islamist armed conflicts have been costly and ineffective in terms of both human casualties and economics. In many cases, attempts to crush militant Islamist movements have been counterproductive, leading to the escalation and/or spread of these conflicts, with additional human lives lost. Twenty years of massive investments in military solutions have not been associated with a decrease in the number of conflicts in which armed Islamist actors are involved – quite the contrary. Furthermore, the war in the Afghanistan/Pakistan war zones alone is estimated to have cost over USD 2,000 trillion, and this amount only reflects the United States' expenditure, not allies' or Afghanistan's funds.[14]

As we demonstrate in this book, external military intervention – which has been one of the primary measures used by the US, Russia, the UK, France, and other countries to counter the ills of Islamist civil wars – has not contributed to sustainable peace but is part of the explanation for why Islamist civil wars have become so intractable. While there has been a gradual winding down of Western military interventions during the first half of the 2020s, the vacuum left by Western withdrawal has partly been filled by other intervening states (including Russia), complicating the resolution of conflicts further, a theme we will come back to in the concluding chapter. Our book enhances our understanding of why some Islamist armed conflicts are open to conflict resolution, whereas others are not. While conflicts over self-defined Islamist claims in general are difficult to resolve, we can identify a few exceptions

[14] Note that this sum does not count the costs for medical care and benefits for the men and women who served, which are estimated at another USD1.1 trillion up to 2050 (Crawford 2019, 13).

to this general trend – examples of mediation, negotiations, and even peace settlements between Islamist radicals and more secular-leaning governments. Our research, thus, comes with important policy implications.

The transnational ideological framing of Islamist conflicts may serve to increase uncertainty regarding the extent and nature of transnational assistance in terms of foreign support. Our analysis lends support to a different approach: *localization*, where efforts focus on preventing Islamist armed conflicts from becoming transnational, or on disconnecting them from their transnational dimensions and networks, and seeking ways to open negotiations and dialogue with locally anchored actors. The international community can help by providing political, economic, cultural, and intelligence support to assist local and national capacities in dealing with Islamist insurgencies, in parallel with efforts to eradicate the underlying causes of insurgencies. Additionally, one implication of our study is that those Islamist civil wars in which the fighting actors isolate themselves from the wider trans-Islamist networks (on the rebel side) and the global alliance structures against radical Islamism (on the government side) should stand a better chance of reaching an end. Third-party actors engaged in preventive efforts could thus seek to prevent conflict actors from joining transnational networks. Breaking away from the global jihad, as well as from the global war against it, could pave the way for more sustainable terminations of civil wars.

OUTLINE OF THE BOOK

The book proceeds in the following manner. In Chapter 2, we lay out our theoretical framework for understanding the intractability of Islamist civil wars and explain why the transnational dimensions create fundamental obstacles to the resolution, termination, and sustainable end of these conflicts. Chapter 3 examines these expectations, showing that Islamist armed conflicts are less likely to terminate and, if terminated, more likely to resume than other conflicts. We also find evidence suggesting that international entanglement in terms of foreign fighters and government support contributes to the intractability of Islamist civil wars.[15] In Chapter 4, we analyze two cases of Islamist civil wars, in Afghanistan and Mauritania, where the international dimensions have fluctuated over time. This chapter explores the conditions under which disengagement from international networks creates some space for conflict termination. In Chapter 5, we explore the prospects for conflict resolution worldwide and find that there is an underutilization of negotiations as well as peace agreements in Islamist-framed conflicts where the transnational dimension is more pronounced. While the chapter focuses on overall trends, there are important exceptions in which civil wars seemingly came to some sort of conflict resolution even though they were framed in Islamist terms. In Chapter 6, we delve into a few of these exceptions. We analyze two cases, Mali and Syria, where Islamist insurgents and opposing governments were able, to some extent, to insulate themselves from the wider transnational networks that typically surround Islamist civil wars. In Mali, we study Ansar Dine, Katiba Macina, and AQIM, in which different mediation attempts were initiated with those parts of the insurgency that are Malian in orientation and character.[16] In Syria, we focus on the case of HTS, which cut ties with both IS and al-Qaeda, enabling its receptiveness to dialogue with external actors. We explore how the parties distanced their conflicts from the global networks of support structures in which they were embedded and how this shaped the possibilities for conflict resolution. Lastly, in Chapter 7, we discuss our main findings and also problematize conflict resolution in Islamist civil wars from a gender and minority

[15] Chapters 2 and 3 draw on and develop arguments and empirics presented in our article Nilsson and Svensson (2021).

[16] The role of AQIM is discussed in both Chapter 4 (Mauritania) and Chapter 6 (Mali).

perspective, draw out the implications for theories of conflict resolution, and identify policy implications based on our work regarding how to end Islamist civil wars. These include prioritizing localization and discouraging external entanglement to create openings for conflict resolution in Islamist civil wars.

2 Our Argument

The Strategic Embeddedness of Islamist Civil Wars

When an armed group raises the banner of Islam in a violent conflict, it invokes a sense of community that goes beyond the nation-state. Although all Islamist conflicts have local roots and homegrown grievances, and the degree to which groups are oriented externally varies, all Islamist groups have the potential to tap into a wider net of transnational connections outside their domestic conflict. Understanding this dual interaction between the local and global dimensions is essential if we are to explain why Islamist conflicts are so intractable.

In this chapter, we argue that Islamist armed conflicts clearly stand out from others: how they are managed by the outside world, as well as how the parties involved in these conflicts relate to the outside world. Here, we develop our argument concerning strategic embeddedness and how the strategic environment of Islamist armed conflicts can help explain why this particular set of civil wars is so intractable. Thus, we cannot understand why Islamist armed conflicts are so difficult to resolve and bring to a close without taking the strategic context into account.

We argue that civil wars fought over Islamist aspirations are less likely to end than other conflicts, as the ideational features of these conflicts can increase the uncertainty regarding the resolve and capabilities of the warring actors. Importantly, these conflicts harbor the potential for transnational support in various forms to the rebels and the governments fighting those groups. Such international support tends to create a high degree of uncertainty in terms of the extent and nature of support, including the potential influx of foreign fighters, monetary assistance from a web of sponsors on the rebel side, as well as a plethora of intergovernmental support structures on the government side. Given that governments and rebels involved in Islamist conflicts are better able to make transboundary appeals for support compared with actors engaged in other conflicts, and that such support tends to be very diverse, there is a higher uncertainty about capabilities and resolve, thereby resulting in great difficulty in bringing these conflicts to an end.

In this chapter, we lay out the different components of our explanation for the intractability of Islamist civil wars. Understanding what makes Islamist civil wars so challenging is necessary to understand what can be done to resolve and end them. We, therefore, explain how the transnational dimension of Islamist civil wars affects the level of uncertainty in conflicts and how it can decrease the chance for termination, increase the risk of recurrence, and reduce the chances for conflict resolution.

THE STRATEGIC EMBEDDEDNESS OF ISLAMIST CIVIL WARS

The Concepts of Islamist and Jihadist

Before outlining our argument in depth, we reflect on some conceptual distinctions. So far, we have discussed certain armed conflicts as *Islamist*, using this as a generic term under which various forms of expressions of political-religious ideologies can be sorted. We have defined Islamism as a political ideology that emphasizes the holistic role of Islam in all dimensions of life, including public life. The tenets of Islam should, from this perspective, be the fundamental principles for society, and from these fundamentals, the practical arrangements for modern life can be meaningfully derived. This definition is in line with how previous research has conceptualized Islamism and Islamist groups. For example, Ahmad defines an Islamist group as a "substate faction that utilizes Islamic ideas, identity, symbols, and rhetoric in its framing, and that espouses political order based on Islamic laws and institutions" (Ahmad 2015, 92). Similarly, Wiktorowicz defines "Islamic activism" as "the mobilization of contention to support Muslim causes" and points out that it can be political and nonviolent (Wiktorowicz 2003, 2). Defining

"Islamist" in this general sense thus encompasses a wide variety of Islamist movements, ideologies, and thoughts. Many Islamist movements rely on nonviolent means and work through the political system (e.g., elections) (Gerges 2009, 277).

When we refer to Islamist armed conflicts in this book, we focus on a smaller subset of Islamist movements that have taken up arms. Previous research sometimes uses the term jihadism to describe the category of cases where Islamists are armed and seek to realize their Islamist aspirations by seizing power (Gerges 2009, 277). While the concept of jihad has an inner, spiritual meaning to describe efforts to persist and strive for a more righteous life (sometimes described as "the greater jihad"), it can also entail the use of violence in the protection and advancement of Islam. Jihadists is a term sometimes used to describe armed Islamists more generally, and sometimes more specifically Sunni Islamist movements, not Shia militant groups (Hegghammer 2014).

In other instances, the terms jihadism and jihadists are reserved for a specific subset of Sunni Islamist movements – those that are linked to the two dominant networks of al-Qaeda and IS. These movements stand out in different ways, but perhaps most pertinently in terms of their interpretation of two central theological concepts: jihad and *takfir*. They emphasize jihad as an individual and religious duty on par with other religious practices, such as prayer and almsgiving. Notably, they argue that the decision to take up arms is primarily left to the individual (an individualization of the authority-making process of jihad). They also differ from mainstream Muslim tradition by using an exclusionary practice (*takfir*) of separating righteous from non-righteous believers and declaring someone as outside of Islam, even if there are heterogeneities within this practice as well (Poljarevic 2021).

Previous research identifies many ways of subcategorizing this quite heterogeneous category of Islamist armed conflicts. One subcategorization is the distinction between armed Shia and Sunni Islamist groups, where Shia Islamist movements often have followed a particular historical trajectory (Valbjørn and Gunning 2020). Previous research also distinguishes between different types of Islamist groups based on their goal types. Hegghammer differentiates between five forms: revolutionaries, nationalists, pan-Islamists (which can be subdivided into two separate categories: classical jihadists and global jihadists), vigilantists, and sectarians (Hegghammer 2014, 10). Others categorize Islamist armed groups depending on their hierarchy of targets: those prioritizing the close enemy (corrupt and illegitimate governments in Muslim countries) and those prioritizing the far enemy (particularly the US) (Gerges 2009). Acknowledging these heterogeneities, our primary focus is to understand Islamist armed conflict. While the conceptual discussion in previous research is helpful for a deeper understanding, we thus aim to examine how Islamist armed conflicts, as one category, compare with other conflicts. We will, however, as part of this book, also examine variations within this broader category, particularly focusing on the transnational dimension of some of these movements. Conceptually, we primarily use the term Islamist armed conflicts to describe the overall phenomenon under investigation. The term jihadist, however, is applied more narrowly to denote conflicts motivated by militant Salafi ideology within Sunni Islam, or to describe the act of taking up jihad as an armed struggle.

The Transnational Dimension in Islamist Conflicts: The Rebel Side

Religion is not only about beliefs and behavior but also about belonging (Freeman and Houston 2010; Marshall 2002; Olson and Warber 2008). This sense of belonging is not easily confined within the borders of contemporary nation-states. The existence of transnational constituencies applies to all religious groups, as religious traditions are among the largest entities beyond states with which individuals identify and associate themselves (Grzymala-Busse 2012). Religious traditions help to shape a sense of identity that transcends national and local identities. This applies to all world faith traditions. In conflicts framed in religious terms, conflict actors commonly have some religious-based connection to external actors. Yet, in Islamist conflicts from 1979 onward, the transnational network has grown and become essential

(Crenshaw 2017; Hegghammer 2010). That year is often seen as a turning point, marked by several key events that sparked the rise of militant Islamism – most notably the Soviet invasion of Afghanistan, which was met with resistance by Islamist rebel groups; the Iranian revolution, along with Saudi Arabia's fear of its spread; and reactions to the Camp David peace accord between Egypt and Israel. These events contributed to the development of Islamist movements and a deepening of transnational ties across different areas of contestation. Thus, political Islamism in various shapes and forms has, since 1979, increasingly manifested itself through various nonviolent but also violent manifestations (Kepel 2006; Maher 2016; Pischedda and Vogt 2025).

The sense of a wider community of believers, the *umma*, is at the core of Islam. Importantly, the *umma* is not a concept that refers to a community of believers within a particular nation-state; it relates to the community of Muslims everywhere. Thus, the concept of the *umma* captures an important aspect of the Muslim faith tradition, transnational solidarity, where identities rooted in faith are expected to outweigh the solidarity and sense of identity linked to other categories of social lives, including states, class, or caste. The idea of the *umma* is vital for peacebuilding and nonviolent solidarity across borders and has been a central motivation behind Muslim communities reaching out to those in need (Abu-Nimer 2003). However, the concept is also crucial in understanding the interconnectedness of Islamist civil wars. Framing a conflict in Islamist terms means that a rebel group has the potential to appeal to a broader constituency. Islamism is not a transnational ideology per se, but rather a class of religious-political ideologies and streams of ideas with many facets and variations. However, it does have transnational aspects, due to the importance of the wider sense of community that does not end at borders. We have seen this in the Muslim Brotherhood-inspired movement that has collaborated across borders in Egypt, Syria, and Palestine; Libya-supported Muslim liberation movements in the Philippines (Mindanao), Indonesia (Aceh), and Chad; as well as the most transnationally developed Islamist networks, al-Qaeda and IS. By launching an explicitly Islamist revolution, rebel groups can both appeal to local tradition and champion local grievances and, at the same time, make a broader appeal that bolsters their chances for external support.

Transnationalization comes in many different forms and is a multilayered phenomenon (Drevon and Haenni 2022; Harpviken 2012; Krause 2022). Beyond the resource mobilization of external support, there are also organizational, tactical, and ideological dimensions of transnationalization (Harpviken 2012). Thus, transnationalization can include the formal pledging of allegiance (which applies particularly to how transnationalization has manifested in the cases of the networks of al-Qaeda and IS). However, it can also entail a more general or looser ideological alignment as well as shared goals and aspirations. Another form of transnationalization is the repertoire of tactics and modus operandi, in which different groups can copy or learn from one another. External support can take many varied forms, for example, tactical collaboration, logistical assistance, the provision of safe havens and space, financial support, and military equipment.

Transnationalization is manifested not least through the persistence of networks of foreign fighters, which were numerically the largest in the Iraqi and Syrian civil wars but also existed in conflicts such as in Somalia, Afghanistan, Libya, India (Kashmir), and Pakistan (Malet 2015). Foreign fighters have been active in other transnational ideological campaigns (including the Russian Revolution and the Spanish Civil War) – we will return to this matter later – but other religious traditions, with the possible exception of Judaism (many foreign Jewish volunteers fought in the 1948 War of Independence), have seen relatively few foreign fighters involved in armed conflicts in the modern era. The foreign fighter movement has grown into an important contemporary trend in Islamist armed conflicts. The presence of foreign fighters in Afghanistan, Chechnya, Somalia, and, in particular, Syria and Iraq has marked and affected the dynamics of these conflicts (Byman 2019), and while foreign fighters participate in many different conflicts, the phenomenon of foreign fighters has become particularly associated with conflicts fought over Islamist aspirations. The global foreign fighter movement was fueled by a creed emphasizing the individual duty to engage in jihad for the protection and advancement of Islam. The goal of establishing the Caliphate originated from the anti-Soviet occupation campaign in Afghanistan and has since spread to many key Islamist civil wars (Byman 2019).

Transnational connections between different Islamist rebel groups and individuals add to the complexity of Islamist civil wars as local actors tend to consider the reputation of the global movement when making strategic decisions.[1] The uncertainty surrounding Islamist civil wars is, therefore, also heightened by local non-state actors perceiving a need to consider how their local decisions affect partners worldwide. It is clear that many Islamist actors see themselves as part of a larger movement. When the Taliban movement was victorious in Afghanistan, local Islamist armed groups celebrated in Syria, Somalia, and Mali. Appearing vulnerable and demonstrating less resolve affect the reputation of Islamist armed actors elsewhere. Governments and groups learn by observing the behavior of other actors engaged in Islamist civil wars. These reputational dynamics may heighten the uncertainty, as the parties need to take into account not only the local context in a given situation of conflict – the costs and benefits of pursuing a violent struggle versus the costs and benefits of pursuing a more peaceful path – but also the broader global repercussions when considering ending their conflict.

The Benefits of the International Dimension for Rebels

Rebel groups are incentivized to appeal to this larger pool of Islamist actors because framing their conflicts in Islamist terms helps them to magnify their ability to be heard and seen and to acquire material and other types of support. Islamist claim-making has a bargaining advantage; making Islamist claims allows a rebel group to appeal to a broader

[1] On reputational dynamics in civil war, see Walter (2009).

constituency to amplify its local demands by appealing to global rhetoric. In this sense, Islamist claim-making functions as a force multiplier, enhancing the capabilities of the rebel side. The prospect of securing external support may be one of the reasons why rebel groups appeal to Islamist demands in the first place. For instance, the armed conflict in Chechnya was Islamized due to the insurgents' need to gain external support (Bakke 2014; Rich and Conduit 2015). By appealing to a constituency beyond the nation-state, a rebel group can enhance its capacity and strength. Once a conflict is framed in Islamist terms, believers from other countries may feel obligated to support the warring actors in the form of financial resources, diplomatic assistance, military equipment, or foreign fighters. For Islamist groups more generally, this makes appeals to Islamist goals and aspirations a means to connect their local struggle to a larger trajectory of solidarity across borders – appealing to the notion of the *umma* – and thereby garner more comprehensive support.

Transnationalization has been an important way for Islamist networks to expand. Compared with other groups, "Islamic organizations are both more likely to make connections and more likely to seek connections with other Islamically inspired organizations" (Asal et al. 2015, 21). Al-Qaeda has, partly because of the lack of other possibilities for expansion, especially after being ousted from its base in Afghanistan, used a franchise model. However, the way in which new fronts have opened up through branching out has varied in form and timing (Mendelsohn 2016). Transnationalization is driven not only by supply from transnational networks but also by demand from local actors. Severe conflict conditions incentivize rebel groups to seek assistance externally; religious ideology has a small but discernible effect on them (Asal and Malet 2024). Other contributing factors that can influence the number of foreign fighters are, for example, group cohesion and how easily accessible the battlefronts are (Duyvesteyn and Peeters 2015). While forming stable alliances has been difficult and is rare among non-state armed groups targeting civilians, al-Qaeda is a network that seems to have been particularly adept at overcoming obstacles to the formation of alliances (Bacon 2015). Terrorist groups have incentives to build relationships with other actors, as alliances can help terrorist organizations bolster their capabilities (Horowitz and Potter 2014). There are also different types of transnational ties; for example, Krause (2022) explores two types – transnational operations and transnational recruitment – demonstrating substantial variations regarding these forms of transnational ties.

Even after becoming transnational, local actors, such as rebel groups, possess a great deal of agency, and the degree and type of transnationalization are constantly negotiated and adapted by local actors interpreting and contextualizing the messaging and forms of the global, transnational Islamist networks (Clausen 2022). Thus, the potential of transnational connections does not imply that local actors are hierarchically steered by external patrons. While there is external influence, local actors maintain agency to shape the interpretation and practice, adding to the complexity and difficulty for governments to ascertain their enemy's true resolve and capacity. Transnationalization is not driven entirely by global networks that establish local footholds or by local actors that internationalize their struggles, but by both these dynamics (although the importance of the local or global agency may differ across contexts).

The Transnational Dimension in Islamist Conflicts: The Government Side

The transnational character of Islamist conflicts is also manifested through support for governments and reflected in counterinsurgency operations against groups fighting over Islamist claims. Whereas previous research on Islamist civil wars tends to focus on the character of the rebel side, including how insurgencies use the existence of extra-worldly rewards (Walter 2017), draw from their transnational pool of recruits (Toft and Zhukov 2015), or discount the cost of conflicts against a longer time horizon (Toft 2006), these explanations do not sufficiently consider the role of the (often more secular-leaning) governments fighting Islamist rebel groups. Governments fighting Islamist rebels are embedded in an international structure of interstate alliances, which can serve to boost their capacity to fight Islamist insurgencies (Byman 2006; Wanandi 2002) as well as facilitate collaboration in governments' counterterrorism activities (Romaniuk 2010). Interstate cooperation is broad (Mendelsohn 2009), and the US has been the leading actor in this alliance, particularly after 9/11; US support to governments combating Islamist armed groups includes countries such as Pakistan, Egypt, Iraq, and the Philippines (Henne 2017). The international alliance structures against radical Islamist actors are multifaceted and entail cooperation in different issue areas, including military, financial backing, law enforcement, and intelligence (Bensahel 2006). Thus, governments engaged in armed conflict against an Islamist actor may solicit support from other states. This strategic environment in which governments fighting Islamist rebels are immersed creates uncertainty about their capabilities. The capacity of challenged governments is potentially amplified by transnational interstate assistance. However, for the conflict actors it is ultimately more difficult to judge the extent to which governments will receive this support. The potential to receive support from the broader network of states can lead actors to overestimate their strength. Even if the actors have terminated their conflict, a return to the battlefield may follow. It can also decrease the rebels' ability to correctly assess the capabilities of the government they are fighting.

The Benefits of the International Dimension for Governments

There are also strategic benefits for governments fighting Islamist armed conflicts. Governments may benefit from engaging groups involved in terrorist violence (Bapat and Zeigler 2016). While the rebel side may help to define whether the conflict is Islamist by raising Islamist claims at the outset of the conflict, the Islamist framing of a conflict offers some opportunities for the government side, as well as for external states that have provided foreign support. During the 1980s, the US supported the Mujahideen in Afghanistan to weaken the Soviet Union and the government it supported in Kabul. At that time, the fight against communism overrode other concerns. However, after 9/11, the strategic international environment shifted dramatically. The fight against radical Islam became a global priority. This provided governments fighting Islamist groups with the possibility to frame their conflict as one of the fronts in the global West-led War on Terror. The vast resources, primarily invested by the US but also by other countries, imply that fighting Islamist actors often has come with significant benefits for the government: economic support, military training (often of a specialized and highly qualified nature), advanced military equipment, informational advantages, but also international prestige, access to key actors in the international arena, and general goodwill. Western-supported regimes also gain political cover, allowing them to deflect potential criticism of their human rights and democratic shortcomings, corruption, internal dissident crackdowns, and inept governance. Authoritarian regimes can covertly justify continuing repressive, corrupt, and exclusionary practices while still retaining support from external actors. In sum, it may be beneficial for states to engage in fighting Islamist armed actors. This applies particularly to so-called weak states, such as Somalia, Nigeria, and Mali. The Global War on Terrorism has, in some cases, incentivized weak states to pursue conflicts with Islamist groups and thus shy away from seeking sustainable solutions, as this may render them worthy of support from wealthy and strategically important external actors such as the US, France, the UK, Russia, and others. The international support structure that weak states have received in combating Islamist armed conflicts may have created incentive structures that spur governments to fight rather than terminate Islamist armed conflicts.[2]

[2] This argument resonates with Bapat (2011), who shows how military aid can incentivize governments to pursue military campaigns against terrorist groups and hinder negotiations. Bapat finds that US military assistance for host countries increases resident terrorist groups' survival by 59%. See also Kim, Li, and Sandler (2019).

Transnational support can also be a double-edged sword for governments, as such assistance may alienate their base and reduce the government's legitimacy, thereby decreasing its domestic support. Collaboration with external actors, such as the US, entails a significant risk for regimes in power (Henne 2017, 52), further enhancing uncertainty of the governments' real capacities.

Moreover, just as Islamist armed actors may consider the reputations of their allied partners in other parts of the world, governments may also do the same. Negotiating with Islamist armed rebel groups may signal a decrease in the resolve of the governments engaged in military campaigns against such groups. The fact that parties seek to maintain a reputation of toughness to deter future challengers has been shown in the study of interstate conflicts (Crescenzi 2007), as well as territorial and ethnic conflicts (Walter 2009). The transnational character of some Islamist civil wars creates reputational dynamics on a different scale. The implication of our argument is that governments seek to maintain a reputation of toughness on an international scale. Governments are allied in the fight against radical Islamists, and this de facto alliance cuts across other intergovernmental alliances. Thus, in the fight against Islamist armed actors, otherwise rival powers, such as China, Russia, the US, Saudi Arabia, and Iran, stand on the same side. They also partly receive support from each other, particularly among weaker states, which creates challenges in terms of reputation. These challenges make concessions difficult, not necessarily because of the dynamics of a local situation, but because of how this is perceived by the outside world and its implications. This adds to the uncertainty about the resolve and capacities of the governments embroiled in fighting Islamist civil wars.

How the Transnational Dimensions Influence Uncertainty

With a higher degree of uncertainty, there is a greater risk of rational miscalculation: The parties may, for example, believe that the other side's resolve is lower than it actually is, which may increase the risk of continuous conflicts. While battlefield experiences serve as costly signals that help parties update their resolve and capabilities, leading to a convergence of expectations (Fearon 1995), this updating process may be hindered or slowed down in highly complex situations. The transnational dimensions in which Islamist armed conflicts are embedded make them more complex, thus complicating this process.

Let us start by explaining how the transnational dimension of the rebels in Islamist civil wars increases uncertainty – making it more difficult for governments engaged in these civil wars to correctly ascertain the resolve and capacities of the rebels. Whereas nationalist conflicts tend to be territorially restricted and have more localized support networks, in Islamist conflicts, the rebels, to a greater extent, may draw support from a larger community not limited to a particular conflict, thus offsetting domestic pressure for settling the conflict (Kalyvas 2018; Toft and Zhukov 2015). The existence of a transnational pool of recruits and a broader international support network increases the potential for conflict intractability, as these factors provide the Islamist rebels with a greater capacity to remobilize. Previous research demonstrates that the involvement of foreign fighters affects conflict outcomes by decreasing the chance for governments to achieve victory (Chu and Braithwaite 2017). It also shows how external support to the rebel side can influence the level of uncertainty, thereby reducing the chance for bargained settlements of conflicts (Sawyer, Cunningham, and Reed 2017). The potential for foreign support creates a structure of uncertainty around the true capability of the rebel groups, increasing the risk that parties may over- or underestimate their strength. Indeed, the potential for heightened capacities through transnational support may enhance uncertainty and increase the risk of a return to the battlefield

Moreover, the global character of the Islamist movement typically creates tensions with local audiences that may challenge or decrease the domestic support base. A key point here is that foreign fighters have the potential to *both* increase and decrease the strength of domestic insurgencies. On the one hand, foreign fighters may contribute weapons, financial support, and military or strategic know-how. However, foreign fighters may also weaken rebel groups, as the introduction of what are perceived as foreign ideas, norms, and practices may alienate local populations (Bakke 2014; see also Svensson et al. 2022). For rebel groups, appealing to Islamist support networks and adopting a more radical Islamist ideology can also become a weakness, as the introduction of new religious practices, stricter interpretations of orthodoxy, and new ways of articulating and manifesting political claims may alienate such groups from local customs and the identities of the domestic constituencies (Crenshaw 2017; Kalyvas 2018). Foreign fighters "bring new ideas about who is the enemy and what the goals are to a conflict, creating divisions among the opposition and weakening popular support" (Byman 2019, 12), which "often undermine the causes they claim to support" (Byman 2019, 9). External support may, therefore, backfire, thus increasing the complexity and uncertainty of the conflict. Hence, the introduction of foreign fighters does not unidirectionally enhance the capacity of the non-state side; it may also weaken it by introducing a new framing of the conflict or a new repertoire of tactics that do not resonate with the domestic base of an insurgency, thereby increasing the risk of a split or an undermining of the insurgency. Hence, the uncertainty about the capacity and resolve of the rebel side increases when they rely on foreign fighters. This should also make it difficult for the government to assess the true strength of the rebels. The tensions between the local constituency and the global context create a fundamental uncertainty about the capabilities of the insurgencies.

As we have suggested, the idea of transnational solidarity, the *umma*, is an important aspect of Islam more generally, and of Islamism more specifically. How this transnational solidarity should be manifested is far from evident, however, and there is room for several types of configurations. While Islamist movements carry the potential for transnationalization, this is not inherent. Islamist movements can focus on the more local or national scene. It is often far from certain whether a group is genuinely local or transnational. This means that there are inherent uncertainties, not only about the potential of foreign fighters, but also about which types of conflicts will become transnationalized and what the potential for the transnational dimension is, which varies across time and space.

Turning to the governments fighting in Islamist civil wars, external interventions and support structures will also affect them and how the rebels *perceive* them. This is important from a bargaining perspective: When governments receive support from external actors, it is more difficult for rebels to judge the level of their resolve – high levels of external support may indicate either low levels of fighting spirit when external actors prop up vulnerable regimes, or a high level of fighting spirit when such support creates expectations of momentum toward victory; either way, they have the potential to obscure the government's genuine internal strength. The amount of support that will be forthcoming will be immensely more difficult to predict. Rebels may, therefore, fight on in the belief that governments are weaker and less committed than they really are.[3]

How Uncertainty Increases the Risk of Intractability

Taken together, we propose that in conflicts where the actors appeal to Islamist claims, there is greater uncertainty about resolve and capabilities, thus increasing the risk of bargaining failure. Theoretically, we should expect actors' divergent assessments of strengths and motivations to converge through warfare – actors communicate their true resolve and strength most credibly by fighting (Fearon 1995). However, the strategic environment surrounding Islamist civil wars, manifested in various types of international networks and alliances, makes it less likely that the expectations will converge. If they do, they can swiftly diverge again. Because the resources of warfare are partly outside the belligerents' own control in Islamist civil wars,

[3] It should be noted that information failure in a bargaining perspective is a type of *rational* misunderstanding that occurs due to the strategic nature of conflict. It should be differentiated from explanations focusing on cognitive biases, such as explanations for intractability focusing on the "secular bias" among governments fighting religious rebel groups; on this see Klocek (2017).

events on the battlefield will play a less substantial role in decreasing the information failure between the parties. Instead, we surmise that Islamist civil wars are situated in a particular strategic context that, due to the potential for external entanglement, creates a higher degree of uncertainty about the resolve and capabilities of the actors. Hence, once the parties have become engaged in an Islamist civil war, they become embedded in a particular strategic environment that makes its sustainable termination more challenging. Islamist civil wars will therefore be less likely than other conflicts to end, and if they do, they will more likely recur. Moreover, the fluidity of international support networks of Islamist insurgencies, as well as the strength of and advantages for governments to link up to the government-based alliance system against radical Islamist groups, create conditions for new groups to reemerge (Choi, Choi, and Yang 2022). Indeed, as suggested by Byman (2018), the defeat of Islamist armed actors may turn out to be illusory as the pool of potential recruits persists, and civil war may be reactivated by new rebel groups that come "roaring back." Thus, even if a rebel group has been defeated on the battlefield, strategic uncertainty prevails. The appeal to Islamist claims has activated a pool of potential recruits and supporters, which can emerge through new manifestations. In conflicts where the warring actors formulate their demands in Islamist terms, this can help the rebels lower the threshold for finding recruits willing to continue the fight, making it easier for new rebel groups to remobilize former fighters or engage recruits. When parties are uncertain about their foe's resolve and capacity, they may end up engaging in costly wars that last longer. Additionally, if these wars end, they are more likely to resume.

How Conflict Resolution Is Possible in Islamist Conflicts

This strategic embeddedness also affects the likelihood of conflict resolution. When parties' expectations of the likely costs and the probability of pursuing violent strategies versus negotiations do not converge, conflict is likely to continue. A vital task of the conflict resolution process is bridging the informational gap between the parties through, for example, mediation (e.g., Gilady and Russett 2002; Kydd 2010; Lundgren 2020). When the parties have reached a convergence of expectations, it can pave the way for a negotiated solution to armed conflicts. However, as we have argued the transnational dimension of Islamist civil wars and support networks increases the uncertainty regarding both capabilities and resolve. The uncertainty surrounding Islamist conflicts makes expectations less likely to converge. For example, the presence of foreign fighters can create divisions in insurgencies and also, in other ways, complicate efforts to negotiate those conflicts (Bakke 2014). This is not surprising, given that "foreign fighters often fiercely oppose any peace deal" (Byman 2019, 13). Similarly, the governmental support structure in the fight against Islamist armed groups will further contribute to making the situation more complex and difficult to ascertain. In situations characterized by informational divides – which we could expect Islamist conflicts to be particularly at risk of – dialogue aiming to resolve conflicts will, therefore, be less likely to occur. Hence, based on this, we expect that negotiations and peace agreements are less likely to occur in Islamist conflicts in general, and this should particularly be the case for those Islamist conflicts that are most ingrained in transnational dynamics.

The intractability of Islamist conflicts can thus be traced back, not primarily to their intrinsic ideological nature, but rather to the fact that this ideology enables a particular strategic environment that impedes the peaceful settlement of conflict. This fundamental insight is critical for understanding the potential role of conflict resolution. The resolution of Islamist conflicts requires a de-transnationalization of the conflict before it can become open to serious conflict resolution attempts. This means that preparing the ground for resolving Islamist conflicts involves detaching and delinking Islamist armed conflicts, on both the government and the rebel side, from the transnational networks in which they are embedded. This enables parties to ascertain each other's strength and resolve more accurately, and based on this, they can make more realistic estimates of what can be achieved and how the war can be brought to an end. The parties' expectations of the war in which they are engaged can converge, paving the way for a common understanding that can lay the basis for a termination of the conflict.

RESPONDING TO COUNTERARGUMENTS

Are Islamist Conflicts Really Exceptional in Terms of Transnationalization?

A counterargument to the one we have outlined is that Islamist civil wars are in no way unique in garnering external support. This is a variant of the *instrumentalist* perspective on religion and conflict. Outside support for civil war actors is a widespread phenomenon (Salehyan 2007) that seems to be an increasing trend (Pettersson and Wallensteen 2015). However, it is not just the occurrence or potential of external support that creates uncertainty, we contend, but also the *diversity* of support. Islamist civil wars are embedded in a more diverse support structure than other types of conflicts. External support structures have existed in many other civil wars, not least concerning the Soviet-backed Marxist rebel groups during the Cold War, which share similarities with many Islamist armed groups (Kalyvas 2018). Neighboring countries have also provided external support to ethnic brethren in ongoing civil wars or assisted rebel groups as a way of weakening a hostile neighboring country (Cederman, Girardin, and Gleditsch 2009; Davis and Moore 1997; Salehyan 2007). However, there are also significant differences in the trajectories of external interventions. The main difference between the support structure of Marxist groups during the Cold War and Islamist groups in more contemporary times is that Islamist support networks are not predominantly state-based. Research on the trends of support to rebel groups shows that the providers have shifted from great powers to non-state actors (Grauer and Tierney 2017). There have been incidents of state support for various Islamist insurgencies, for example, from Libya,

Sudan, Pakistan, and Saudi Arabia. Still, there is also a wide variety of non-state groups, organizations, and individuals that have provided backing to Islamist armed actors. While states offer a wide range of support to rebels in Islamist conflicts, such as military aid or arms transfer, state-based interventions in the form of troops on the ground in support of the rebels are extremely rare in Islamist conflicts.[4] Examples of non-state networks of support include al-Qaeda, which received substantial backing from individuals and groups within Saudi Arabia, even though the government did not actively assist the Islamist group (Byman 2005). The non-state, networked support structure of Islamist groups makes their true strength more difficult to grasp, as their support can come from a plethora of actors in a larger web. The "malleable resiliency" that Islamist armed groups show is due to the West confronting "a networked enemy" (Hoffman 2006, 429). The global network of interconnected armed Islamist groups is transnational, decentralized, and informal, implying that the networks are exceedingly fluid in character. Importantly, as the rebel groups' strength can depend on the extent to which other actors in this network provide support, the capacity and resolve of the rebels are not necessarily revealed on the battlefield.

Is It Ideology or Strategy?

Religious convictions and beliefs may or may not be held by the ideological rebel entrepreneurs making religious claims (Gunning and Jackson 2011), and their followers may or may not share these beliefs. Yet their appeal can nevertheless provide strategic benefits and complicate the bargaining process (Walter 2017). According to Walter (2017),

[4] In fact, during the studied time period (1975–2013, see large-N analysis in Chapter 3), there is only one instance of a state-based intervention with troops on the ground where an external state intervened in an Islamist conflict on the side of the rebels, namely, the conflict between the Taliban government and the so-called Northern Alliance in Afghanistan in 2001, where Iran intervened with troops on the ground. Thus, in this case, it was the government side (the Taliban) making the Islamist claim, whereas the non-state alliance was comprised of both Islamist and secular-leaning groups.

there are strategic benefits to appealing to extremist ideologies, as it can help rebels overcome collective action problems. In particular, using extremist ideologies for mobilization efforts provides nonmaterial private rewards for the recruits (Berman and Laitin 2008). Hence, while normative commitments may play a role, the claims are likely also to have instrumental value (Sanín and Wood 2014). Our argument can thus be seen as a way of understanding the strategic benefits that Islamist ideology can create (Walter 2017). Our argument takes seriously the religious nature of these conflicts by showing how these conflicts impact the strategic nature – the bargaining process – of armed conflicts. The key religious aspect explaining the intractability of Islamist conflicts lies in the particularities of their international character. Other religious aspects of these types of conflicts, including the absolutistic worldviews, increase their intractability and create obstacles to finding a solution. However, these challenges can be managed once they are decoupled from the transnational network, allowing these types of conflicts to be resolved through conflict resolution.

Does This Really Apply to All Islamist Civil Wars?

Our argument suggests an inherent potential for transnationalization in all Islamist civil wars. It is important to clarify that we do not assume that all armed actors making Islamist claims have a transnational constituency and support structure. Rather, it is the existence of this potential that increases uncertainty. Some Islamist groups are clearly transnational – IS, al-Qaeda, and groups associated with their networks – but even those groups more concerned with local territorial issues or those fighting primarily for regime change are embedded in a larger globalized network connecting local theaters of conflict. These connections include the potential of foreign fighters but go beyond broader support and solidarity networks. Groups can also change over time in terms of their transnational connections. The same applies to governments: The potential for support from other states increases the uncertainty regarding their capabilities, making a relapse into conflict more likely. The support structure surrounding

Islamist civil wars is tenuous, increasing the bargaining uncertainty. Indeed, there has been a significant variation in terms of the degree to which Muslim states have collaborated with, for example, the US in counterterrorism efforts (Henne 2017). From the perspective of strategic uncertainty, the actual transnationalization is not necessarily the key impediment to the termination of conflicts. Instead, conflicts are embedded in a strategic environment in which the existence of transnationalization can create the risk of parties continuing to fight.

At the same time, the *degree* of the transnationalization of Islamist conflicts can also be important from the perspective of strategic uncertainty. Within the category of Islamist armed conflicts, those conflicts in which rebel groups and governments can credibly signal their local orientation will be more likely than other Islamist conflicts to be terminated sustainably. We, therefore, expect that transnationally interconnected Islamist conflicts should be less likely to see conflict resolution attempts, such as peace negotiations. Moreover, our argument implies that Islamist conflicts where conflict parties have insulated themselves from global campaigns for or against radical Islam will more likely reach settlements and resolve their conflicts. Once rebel groups or governments disassociate from the transnational arena and focus on domestic issues, the chance of resolving these conflicts increases.

THE CAUSAL CHAIN

Before closing this chapter, some potential endogeneity concerns should be addressed. The argument laid out in this chapter suggests that Islamist claims raised in insurgencies lead to an increased likelihood of external support (on the side of the government or rebels) and that the risk that such external support is forthcoming (or not) increases the strategic uncertainty, which in turn increases the risk that these conflicts become intractable. The steps in the causal chain laid out are, thus, from claims to support to intractability, and uncertainty is the key mechanism linking support to intractability. Can this chain be reversed?

Is it the lack of termination that causes external actors – governments supporting governments, foreign fighters supporting rebel groups – to intervene with their support in conflicts, rather than external support causing intractability? Previous research on external intervention has dealt with this question extensively and has shown, for example, that external intervention generally leads to more prolonged and more intractable conflicts (Aydin and Regan 2012; Karlén 2016; Regan 2002), that the presence of foreign fighters decreases the likelihood of government victory (Chu and Braithwaite 2017), and that conflicts in which rebels receive external support are more likely to experience a relapse of civil war (Karlén 2017). Hence, ample research demonstrates that conflicts in which warring actors receive external support tend to be more intractable.[5]

Going one step further back in the causal chain, could it be that actors frame their conflicts in the name of Islam to generate support from outside actors? There is much merit to this potential counterargument, and we shall explore this more closely in the empirical analysis of this book, both quantitatively and by tracing causal chains more precisely in a few cases, aiming to establish the time order between the making of claims and the supply of external support. In general, we expect external involvement to occur after a conflict has started and the demands for change have been raised. As emphasized by Byman, "the foreign fighters *never* begin the conflicts they participate in and only later play a prominent part" (Byman 2019, 10). Moreover, even if actors have framed their conflicts instrumentally to receive external support, the interconnection between issue framing and external support enhances strategic uncertainty, reducing the chances for termination and conflict resolution.

SUMMARIZING THE ARGUMENT

In this chapter, we argued that the external strategic environment creates specific bargaining obstacles for the termination and resolution of Islamist armed conflicts. These obstacles, it should be underlined,

[5] At the same time, these are complex relationships, and some research also shows that external support can increase the likelihood of particular outcomes, such as victory (see Karlén 2016 for an overview of the findings).

are found on both the government and the rebel side, and it is these obstacles – relating to the internationalization of Islamist armed conflicts – that make these conflicts particularly difficult to bring to an end. Our argument is both structural and probabilistic – that is, we focus on the general conditions that impede conflict resolution and termination in civil wars. We suggest that the level of uncertainty created by the transnational environment in which Islamist conflicts are embedded is one of the main obstacles to conflict resolution, generally speaking. It is thus the transnational nature of Islamist conflicts that makes them intractable. However, it is not a deterministic relationship, and that is why we need to analyze larger trends to explore whether Islamist conflicts, as we expect, stand out from other civil wars from a conflict termination and resolution perspective, and whether this is driven by the transnational nature of these conflicts.

In sum, we have applied a bargaining perspective to Islamist armed conflicts, highlighting the increased risk that information cleavages cannot be overcome during a civil war. We argue that the ideational features of Islamist claims can serve to heighten the uncertainty regarding the capabilities and resolve of both the government and the rebel side. Based on our previous discussion, we can formulate seven testable hypotheses. First, we expect Islamist conflicts to be more difficult to terminate than other types of conflicts. Second, even if the parties have stopped fighting, the heightened uncertainty should increase the risk that bargaining failures occur and war breaks out again. Thus, we expect that Islamist conflicts are more likely to recur compared with other conflicts. Third, even if the previously active groups stop fighting following termination, Islamist armed conflicts should be more likely than other conflicts to see new groups emerging. We explore these expectations in Chapters 3 and 4. Fourth, we further expect that peace negotiations will be rare in Islamist armed conflicts in general because of the uncertainty generated by the external support associated with Islamist claim-making in armed conflicts. Fifth, we similarly expect peace accords to be less likely in Islamist civil wars than in other conflicts. Sixth, while we expect the potential of transnationalization to be enough to create obstacles to the resolution and sustainable termination of Islamist armed conflicts, we also expect the degree of transnationalization to matter; those Islamist conflicts with a more pronounced transnational dimension should be particularly resistant to negotiations. Seventh, and lastly, we also expect such conflicts to be less likely to see peace accords signed. We focus on evaluating these expectations in Chapters 5 and 6.

3 Global Evidence of Intractability

Termination and Recurrence

In the previous chapter, we laid out the core claim of this book, arguing that due to the transnational nature of Islamist conflicts, there is a higher degree of uncertainty around resolve and capabilities, making these conflicts more intractable and more difficult to resolve than other types of conflicts. In this chapter, we assess a few central implications of our argument concerning termination and recurrence. Our focus here is on larger empirical trends across cases worldwide, and in the following chapter, we analyze the causal processes behind these patterns in more depth. Based on novel data regarding religious dimensions in conflict, we explore the association between Islamist claims and conflict termination before assessing whether these conflicts are more likely to recur. We demonstrate there is ample evidence to suggest that Islamist conflicts are indeed less likely to terminate, and if they do come to an end, they are more likely to restart.

MEASURING THE IMPACT OF ISLAMIST CLAIMS ON CONFLICT TERMINATION AND RECURRENCE

Data and Dependent Variables

To evaluate our claims, we rely on dyadic data regarding intrastate armed conflict, defined as an incompatibility over government and/or territory between a government and a rebel group, resulting in at least 25 battle-related deaths in a calendar year. To focus on armed conflicts with 25 battle-related deaths or more is in line with other studies on termination and recurrence, which increasingly focus on both high- and low-intensity conflicts in their analyses (e.g., Cunningham, Gleditsch, and Salehyan 2009; Karlén 2017; Kreutz 2010; Nilsson 2008a). The data come from the UCDP Dyadic Dataset v4–2016 (Harbom, Melander, and Wallensteen 2008; Melander, Pettersson, and Themnér 2016). We rely on dyadic data, as there are important variations within conflicts, both in terms of which conflict party makes Islamist claims and which conflict dyads terminate and (potentially) recur. Our analysis focuses on the period 1975–2013, as this is the period for which we have data for all variables included in our main models.

We construct two datasets, one to study termination and one to examine recurrence. In the dataset in which the interest lies in termination, the unit of analysis is the dyad-year, and we follow each government–rebel dyad until the dyad terminates for at least one calendar year or more, or the observation period ends. The dependent variable *Termination* is coded 1 if the conflict activity for the dyad in focus has dropped below 25 battle-related deaths for at least one year and is coded 0 otherwise (e.g., Karlén 2017; Kreutz 2010). We base this on the UCDP conflict termination dataset version 2-2015 (Kreutz 2010), which includes information on whether the conflict has terminated for at least one year and how it terminated. While conflicts may end in several ways, such as through a peace agreement or a military victory, theoretically, we are interested in termination through any of these pathways and thus consider all terminations (and explore different types of terminations in alternative specifications as well as later in the book). For our statistical analysis, we rely on a Cox proportional hazards model.

In our recurrence dataset, the unit of analysis is the dyad-termination-year, and we focus on all intrastate armed conflicts that have terminated for at least one year and then follow each government–rebel dyad until the observation period ends or there is a recurrence of armed conflict. Since we are interested in the survival of peace up to an event (recurrence of conflict), we employ a Cox proportional hazards model here. *Recurrence* is coded 1 if the government and rebel group become active again (meaning they reach the count of 25 battle-related deaths). To allow us to specifically explore recurrence involving new, previously inactive armed actors, we also created the variable *Recurrence-new*, which is coded 1 if a *new* government–rebel dyad reaches 25 battle-related deaths (i.e., a dyad previously not fighting in the armed conflict over the same overarching issue, e.g., government or territory). Since some dyads may experience repeated recurrences – and the patterns surrounding the first recurrence may be different for dyads that experience a backslide to violence, for example, the fourth time – in our statistical analysis, we account for repeated events by stratifying the analysis on each dyad episode.[1]

Independent and Control Variables

To study Islamist armed conflicts, we rely on the RELAC dataset, a data collection on religious dimensions of armed conflict (Svensson and Nilsson 2018). We use the measure *Islamist claim*, which is coded 1 if the rebel group has self-proclaimed Islamist aspirations at the outset of the conflict, for example, advocating for an increased role of Islam in the society or the state, and 0 otherwise. As mentioned in Chapter 1, according to the UCDP's criteria, the incompatibility is a key part of the definition of an armed conflict, and our understanding of what constitutes an Islamist armed conflict closely aligns with those criteria when focusing on Islamist claims. Rebel groups making such claims include, for example, IS in Syria and Iraq, MILF in the Philippines, Hamas in Israel–Palestine, and the Patani insurgents in Thailand. As mentioned, the category of Islamist armed conflicts thus captures a diverse set of actors, and later in this book, we discuss and analyze variations within this broader category of Islamist armed conflicts, paying particular attention to the transnational dimension. Here, however, we focus on this broader category. Notably, our measurement of Islamist claims does not specify whether the demand is the only or the most important demand. Thus, rebel groups may also make other claims, but we focus here on whether any type of Islamist claim was announced at the start of the conflict. Ideally, we

[1] Please note that when studying recurrence via new groups, we stratify the analysis on the dyad episode of the previous active groups, as this is likely to influence the behavior of any new groups that emerge. We receive the same results without stratification.

would like to know to what extent these claims might have shifted over time, but since no such data are currently available, we focus on the claims made at the beginning of the conflict. We will delve deeper into these temporal dynamics as part of our case illustrations in this book.

In terms of controls, we seek to account for factors that could influence both our dependent variables – termination and recurrence – and our independent variable, Islamist claims. Hence, we begin by identifying several factors before the start of the armed struggle that could influence the prevalence of Islamist armed conflicts as well as the likelihood of termination and recurrence. Karakaya (2015) finds youth bulges and oil rents to be important factors in explaining the prevalence of intrastate conflicts in Muslim-majority countries. To account for such dynamics, we created the variable *Muslim majority*, coded 1 if the majority of the population in a country identifies with the Islamic faith and coded 0 otherwise. Here, we employ data from Gleditsch and Rudolfsen (2016), originally from the Pew dataset (Pew 2012). We include the variable *Youth bulge*, measured as the number of individuals aged between 15 and 24 as a share of the adult population above 15 in the country. The data on youth bulges come from the United Nations (United Nations 2017; Urdal 2006). To account for income from oil, we introduce a control for *Oil*, measured as the value from oil in nominal value, logged (Ross and Mahdavi 2015). These variables are all measured one year prior to conflict onset.

We also account for various features of the conflict that could potentially influence the likelihood of rebels framing their demands in Islamist terms, as well as termination and recurrence. The variable *Territory* is coded 1 if the armed conflict is fought over territory rather than government and is based on data from the UCDP (2015). We also consider the rebels' strength, as this could influence both the type of claims made and the intractability of the conflict (Cunningham, Gleditsch, and Salehyan 2009; Nilsson 2008b). The measure *Strong rebels* is coded 1 if the rebel group is at parity or stronger than the government and coded 0 if the groups are weaker or much weaker. The coding is based on the Non-State Actors in Armed Conflict (NSA) dataset (Cunningham, Gleditsch, and Salehyan 2009, 2013). These variables form part of our main models.

Since armed conflicts over Islamist claims may take on certain dynamics once the conflict has been framed in such terms, we also explore some potential pathways through which armed conflicts over Islamist aspirations may influence termination and the recurrence of conflict. Hence, we account for aspects related to the transnational dimensions in terms of support structures, as well as factors associated with the postwar context. We do not view these factors as potential confounders (since Islamist claims are measured at the outset of the conflict), but their inclusion can possibly help us understand if the Islamist conflicts are following a certain trajectory in terms of their path toward recurrence.

We theorize that conflicts over Islamist claims are more likely, on average, to take on transnational dimensions, such as a higher likelihood of an influx of foreign fighters. To explore this pathway we account for the presence of foreign fighters, relying on data from Chu and Braithwaite (2017), which in turn is based on Malet (2013). The variable *Foreign fighters* is a dummy variable, coded 1 if foreign fighters were involved in the rebel struggle against the government and coded 0 otherwise. Admittedly, there is likely variation in the number of foreign fighters across these cases; however, this is the best data source available with uniform coverage across the globe, and we believe it can serve as a proxy for the relationship we are interested in. We also theorize that military support on the government side is a potential pathway that could increase uncertainty. To capture such involvement, we created the variable *Government support*, coded 1 if a government receives troop support from another state (Melander, Pettersson, and Themnér 2016).[2] Additionally, since the

[2] We also check for the robustness of our results using information about other types of support; for example, regarding government support, we also use data on secondary support beyond troops on the ground. See Appendix, Table A8.

type of termination may influence recurrence, we introduce several variables that capture different outcomes, including *Peace agreement*, *Ceasefire*, *Rebel victory*, *Government victory*, and *Low activity* (Kreutz 2010). Finally, in the recurrence literature, third-party security guarantees in the form of peacekeeping troops have been shown to be of importance to reduce the risk of recurrence. Since civil wars over Islamist aspirations may be less likely to see this form of intervention, and peacekeepers may reduce the risk of recurrence, we account for the presence of a *Peacekeeping* operation in the country, relying on data from Hegre, Hultman, and Nygård (2019).

RESULTS AND ANALYSIS

We now turn to our results and analysis. We begin by providing some brief descriptive statistics of our data. Summary statistics for all variables are provided in the Appendix, Tables A1–A2. Our termination dataset contains 386 rebel–government dyads; 64 rebel groups made Islamist claims at the start of the conflict, whereas 322 did not. The vast majority of all conflict dyads (367 out of 386) are terminated at some point in time, that is, violence drops below 25 battle-related deaths in a year or more. However, as we return to when discussing our results on recurrence, many of the conflict dyads terminated for one year or more experience repeated cycles of violence.

The distribution of Islamist armed conflicts is skewed over time: None of the intrastate armed conflicts in 1975 were Islamist, whereas in 2015 the majority were fought over Islamist claims (Nilsson and Svensson 2017). It is, therefore, important that we correctly estimate and consider the time dimension. We rely on a Cox proportional hazards model, as it allows us to specifically focus on the time up to an event (termination or recurrence) while accounting for time-varying covariates and provides a way of estimating right-censored data (considering that some dyads may have yet to experience an event). We do not have strong theoretical expectations of the failure rate over time, and in such a case, a Cox proportional hazards model, which is more flexible, is preferable over a parametric model (Box-Steffensmeier and Jones 2004). Moreover, since some of the dyads may experience repeated events, we consider this by stratifying our analysis on each episode. In addition, we present our main results relying on alternative survival models, including a Weibull model and an exponential model. The results remain robust (see Appendix, Tables A3–A5).

We theorize that conflicts fought over Islamist aspirations are characterized by higher uncertainty, which, on average, should increase the risk of bargaining failures and a continuation of conflict. Our first hypothesis proposes that armed conflicts over Islamist claims are less likely to terminate. Figure 3.1 displays the Kaplan-Meier survival estimates for the two categories of interest: dyads fighting over Islamist claims vs. those not fighting over Islamist claims (i.e., showing the percentage of cases that have yet to experience termination at a given point in time).[3] As shown in Figure 3.1, the dyads fighting over Islamist aspirations do not terminate at the same rate as those dyads fighting over other types of claims. The

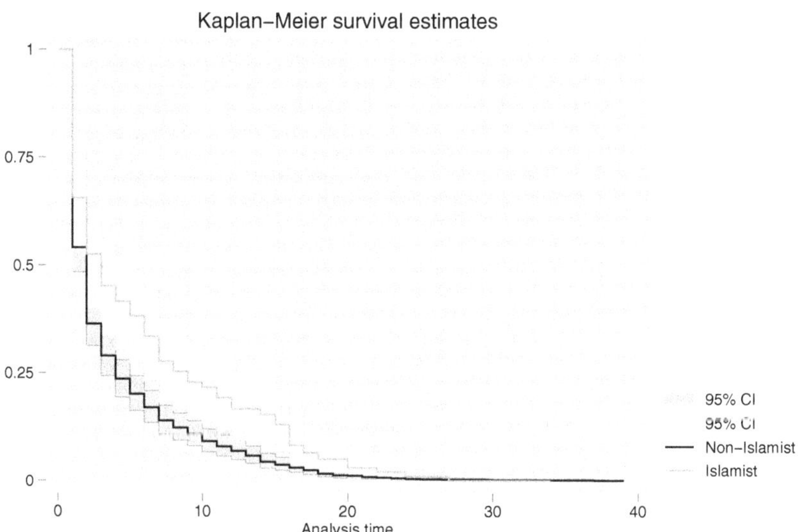

FIGURE 3.1 Survival estimates: Islamist conflicts and termination.

[3] The figures are created using the scheme plottig (Bischof 2017).

results for our Cox proportional hazards model on termination are presented in Model 1, Table 3.1. The hazard ratios are interpreted relative to 1, and a value above 1 indicates an increased likelihood of termination, whereas a value below 1 shows a reduced likelihood of termination. In line with Hypothesis 1, we find that warring actors who fight over Islamist aspirations are 29% less likely than other actors to stop fighting. Notably, this result is obtained while controlling for various country characteristics, such as the presence of youth bulges, whether a country is a Muslim-majority country, and whether the conflict is fought over government or territory.

Having established that conflicts over Islamist claims are less likely to be terminated, we explore if there is a higher risk of

Table 3.1 *Islamist conflicts and the risk of termination and recurrence. Cox proportional hazards models*

	Termination (1)	Recurrence (2)	Recurrence-new (3)
Islamist claim	0.706	1.730	1.718
	(0.095)**	(0.351)**	(0.420)*
Territory	0.962	2.288	0.560
	(0.110)	(0.506)**	(0.147)*
Strong rebels	1.126	0.914	1.066
	(0.153)	(0.330)	(0.295)
Oil_{log}	1.003	1.019	0.981
	(0.004)	(0.010)†	(0.011)†
Youth bulge/adult pop.	1.016	1.042	0.977
	(0.012)	(0.020)*	(0.030)
Muslim majority	1.074	0.869	0.997
	(0.110)	(0.178)	(0.231)
N	1,657	6,194	6,194
Subjects	309	306	306
Failures	433	149	71

Note: †$p < 0.1$; *$p < 0.05$; **$p < 0.01$. Robust standard errors in parentheses clustered on dyad. Note that for Model 1, the unit of analysis is dyad-year; in Models 2–3, it is dyad-termination-year.`

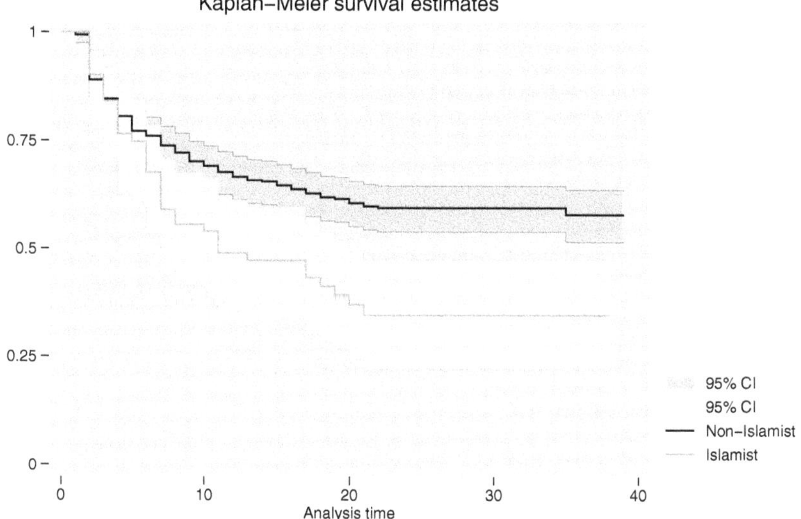

FIGURE 3.2 Survival estimates: Islamist conflicts and recurrence.

recurrence in comparison with other types of conflicts. We begin by looking at some descriptive statistics in our recurrence data. Of the 367 rebel–government dyads in our dataset, 53 were fighting over Islamist aspirations, whereas 314 were not. Recurrence seems to be slightly more common in Islamist armed conflicts: 38% (20 out of 53) compared with 25% (78 out of 314) for non-Islamist armed conflicts. Figure 3.2 displays the Kaplan-Meier survival estimates for recurrence for Islamist and non-Islamist claims (i.e., the percentage of cases yet to experience recurrence at a given time). The recurrence patterns are initially similar, but after a few years, a higher proportion of the Islamist conflicts recur. This provides some initial support for our second hypothesis.

The results for our Cox proportional hazards model on recurrence are presented in Models 2–3, Table 3.1. Conflicts in which the government and a particular rebel group are fighting over Islamist claims show an increased risk of recurrence compared with conflicts fought over other types of claims (see Model 2, Table 3.1). The hazard ratio is above 1 and statistically significant at the 99% level. This effect is also significant in substantive terms: The risk of recurrence increases by 73% when the armed conflict is fought over an Islamist claim, compared with other armed conflicts.

Since we also theorized about the possibility that new Islamist groups, and not just previously active actors, may mobilize and take up arms following a termination, we explore this empirically. In this analysis, we focus specifically on recurrence via new actors who have not been active previously. In line with our theory, we find that when conflicts are fought over Islamist claims, the risk that *new* armed actors emerge increases by 72%, an effect that is statistically significant at the 95% confidence level (see Model 3, Table 3.1). However, we do not know whether the new emerging groups are also necessarily fighting over Islamist claims. A closer inspection of the events of recurrence reveals that when focusing on *Recurrence-new*, out of 80 instances of recurrence, 23 involve a new rebel group fighting over an Islamist claim. This represents about 29%, compared with 20% when we focus on instances of *Recurrence* involving a previously active group. Hence, the proportion of events of recurrence involving an Islamist actor is even higher when we only look at recurrence involving new groups. In sum, the results support our second and third hypotheses. As robustness, instead of relying on a one-year drop in fighting to determine if termination has occurred, we require the fighting to have terminated for at least two years. When doing so, we find that our main results for termination and recurrence are robust (see Appendix, Table A6).

In addition, we also seek to explore two potential pathways as to why Islamist conflicts are so intractable – the presence of foreign fighters and government support. Our theory emphasizes the transnational dimension of Islamist civil wars, and one manifestation is the increased uncertainty relating to the potential influx of foreign fighters. Another is the uncertainty arising from the plethora of intergovernmental support structures on the government side. There is descriptive evidence of the connection between the

Islamist character of civil wars and the presence of foreign fighters and government support. Of the rebel groups fighting over an Islamist claim, 47% see the involvement of foreign fighters, whereas the corresponding figure for rebels in other types of conflicts is 17%. Similarly, government support is forthcoming in 44% of the Islamist conflicts, whereas for non-Islamist conflicts, only 15% see government support.

As a first cut, to begin to tease out these mechanisms, we include these measures in the multivariate analysis (see Models 1–3, Table 3.2) to shed light on potential pathways. When focusing on termination, we find some support for our conjectures that foreign fighters and government support may act as potential pathways. When interpreting the results, it is important to keep in mind that the government support we focus on here is interventions with troops on the ground, hence not capturing other forms of government support, such as financial support or arms transfers. Both foreign fighters and government support are in the expected direction and significant at the 95% level, whereas the effect for Islamist claims is in the expected direction but no longer significant (see Model 1). This suggests not only that Islamist claims have a direct impact on termination but also that the presence of foreign fighters and government support may serve as potential pathways. Turning to our results regarding recurrence, in Model 2, Table 3.2, *Islamist claim* is still statistically significant at the 90% level. But the effect is reduced to some degree (from 73% down to 48%), and the hazard ratio for foreign fighters is in the expected direction and statistically significant. The coefficient for government support is not precisely estimated. The corresponding results for new groups show a reduced effect for Islamist claims that is no longer significant, whereas government support and foreign fighters are statistically significant and in the expected direction (see Model 3). Thus, in line with our expectations, foreign fighters and government support act as potential pathways, although the results are less clear-cut for government support. Using alternative measures

Table 3.2 *Islamist conflicts and the risk of termination and recurrence: exploring the pathways. Cox proportional hazards models*

	Termination (1)	Recurrence (2)	Recurrence-new (3)
Islamist claim	0.835	1.482	1.349
	(0.111)	(0.332)†	(0.327)
Territory	0.850	2.580	0.684
	(0.099)	(0.572)**	(0.185)
Strong rebels	1.182	0.856	0.943
	(0.169)	(0.306)	(0.257)
Oil_{log}	1.000	1.022	0.984
	(0.004)	(0.010)*	(0.011)
Youth bulge/adult pop.	1.015	1.048	0.976
	(0.012)	(0.020)*	(0.030)
Muslim majority	1.134	0.794	0.874
	(0.118)	(0.165)	(0.211)
Foreign Fighters	0.747	1.831	1.864
	(0.085)*	(0.420)**	(0.445)**
Government Support	0.662	0.805	1.888
	(0.101)**	(0.214)	(0.457)**
N	1,657	6,194	6,194
Subjects	309	306	306
Failures	433	149	71

Note: †$p < 0.1$; *$p < 0.05$; **$p < 0.01$. Robust standard errors in parentheses clustered on dyad. Note that for Model 1, the unit of analysis is dyad-year; in Models 2–3, it is dyad-termination-year.

of secondary support yields a similar picture (see Appendix, Table A8).[4]

We want to mention that our argument does not imply a conditional effect. We expect Islamist claims to create uncertainty about external support, which enhances uncertainty even if such support is not always materializing or forthcoming. For transparency, we

4 While this analysis is in line with our expectations, future research should explore these potential pathways in more detail, for example by relying on mediation analysis.

nevertheless explore whether Islamist claims are conditional on foreign support (see Appendix, Table A7a–d). This analysis does not show a conditional effect on termination or recurrence. Thus, the impact of Islamist claims is not amplified through the presence of foreign fighters or government support. However, we find some evidence suggesting that Islamist claims are significant in the presence of government support, but the effect is only significant at the 90% level. Generally, while we find little evidence suggesting that the impact of Islamist claims on termination or recurrence is conditional on the presence or absence of foreign support, there should be some caution in interpreting these results, as such an analysis demands more data. Overall, we do not see these alternative specifications providing a direct test of our theoretical argument, which expects an effect of Islamist claims on termination and recurrence driven not only by the actual occurrence of foreign fighters and government support but also by the strategic context created by such claim-making.

These results are thus well in line with the theory we have put forward and remain stable across various robustness tests. Since we use a Cox proportional hazards model, we test for violations of the proportional hazards assumption using the Schoenfeld residuals. Still, neither the individual nor the global tests for our main models show any violations (Box-Steffensmeier and Jones 2004). Islamist conflicts have become more frequent in recent years, which could be a cause for concern. Yet survival analysis is particularly suitable to address issues relating to time, including right-censoring, but we have nevertheless taken some additional measures to ensure that the analysis is not influenced by the time dimension. A closer look at the data shows that after 15 years, there are 25 dyads with Islamist claims out of a total of 53 dyads in the recurrence analysis (i.e., close to 50% of the cases are still contributing to the analysis at this point). Moreover, we also control for other factors such as economic development measured as GDP per capita (logged), type of political regime using a dummy for anocracy (these are political systems that fall between democracies and autocracies), and size of the population (logged), and we find overall that the results are robust across different specifications (see Appendix, Tables A9–A11).[5] More specifically, when analyzing termination and recurrence, our results remain the same, but when focusing on the recurrence of new groups and controlling for anocracy, *Islamist claim* is no longer significant. However, this result should be interpreted cautiously as some data on anocracy are missing. Thus, taken together, we find strong support for our conjectures, but the evidence is less clear-cut when explaining the recurrence of new groups.

ALTERNATIVE EXPLANATIONS

We now move on to consider some alternative interpretations of our findings. One possibility is that we should expect similar findings for rebel movements that share the characteristics of Islamist civil war and that it is not something particular about Islamist conflicts. This would be in line with the instrumentalist perspective. Kalyvas (2018) points out the similarities with revolutionary rebels in general, such as groups fighting with a leftist ideology. Islamism and leftism represent the two main transnational revolutionary movements during the studied time period. Islamist and leftist groups are similar in the sense that they mobilize based on a revolutionary ideology, harbor ideas that may alienate the local population, and belong to transnational social movements. To explore whether Islamist and leftist revolutionaries follow a similar empirical trajectory regarding termination and recurrence, we created the variable *Leftist*, which captures whether the rebel movement fought over explicit leftist demands.[6] During the time period under

[5] Data on the type of political system comes from Polity2 (Marshall, Jaggers, and Gurr 2015), and anocracy is a dummy variable capturing the regimes that receives a score between –5 and +5 on the Polity2 scale (the full scale ranges between –10 and +10). For GDP per capita, we rely on data from the UN statistics division (United Nations 2015), and population is based on the World Bank World Development Indicators, taken from Ross and Mahdavi (2015).

[6] We use an updated version of a dataset (Fjelde and Nilsson 2019) created by Forsberg and Karlén (2013), which in turn is based on Kalyvas and Balcell (2010); the Terrorist

study, there are 61 groups with a leftist ideology and 321 groups that do not harbor such ideas. Overall, we find some similarities with Islamist groups and some notable differences. Firstly, our results show that conflicts over a leftist ideology are indeed less likely to terminate (see Appendix, Model 1, Table A12). Yet, when exploring if conflicts over a leftist ideology are more or less likely to recur, the tests for proportional hazards showed violations for the *Leftist* covariate. To address this issue, we follow the advice of Box-Steffensmeier and Jones (2004) and interact this variable with the log of time (*Leftist*log(_t)*). Thus, the risk is not stable over time (see Appendix, Model 4, Table A12). Therefore, we also used alternative survival models – a Weibull and an exponential model – but *Leftist* is not significant (not reported here). When focusing on recurrence involving new groups, *Leftist* is only significant at the 90% level (see Table A13). Hence, while there is some evidence that conflicts over leftist ideologies are less likely to terminate, in terms of recurrence, we find some differences between leftist and Islamist conflicts. Importantly, when we study the pathways we identified – foreign fighters and government support – we find that the leftist conflicts stand out compared with the Islamist conflicts. Whereas we found that a higher share of the Islamist conflicts see both foreign fighters and government support compared with non-Islamist conflicts, the leftist conflicts see foreign fighters in 18% of cases, compared with 22% in the non-leftist conflicts, and 13% see government support compared with 21.5% in the non-leftist conflicts. Hence, if anything, the patterns seem to go in the opposite direction. Indeed, when adding foreign fighters and government support to the multivariate analysis, the results for *Leftist* remain the same (see Table 3.3). We can thus conclude that while the Islamist and leftist conflicts, to some extent, see

Organization Profiles dataset by the National Consortium for the Study of Terrorism and Responses to Terrorism (2013); the Minorities at Risk Organizational Behavior Database (Asal, Pate, and Wilkenfeld 2008); and the UCDP Encyclopedia.

Table 3.3 *Leftist conflicts and the risk of termination and recurrence: exploring the pathways. Cox proportional hazards models*

	Termination (1)	Recurrence (2)	Recurrence-new (3)
Leftist	0.598	5.032	1.553
	(0.070)**	(2.136)**	(0.407)†
Leftist × ln(time)	–	0.467	–
		(0.101)**	
Territory	0.738	2.919	0.767
	(0.086)**	(0.606)**	(0.207)
Strong rebels	1.085	0.919	1.010
	(0.168)	(0.326)	(0.287)
Oil_{log}	1.002	1.023	0.985
	(0.004)	(0.010)*	(0.011)
Youth bulge/adult pop.	1.015	1.055	0.981
	(0.013)	(0.021)**	(0.031)
Muslim majority	1.015	0.866	1.010
	(0.102)	(0.168)	(0.232)
Government Support	0.583	2.099	1.943
	(0.086)**	(0.431)**	(0.467)**
Foreign Fighters	0.687	0.888	2.024
	(0.081)**	(0.235)	(0.493)**
N	1,657	6,193	6,193
Subjects	309	305	305
Failures	433	149	71

Note: †$p < 0.1$; *$p < 0.05$; **$p < 0.01$. Robust standard errors in parentheses clustered on dyad.

similar patterns in terms of their intractability, we do not find the pathways to be the same.

It is also conceivable that the findings reflect something about Muslim group identities rather than the claims per se. Our theoretical argument emphasizes the strategic incentives that arise from mobilizing based on Islamist claims and counter-efforts against such uprisings. The effect we expect is related to the particular strategic dilemmas in Islamist civil wars, which we argue arise when rebels frame their aspirations in Islamist terms, rather than to the identity aspect of Muslim conflicts in general. Hence, in contrast to the arguments made about "Muslim exceptionalism" and conflict, we do not expect Muslim identity to matter.[7] To explore this, we account for *Muslim identity*, which is a dummy variable capturing whether the religious majority of the constituency of the government or the rebel group comes from the Muslim faith tradition. This variable thus captures both armed conflicts where Christians are fighting Muslims, such as in Chad between the government and the Armed Forces of the Federal Republic (FARF), and armed conflicts where Muslims are found on both sides of the conflict, for example, in the conflict over government power in Iraq, where the conflict is fought between Sunni Muslims on one side, and Shia Muslims on the other. The variable is based on data from the RELAC dataset (Svensson and Nilsson, 2018). When we consider the effect of Muslim identity, the results regarding Islamist claim-making still holds, and there is no evidence that conflicts fought over a Muslim identity have a higher likelihood of termination or recurrence by the same actor (see Appendix, Table A12). Yet we do find that this factor seems to be associated with recurrence via new actors, but only at the 90% level, and *Islamist claim* is then no longer significant (see Appendix, Table A13). Taken together, the evidence instead suggests it is the Islamist claim-making, and not the Muslim identity dimension, that drives the increased risk of intractability. Since our conceptualization of Islamist civil wars focuses on Islamist aspirations as such, this lends support to the notion that it is the ideas that matter rather than the identity. However, as previously noted, we do not make any assumptions regarding the sincerity of the claims and whether the rebels, leaders, and followers believe in these ideas or whether they serve other purposes.

[7] For an overview on the Muslim exceptionalism discussion, see Fish, Jensenius, and Michel (2010), Fox (2007), and Karakaya (2015).

The notion of uncertainty created by the strategic context of Islamist armed conflicts is central to our argument rather than the intensity of religious beliefs associated with Islamist conflicts. To tease out whether it is the *religious* dimensions of conflicts more broadly that make conflicts intractable or whether the intractability is more restricted to Islamist conflicts (as our argument suggests), it is worth examining whether our findings apply to non-Islamist religious conflicts that are fought over religious claims, such as conflicts involving militant Sikh or Christian rebel groups. Yet we find no similar effect as regards those religious conflicts that do not concern Islamist aspirations (see Appendix, Table A12 and A13). However, since most religious conflicts are fought over Islamist claims, it must be noted that these non-Islamist religious conflicts are very few, and it is thus challenging to identify significant effects.

Another possibility is that Islamist armed conflicts are more fragmented than other types of conflicts, which makes these conflicts more intractable. To explore this, we add the number of rebel groups involved in the conflict to the three main models (see Appendix, Table A14). We find that our results concerning Islamist claims and termination, as well as recurrence, are robust. When examining the recurrence of new groups, however, *Islamist claim* is no longer significant, and in already fragmented conflicts, there is an increased risk of new groups emerging. This does not make the finding spurious, but it says something about *why* we see an increased risk of new groups emerging in Islamist conflicts.

Finally, to further explore potential pathways as to why Islamist conflicts are so intractable, we assess if the way the conflicts are fought could matter (see Appendix, Table A15). However, the results remain the same when accounting for factors related to how the war was fought, including the intensity and duration of the conflict. Subsequently, we look at the postwar context, studying the type of termination and the presence of peacekeepers, but our main findings remain the same (see Models 1–2, Table 3.4). Notably, we

Table 3.4 *Islamist conflicts and the risk of recurrence: exploring alternative pathways via types of termination and peacekeeping. Cox proportional hazards models*

	Recurrence (1)	Recurrence-new (2)
Islamist claim	1.656	1.711
	(0.335)*	(0.412)*
Territory	2.061	0.476
	(0.461)**	(0.130)**
Strong rebels	1.204	1.181
	(0.479)	(0.370)
Oil_{log}	1.022	0.984
	(0.011)*	(0.011)
Youth bulge/adult pop.	1.035	0.986
	(0.020)†	(0.030)
Muslim majority	0.849	0.868
	(0.177)	(0.206)
Peacekeeping presence	0.737	1.576
	(0.117)†	(0.335)*
Ceasefire agreement	1.518	0.926
	(0.533)	(0.467)
Government victory	0.533	0.506
	(0.236)	(0.293)
Rebel victory	0.507	1.419
	(0.343)	(0.701)
Low activity	1.853	1.922
	(0.525)*	(0.637)*
N	6,144	6,144
Subjects	304	304
Failures	149	69

Note: †$p < 0.1$; *$p < 0.05$; **$p < 0.01$. Robust standard errors in parentheses clustered on dyad. Peace agreement is the reference category when evaluating different types of termination.

find no evidence that Islamist conflicts are more likely to recur due to how they have terminated, nor in terms of the guarantees received in the form of peacekeeping troops on the ground.

EXTENDING OUR ANALYSIS

As we move this chapter toward a conclusion, we would like to take the opportunity to reflect on the actuality of our argument. So far, our statistical analysis has, due to data access issues on a few variables, been restricted to the period 1975–2013. In this section, we present some descriptive analyses illustrating that the problem we have focused on in this book is still pertinent even when taking into account developments in recent years. Our aim here is thus not to replicate our previous analyses, but rather to present some general patterns regarding the termination and recurrence of Islamist conflicts when including more recent years.

To shed light on the intractability of Islamist conflicts in recent years, we provide descriptive analyses covering the period from 1975 up to 2023, which we compare with the period previously analyzed, from 1975 up to 2013. This can provide us with insight into the broader patterns of intractability, also covering more recent times. Drawing on the UCDP dyadic dataset version 25.1 (Davies et al. 2025), an updated version of the RELAC dataset (Svensson and Nilsson 2018), and the UCDP conflict termination dataset version 4-2024 (Kreutz 2010), we analyze the patterns regarding termination and recurrence (see Table 3.5). As noted earlier in this chapter, terminations refer to instances where the armed conflict results in fewer than 25 battle-related deaths in a calendar year, focusing on each government–rebel dyad. Hence, some conflicts may persist at a lower level of activity or temporarily cease activity to later resume above this level. As shown in Table 3.5, when focusing on the earlier period, the share of Islamist conflicts that terminated is 80%, which remains the same when including more recent years. Turning to the non-Islamist conflicts, we observe the same pattern. During the earlier period, the share that eventually terminated is 97%, and when considering the extended time period, it remains at 97%. Thus, also for this category, the patterns are stable. Here, it is important to keep in mind that there is right-censoring in our data, and more recent

Table 3.5 *Proportion with terminations and recurrence, Islamist vs. non-Islamist conflicts*

	Termination		Recurrence	
	1975–2013	1975–2023	1975–2013	1975–2023
Islamist conflicts%	80	80	36	31
Non-Islamist conflicts%	97	97	26	28

conflicts may not yet have terminated (but may do so at a later stage). Yet our focus is on the comparison between Islamist and non-Islamist conflicts, and based on this evidence, the patterns of termination suggest that what we observed for earlier periods are as relevant when extending the period to include more recent years.

We now turn to the patterns regarding recurrence. For the government–rebel dyads that have seen a termination for one year or more, we study whether these again become active in terms of reaching 25 battle-related deaths or more (for this analysis, we focus on whether the same conflict dyad becomes active again). For the earlier period, the share of Islamist conflicts that recur is 36%, whereas for the longer time period, the share decreases to 31%. Hence, when considering an extended time period that includes more recent years, Islamist conflicts are about as intractable as before in terms of their recurrence, but we notice a decline. The non-Islamist conflicts see a slight increase, from 26% to 28%. Hence, regarding recurrence, the evidence suggests that Islamist conflicts are somewhat less likely to recur, whereas non-Islamist conflicts are somewhat more likely to recur than before. Overall, though, the patterns are fairly stable, in particular in terms of termination, and Islamist conflicts continue to pose a challenge in terms of their intractability.

An important part of our explanation centers on external support to both the government and the rebel side, and the fact that Islamist conflicts tend to attract military support. As part of our global analysis presented earlier in this chapter, we focused on state

Table 3.6 *Proportion with state troop support to the government or rebel side, Islamist vs. non-Islamist conflicts*

	Government support		Rebel support	
	1975–2013	1975–2024	1975–2013	1975–2024
Islamist conflicts%	34	34	0	1
Non-Islamist conflicts%	11	15	6	6

support to the government side and external support in the form of foreign fighters to the rebel side. Do these patterns remain relevant in more recent years? Data availability problems hinder us from arriving at a definitive answer to that question. While we do not have access to data on the more decentralized support in the form of foreign fighters, we still present here some patterns focusing on state support in the form of foreign state troops on the ground, either on the government or the rebel side, for each conflict dyad (see Table 3.6).

When we study government support for the earlier time period, the share of Islamist conflicts that received military troop support on the government side is 34%, which remains the same when including more recent years. The corresponding figures for non-Islamist conflicts are 11% compared with 15%. Hence, the general trend persists, and if anything, non-Islamist conflicts see a slight increase in state support for the government side. Next, we study troop support by foreign states to the rebel side. We noted earlier that this type of military intervention on the rebel side is a rare phenomenon in Islamist conflicts, and that the type of external support in these conflicts tends to be more decentralized or take other forms than by deploying foreign troops on the ground. Hence, while states also provide support to the rebel side, sometimes as part of regional power struggles, this may also be in the form of financial support, arms transfers, or other forms of military support. Having said this, when focusing on state support to the rebel side in the form of troops on the ground in the Islamist conflicts, there are no such cases for the limited time period, and only 1% for the extended time period. For non-Islamist conflicts, the patterns are also stable; the share is 6% regardless of the time period studied. Thus, when it comes to military support in the form of foreign troop support on the ground, the patterns are very similar. We can, therefore, conclude that overall, the patterns regarding intractability, as well as external support structures, persist when we consider a longer time period.

WHAT DO WE KNOW ABOUT THE GLOBAL PATTERNS OF INTRACTABILITY?

In sum, we find strong support for our theoretical conjectures regarding the global patterns of conflict termination and recurrence. When a conflict is framed in Islamist terms, it is less likely to be terminated and more likely to restart. We find support for our expectations regarding the transnational dimension of these conflicts. Our results show that the degree of internationalization matters – specifically, we find some evidence that the presence of foreign fighters on the rebel side and secondary support on the government side make these conflicts more intractable. In our analysis, we have ruled out some competing explanations for the religious dimension more broadly, and we also nuanced the claim that Islamists are merely the new revolutionaries: While we find some similarities with the leftist movement, our results show that Islamist armed conflicts follow a distinct trajectory in terms of intractability. Our evidence also suggests that it is militant Islamism, not Muslim identity, that is associated with a higher risk of conflict intractability. The analysis presented in this chapter provides a general test and an overview perspective of the global trajectory. However, we need to look more closely at the cases to understand how the theoretical mechanisms we suggested actually work. That is what we turn to next.

4 The Intractability of Islamist Civil Wars

Afghanistan and Mauritania

Studying global patterns, we have shown that Islamist conflicts stand out in two fundamental ways: their intractability and the level of external support. We suggested that these two are connected: The involvement of external actors makes it exceedingly difficult for governments and rebels to correctly judge the other side's strength and resolve, and inherently challenging to credibly communicate information about their own side's strength and resolve. This is not only a matter of external involvement, which is also present in non-Islamist armed conflicts. Instead, Islamist conflicts are driven by a specific type of constellation of external involvement typically associated with Islamist conflicts. This includes government-to-government military support from great powers and a decentralized, dispersed transnational network providing support to Islamist insurgents. This strategic context deepens the structural uncertainties and makes it harder to correctly assess each side's capabilities and resolve, thereby making these conflicts more intractable than others. To explore our explanation in depth, we provide two case illustrations – Afghanistan and Mauritania – which display an intriguing variation regarding their degree of intractability.

In this chapter, we explore whether our explanation can help us understand why the conflict in Afghanistan became so intractable and why it came to an end in 2021. Afghanistan is perhaps one of the Islamist conflicts in which the transnational dimension plays out most starkly. A twenty-year-long American-led international military intervention sought to target and defeat the Taliban for their role in hosting the transnational al-Qaeda network responsible for the 9/11 attacks on America's homeland. It is an important case to study because it helps us understand how the transnational dimension – most notably in terms of support from external actors – can increase uncertainty about capabilities and resolve, thereby enhancing intractability. As part of this chapter, we will contrast this with the case of Mauritania, which has a very different trajectory. We selected these two cases as they had strikingly similar initial developments and conflict characteristics but remarkably different trajectories. In particular, although both Afghanistan and Mauritania have been targets, bases, and territories of recruitment for transnational Islamist armed groups, Mauritania has experienced a surprisingly short-lived Islamist armed conflict; after a brief outbreak, the conflict was contained and terminated in 2011, whereas the conflict in Afghanistan dragged on for many years. We will see how the insulation of Mauritania from the broader regional battle for and against radical Islamist actors helps explain why the conflict ended relatively quickly.

THE ISLAMIST CIVIL WAR IN AFGHANISTAN: INTERNATIONALIZED AND INTRACTABLE

We begin by tracing the roots of the Afghanistan conflict's transnational nature before we explain how this transnational dimension created a strategic setting of uncertainty surrounding capabilities and resolve, which we argue can contribute to a better understanding of the war's intractability. We then explore how the US withdrawal turned the tables and how disengagement from transnational links and networks paved the way for the termination of the conflict in 2021.

The Transnational Nature of the Afghanistan Conflict

The Afghanistan war played a fundamental role in shaping and creating the conditions for the emergence and dispersion of the global movement of armed Islamist actors with transnational aspirations. When the Soviet Union invaded Afghanistan in 1979 in support of the challenged local communist leadership, the main resistance actors were Muslim fighters (Mujahideen), who took up the fight against the foreign occupation force. The Soviet invasion was a breaking point in terms of transnational Islamism. In solidarity with their Afghan brothers, thousands of young Muslim men traveled to the Afghan mountains to join what was seen as a righteous defense struggle against the Soviet invasion. The Mujahideen movement was a network of rebel groups fighting against the occupation, a conflict that pitted the Soviet Union, a secular and explicitly atheistic state, against a number of Islamist rebel groups with diverse leanings and ideological perspectives. The rebels received US support to counter the Soviet Union's expansion and engage it in a costly insurgency. The insurgency also received support from Pakistan and Saudi Arabia (as well as resourceful actors and individuals in the wider Gulf). The war in Afghanistan became the focal point for the emerging transnational armed Islamist movement. It allowed these actors to unite under a common banner against a joint foe: the secular Soviet Union and its invasion of a Muslim country. The Afghanistan campaign provided a basis for transnational mobilization on an unprecedented scale. The anti-Soviet campaign can thus be seen as the birthplace of the global jihadist struggle, as many jihadist fighters from all over the Muslim world fought shoulder to shoulder against a common enemy. Among the fighters taking up jihad was Osama bin Laden, who later came to form the al-Qaeda network. Muslim men (overwhelmingly) traveled to Afghanistan to take up jihad, the violent struggle against perceived enemies of Islam, and to establish an Islamic state governed by Sharia law. A key person in the development of the internationalization of this transnational armed Islamist movement was Abdullah Azzam. A Palestinian ideologue and thinker, Azzam saw the Afghanistan campaign as a chance to create a Sunni counterpart to the 1979 Iranian revolution. He masterminded and set up the organizational infrastructure of the international recruitment campaign, supplying Muslim men to the Afghanistan front. Through the experience of the conflict, the movement of interconnected transnational armed Islamist actors was formed, its ideological dimensions developed, and its tactical and military skills enhanced (Gerges 2009; Hegghammer 2010, 2020; Rashid 2022; Stenersen 2017).

After Soviet forces withdrew at the end of the 1980s, the various Afghan warlords turned on one another. Thus, the end of Soviet occupation did not bring about peace in Afghanistan. Instead, a fierce power struggle between various rebel factions created a chaotic and violent context, marking the period up to 1994 as one of turmoil and civil war. In this era of anarchic turbulence, a highly organized student movement cultivated in neighboring Pakistan established itself with the tacit approval of its government. In 1996, the Taliban movement was able to topple the regime and gain power, which they held on to, implementing a harsh system of governance. Initially, many citizens welcomed the Taliban movement for its efforts to establish order in chaotic Afghanistan. However, this came at a significant cost to religious minorities – predominantly the Shia Hazaras, who faced severe repression – and Afghan women, whose freedoms and human rights were profoundly curtailed (Hamid and Farrall 2015). The largely internationally unrecognized Islamic Emirate of Afghanistan persisted until it collapsed during the American-led invasion in late 2001 (Byman 2019).

Al-Qaeda maintained its presence and close contacts in Afghanistan after the military resistance campaign against the Soviet invasion. Once the Taliban established their emirate, it provided al-Qaeda with a better position and opportunity in Afghanistan. The Taliban and al-Qaeda were fundamentally different – the former was essentially a nationalist movement of mass mobilized madrasa students from Pakistan and the borderlands who aspired to achieve regime change in Afghanistan, whereas the latter was a transnational network consisting of a global Islamic avant-garde focused on revolution in the wider Muslim world, aiming to liberate Muslim lands from foreign occupation and intruders (Sheikh and El-Jaichi 2022, 14). Nevertheless, despite their fundamental differences, the connections between the two organizations were many and multilayered. They included ideological affinity within the broader corpus of jihadist thought and imaginaries that entailed visions of governance defined by Quranic law, an emphasis on what was seen as the religious duty to defend the Muslim faith and peers, and a joint idea of the enemy in the decadent West and its puppet regimes in the Muslim world (Stenersen 2017).

The linkages between the Afghan Taliban and al-Qaeda are intricate and go back decades (Elias 2021; Jones 2008; Rashid 2012). However, they "remain two distinct entities, with different memberships, ideologies and objectives. The interactions and contacts that do exist between the two groups are found in three main forms: personal/individual ties, the commonality of a shared religious belief, and their circumstances (a shared location and enemy)" (Van Linschoten and Kuehn 2012, 327). Transnational ties developed gradually. Social and family ties were cultivated through intermarriages and friendships developed over the years, and they engaged in tactical or strategic collaboration in military affairs. Social and family bonds were also upheld by the cultural code of hospitality, which is fundamental in Pashtun society. Accepting someone as a guest requires that the host also offer protection. Al-Qaeda was received as an honorable guest, and the Taliban felt culturally obligated to protect them (Rashid 2022, 140).[1]

The al-Qaeda movement began targeting the US ("the far enemy") after the US-led intervention during the Kuwait War of 1991, when the American military presence on Saudi Arabia's territory was seen as highly provocative. The US was perceived as the main backer of the allegedly corrupt and illegitimate Saudi government and other Arab allies ("the near enemy"). One of the first major al-Qaeda attacks was the simultaneous bombings of the American embassies in Kenya and Tanzania in 1998 (Gerges 2009; Sheikh and El-Jaichi 2022).

The Taliban movement was founded in the early 1990s in the Pashtun-dominated areas of western Pakistan by the cleric and warlord Mulla Omar. Rooted in the Pashtun ethnic context, the Taliban movement had a basis in the Deobandi religious ideology,

[1] On the *Pashtunwali* code of honor, see also Atran (2010).

emphasizing a strict interpretation of Sharia law as the judicial and constitutional basis for the Afghan emirate to which they aspired. The Taliban started as a religious movement but gradually became more militant. The religious schools in Pakistan – madrasas – were the cradle of the Taliban movement. The movement provided young boys with a social network that included housing, food, and religious training. Pakistan was critical in cultivating and maintaining the Taliban movement (Sheikh 2016).

With the 9/11 attacks on the World Trade Center in New York City and the Pentagon in Washington DC, followed by a failed attempt on the White House, the fight against al-Qaeda became a paramount concern for the US. Identifying Afghanistan as the host of the al-Qaeda network, US President George W. Bush demanded the immediate and unconditional surrender of the top leadership of al-Qaeda, including Osama bin Laden. However, the Taliban was not ready to hand over bin Laden unless the Americans could provide "solid evidence of bin Laden's guilt first" (Radio Free Europe/ Radio Liberty 2001; Sheikh et al. 2026). Instead, the Taliban proposed, for instance, to examine the evidence against bin Laden in a Muslim court inside Afghanistan, which the Americans deemed unacceptable (The Guardian 2021). Following 9/11, a US-led intervention targeted the al-Qaeda sanctuary in Afghanistan. The invasion, launched after the Taliban refused to hand over bin Laden unconditionally, saw America partnering with Afghan warlords who had been defeated or forced to retreat by the Taliban. Allied with local anti-Taliban forces, including the Northern Alliance, the US-led intervention ousted the Taliban from power in Kabul in 2001. After being nearly defeated as a military force, the Taliban remobilized from bases in the Pashtun heartland and their more restricted sanctuaries in Pakistan with a new focus: fighting the American-led intervention in Afghanistan (Rashid 2022; Sheikh et al. 2026). Thus, the war in Afghanistan was not only transnationalized on the rebel side but, from 2002 onward, also on the government side, through the American-led intervention.

How the Transnational Nature of the Afghanistan Conflict Created Intractability

Attempts to end the conflict were built on the premise that the Taliban would sever ties with the transnational al-Qaeda network. The intransigence of transnational actors obstructed attempts to establish dialogue: "The extensive Taliban links with international jihadi allies impinge on strategic decision-making because these groups are inimically opposed to any settlement in Afghanistan short of a Taliban victory" (Farrell and Semple 2015, 99).

It was difficult for non-Taliban actors in Afghanistan to ascertain whether a link between the Taliban and al-Qaeda existed, as well as the depth and degree of any connection. Even after the 2020 Doha agreement had been reached, differing perspectives persisted. For example, a UN report from May 2020 revealed that the Taliban had not yet cut ties with al-Qaeda and that they were in contact with al-Qaeda during the negotiations:

> Relations between the Taliban, especially the Haqqani Network ..., and Al-Qaida remain close, based on friendship, a history of shared struggle, ideological sympathy and intermarriage. The Taliban regularly consulted with Al-Qaida during negotiations with the United States and offered guarantees that it would honour their historical ties. Al-Qaida has reacted positively to the agreement, with statements from its acolytes celebrating it as a victory for the Taliban's cause and thus for global militancy. (United Nations Security Council 2020, 3)

As part of the 2020 Doha agreement, the Taliban agreed "not to allow al-Qaeda or any other extremist group to operate in areas under their control." At the same time, "they do not appear to have publicly rejected al-Qaeda either" (El-Bay 2021). Thus, it remained difficult to ascertain the extent to which the Taliban upheld secret ties – the potential for transnational ties continued to create uncertainty.

Intractability and the Transnational Dimension

We have argued that the transnational dimension in the form of external interventions and involvement creates strategic uncertainty in Islamist armed conflicts, making it more difficult to end such conflicts. This perspective can help us understand the Afghanistan war – an intractable conflict drawn out over decades. Why did military encounters not reveal sufficient information about the parties' capabilities and resolve to find a mutually acceptable bargain short of continued destructive conflict? Our analysis suggests that the military intervention on the side of the government, along with the connection between the rebels and al-Qaeda, made it difficult for the Kabul government and the Taliban movement to accurately assess one another's capabilities and resolve. In particular, there was strategic uncertainty about the fighting spirit and capacity of the American protégé – the government in Kabul. The Afghan government was propped up by a multilateral government-to-government support structure.

The sheer size of the military and economic investment in Afghanistan by the US and its Western allies created an incentive structure for corruption. Afghan army figures were routinely inflated to generate more financial support and influence. "Ghost soldiers," who existed only on paper, helped secure funding for higher-ups in the military hierarchy, and there were reports of low government morale (BBC 2021; Rasmussen 2016). The Afghan state army had been receiving substantial support from the US and its allies, and training programs for Afghan soldiers had been in place for many years (Wintour 2021). Yet genuine public support for the government was obscured under the blanket of Western intervention.

The extent of the information failure – the discrepancy between expectations and their true resolve and capabilities – became apparent when the US withdrew from Afghanistan in August 2021. While the government in Kabul might have expected the Taliban forces to be strengthened by the American withdrawal (as well as that of other countries that had fought alongside the US), the rapid speed of the takeover was probably unforeseen. Even the US, with its world-leading intelligence resources, struggled to accurately estimate the strength of the Taliban, particularly in failing to appreciate the weaknesses and lack of fighting spirit within the Afghan military. President Joe Biden asserted that a military takeover by the Taliban was avoidable, stating that "the Afghan troops have 300,000 well-equipped [soldiers] and an air force against something like 75,000 Taliban," and later claimed that "the Taliban overrunning everything and owning the whole country is highly unlikely" (Biden 2021).

When the blanket of support was lifted, it became apparent just how low the degree of interest was among the Afghan military in fighting for its government. According to an American official evaluation report, the "single most important factor" in the collapse of the Afghan military forces "was the U.S. decision to withdraw military forces and contractors from Afghanistan" (SIGAR 2022). The American withdrawal undermined the morale of the Afghan soldiers, who could no longer rely on American airstrikes that had empowered the Afghan forces. Moreover, the Afghan soldiers could no longer count on the Americans to ensure that the Afghan government would pay out salaries to its military personnel (SIGAR 2022). While the Taliban movement communicated over and over again that the government lacked legitimacy and would not be able to stand on its own feet once the American intervention was over, such messages were likely not deemed credible by the government, the Americans, and their Western partners because the Taliban had strategic reasons to pursue precisely this messaging. Even in the wake of the American withdrawal, President Ashraf Ghani communicated that the withdrawal would strengthen, not weaken, the Afghan force and portrayed the withdrawal as something happening on his initiative (Adili 2021).

De-transnationalization and Conflict Termination

Once the conflict de-transnationalized, it ended quickly. The Taliban officially broke its ties with the al-Qaeda movement through the

2020 agreement, in terms of its commitment to not allow al-Qaeda to use Afghanistan to launch attacks. Still, as we discuss later, the break was not entirely clear-cut. The US withdrew in 2021, and the government of Afghanistan was left alone to fight the Taliban forces. On the verge of the American withdrawal, the Afghan government's military withered and collapsed. The Afghan case is illustrative of an information failure, with parties' expectations not converging, upheld over time due to ambivalence regarding the future presence of external actors (al-Qaeda on the rebel side and the US on the government side). Uncertainties around the ties and how they would form in the future were at the core of the conflict, and they help explain why the parties could not manage to escape their intractable strife. The case of Afghanistan also demonstrates how disengagement by the external actors preceded and led to the war's end: In the Doha agreement, the parties agreed to a US withdrawal, and the Taliban committed to deny al-Qaeda the use of its soil for military attacks. The disassociation between al-Qaeda and the Taliban, as well as between the government of Afghanistan and the US, led the parties to reveal their military capacities and their will to continue fighting, resulting in a swift termination of the conflict.

The de-transnationalization processes were not due to the primary parties symmetrically disengaging from their foreign patrons. Instead, the shift was brought about through an accommodation between one of the primary parties (the Taliban) and one of the secondary actors (al-Qaeda). On February 29, 2020, the Taliban signed the Doha agreement with the US to start peace talks between the Taliban and the Afghan government (for a critical assessment of this agreement, see Maley and Jamal 2022; see also Semple, Raphel, and Rasıkh 2021). This agreement stipulated that the US and its allies would withdraw from Afghan soil and that the Taliban would "not allow any of its members, other individuals or groups, including al-Qa'ida, to use the soil of Afghanistan to threaten the security of the United States and its allies" (The Doha Agreement 2020, III). While the US sought to achieve a clear break between the Taliban and al-Qaeda, the agreement was less clear-cut. In the agreement, the Taliban committed themselves to not allowing al-Qaeda to use Afghanistan as a basis for launching operations or attacks against the US and the rest of the world. However, the Taliban did not commit to a total break in all types of contact with the al-Qaeda network.

The disassociation between al-Qaeda and the Taliban, in conjunction with the American commitment to withdrawal, made the peace process of 2020–2021 – the Doha rounds – possible. Yet the peace process in Doha made no significant gains beyond addressing some procedural issues. While the split between the Taliban and al-Qaeda was not definitive, it served as a prerequisite for progress in peace talks. It was a requirement of the government's leading external supporter, the US, and enabled the US to enter into talks with the Taliban and commit to withdrawing from Afghanistan. De-transnationalization emerged as an outcome of the process and was a key condition for the deal.

The US withdrawal was the key reason for the termination of the civil war in Afghanistan in 2021. There are several reasons why the US decided to withdraw, and it goes beyond the scope of this book to seek to explain that decision. Yet the shift in priorities, with an emphasis on defeating the even more radical IS, which was also fighting the Taliban (Bunzel 2021), opened up space for reconsideration in the US–Taliban relationship, following the classical realist logic that my enemy's enemy is my friend. The US withdrawal from Afghanistan was also partly driven by American domestic concerns about continuous, costly American engagement. War weariness was a factor behind the decisions of both Trump and Biden to withdraw. The plans to exit Afghanistan were not new; already under President Barack Obama, plans had been made for American disengagement (Gardner 2009). While Obama tried to create a better position for an eventual withdrawal through the so-called Surge, a military offensive against the Taliban, it did not succeed in pacifying the insurgents. Public opinion is also part of the explanation behind the American withdrawal, yet it is insufficient. The American intervention was growing unpopular, and still, the US stayed in Afghanistan. It was only after the Taliban severed its ties with al-Qaeda in terms of its commitment not to allow al-Qaeda to operate from Afghanistan that the US decided to withdraw. While the US had tried to achieve this under three presidencies (Obama, Trump, and Biden) (Sheikh et al. 2026, 6),[2] the withdrawal did not take place until an agreement was reached between the Taliban and al-Qaeda, where the latter was restricted from using Afghanistan as a base for attacks on the US and its allies. Again, the transnational dimension is central to understanding the termination of the conflict.

With the US withdrawal and cessation of government support, the conflict was isolated from the Global War on Terror. The final decision to withdraw was made by President Trump in 2020 (Shane 2022), and as mentioned the key factor behind the US withdrawal was the break with al-Qaeda. Secretary of State Mike Pompeo stated that the Taliban, "for the first time, have announced that they are prepared to break with their historic ally, al-Qaida, who they've worked with to much the detriment of the United States of America. You can see; go read the document. The Taliban have now made the break" (CBS News 2020). The decision to withdraw was later confirmed and re-specified by President Biden in April 2021 (Ryan and DeYoung 2021; The White House 2023). Both the Taliban and the US had strong preferences for an American withdrawal, but for different reasons. Notably, de-transnationalization on the rebel and government sides was a mutual and negotiated process: The al-Qaeda–Taliban split would not have happened if the US had not committed to withdrawing, and vice versa.

Was strategic uncertainty the driving force in the dynamic of the intractability of the Afghanistan war? For example, if there had been little ambiguity regarding Western powers, would that have led the Taliban to stop fighting? It is, admittedly, inherently difficult to

[2] For background on the history of the peace efforts, see, for example, Sheikh and Khan (2019) and Suhrke, Harpviken, and Strand (2002).

provide evidence that uncertainty (of resolve and capability) is the key causal mechanism at play in this case. The two large unknowns that permeated the conflict were the nature of the al-Qaeda–Taliban relationship and the staying power of the Western backers, primarily the US. The uncertainty regarding the al-Qaeda–Taliban relationship was there from the outset. There were "significant knowledge deficits" regarding the strength and organization of al-Qaeda among the key American decision-makers, which influenced the decision to go to war (Sheikh et al. 2026). The uncertainty about whether the Taliban was a truly nationally rooted movement or more of a branch of the transnational network of armed Islamist groups was at the core of this. The ambiguity of Western support for the Afghan government created different expectations of the outcome of the war in Afghanistan. The Taliban continued to fight, presumably because they expected that Western support would be withdrawn and weaken the regime to such an extent that it would collapse. The government of Afghanistan, on its part, continued to fight, likely expecting the US to maintain its support. When the situation was clarified, with the different sorts of de-linking on both sides, the conflict was promptly brought to an end. The Afghanistan case thus illustrates that it is more likely that the parties' expectations will converge if both sides can ascertain the impact of external factors, such as the size, type, and duration of outside support. A de-transnationalization of the conflict makes such convergence more likely to occur.

The nature of the American disengagement shaped the *type* of conflict termination that took form. The Afghan war ended, not through a negotiated settlement, but through rebel victory. The Doha agreement was a deal made over the heads of the Afghan government, the US ally. Sidelining its allied partner, the US left one of the key stakeholders out of the deal-making process, with severe consequences. The Doha agreement was signed on February 29, 2020, and the parties agreed that intra-Afghan negotiations would be initiated within a few weeks and no later than March 10. But the Taliban escalated their demands, following disagreements on prisoner exchange, and did not meet the deadline. The US, however, went ahead with its plans for disengagement (Sheikh et al. 2026). Thus, while the Doha agreement stipulated intra-Afghan negotiations toward a power-sharing arrangement between the government and the Taliban, it did not provide guarantees or mechanisms to ensure that the parties would adhere to their commitments. And when the Taliban evidently did not follow through on this part of the agreement, they could do so without the agreement being jeopardized.

At the time of writing, Afghanistan is anything but a prosperous and free society. After their joint enemy – the government of Afghanistan – was defeated, the IS-K (Islamic State – the Khorasan province) continued their fight against the Taliban, the new government of Afghanistan (as mentioned earlier, one of the reasons the US sought to ease the relationship with the Taliban was their enmity with the IS), implying that Afghanistan was still in conflict, albeit at a substantially lower level. Importantly, once the Taliban took power, the situation for women in Afghanistan worsened considerably; they were marginalized from political life, denied access to education, and restricted in their movement. Hence, while the conflict in Afghanistan has ended, it is crucial to keep in mind that violence and various forms of transgression have continued, with some groups suffering the consequences more than others (we will return to this issue as part of the concluding chapter). Having shown how transnational support influenced the dynamics of intractability and termination in the Afghanistan case, we now turn to the case of Mauritania, which, despite some similarities in terms of challenges by Islamist groups, experienced a very different trajectory.

THE ISLAMIST CIVIL WAR IN MAURITANIA: INSULATED AND BRIEF

Most of the countries in the Sahel region of West Africa were hit hard by the regionally interconnected Islamist armed conflicts of the 2010s and onward. One country, however, stands out. Mauritania was embroiled in an Islamist armed conflict, with the al-Qaeda branch spreading its influence throughout the region. However, the country managed to terminate the conflict in 2011. The lack of Islamist violence in Mauritania is a "remarkable turnaround, given the spate of violence that shook the country from 2005 to 2011" (Wehrey 2019, 10). Whereas there are many particularities with the case of Mauritania, making it difficult to generalize to other Islamist civil wars (Oxford Analytica 2023), it is noteworthy as it illustrates how the conflict was disentangled from the broader international struggle and thereby could be brought to an end. Mauritania has been identified as a particularly interesting case in this regard, especially when compared with the fate of neighboring countries: "Mauritania managed to escape the fate of Mali following the collapse of 2012, where irredentism, armed jihadism, and lingering praetorianism combined to all but destroy a once-thriving democracy ... sparing Mauritania from any serious terrorist attack after 2011" (N'Diaye 2021, 16). Thus, Mauritania has been identified as a case "of more limited jihadist mobilization than one might expect amid the wider regional turmoil" (Thurston 2020, 23). When the US State Department's Under Secretary for Political Affairs, Victoria Nuland, visited Mauritania in 2022, she called it an "island of stability in a very, very rough neighborhood" (AFP 2022).

Compared with Afghanistan, Mauritania is on the other end of the spectrum. The civil war between Islamist actors and the government was relatively brief. According to the UCDP, AQIM made their first statements regarding the conflict following a coup in 2008, where they proclaimed their goal to overthrow the new military regime, but the conflict did not cross the threshold of 25 battle-related deaths until 2010 (UCDP 2024). Yet, since 2011, Mauritania has managed to avoid an increase in attacks by Islamist armed actors (Kone 2019). After the conflict was terminated, it did not recur. In this sense, Mauritania is not representative of the general trajectory of Islamist conflict when it comes to conflict termination: "Mauritania is a rare bright spot amid regional tumult"

(Boukhars 2016, 1). How did the Islamist civil war in Mauritania avoid the intractability seen in many other Islamist civil wars?

Attempts at Transnationalization

Mauritania was identified early on as a potential country for expanding the transnational jihad. When AQIM sought to establish itself in the Sahel region, its strategy was to develop local cells of armed Islamist fighters. One country where they planned to do so was Mauritania, which was described as AQIM's "first target" (Ibrahim 2021), drawing on militants trained in AQIM's camps in northern Mali. The group originally started as a breakaway faction of Groupe Islamique Armé (Armed Islamic Group, GIA), which fought in the Algerian civil war. For many years, it was known as the Salafist Group for Preaching and Combat (GSPC), and only later was it rebranded as AQIM (Boukhars 2020; UCDP 2024). When violence by Islamist armed actors initially occurred in Mauritania in June 2005, it was the group GSPC that engaged in the violence, which resulted in the deaths of 15 government soldiers and nine of the attackers (Kone 2019; Wehrey and Boukhars 2019). As highlighted by Wehrey and Boukhars (2019, 29) "over the next six years, Mauritania would be rattled by fourteen attacks on its soil, conducted by Mauritanian GSPC and AQIM cells, operating out of northern Mali".

Why was Mauritania selected as a potential area for transnational Islamist armed actors to gain a foothold in the Sahel? Several factors contributed to Mauritania being perceived as a logical first target for Islamist militants seeking to broaden their regional base from Algeria. Traditionally, Mauritania is a country known for its austere religious tradition. The madrasas had a major influence, particularly in educating children from the lowest-income families in Mauritania (Boukhars 2016, 10). While the rest of the region is shaped by the French-type secular *laïc* model, Mauritania is the only country in West Africa where Islam is the state religion (Thurston 2021). In a country traditionally divided between sub-Saharan Africans and Arab-descended Moors, Islam served as a unifying identity across racial divides (Elischer 2019, 209). There has been significant Salafi political influence in Mauritania (Elischer 2019), which, from the perspective of the Islamist armed actors, could be seen as fertile ground for their movement. The prevalent attitudes toward militant Islamist worldviews in Mauritania were not as negative as in other Muslim countries. For example, Mauritania stands out compared with a range of other Muslim countries in popular attitudes toward IS. In Mauritania, only 62% of the population was very hostile toward IS, whereas the corresponding figures in Tunisia, Iraq, and Lebanon were above 90%. In terms of self-reported positive attitudes toward IS, Mauritania showed the highest share (20%) in comparison with a set of other Middle East and North Africa (MENA) countries (Lia 2016, 77), indicating that at least part of the population was receptive to radical Islamist ideologies in support of armed Islamist actors. This ideological context was something that Islamist armed actors seeking to mobilize against the government could capitalize on: "Ideologically ... militant jihadism has drawn on long-standing Islamic traditions in the country" (Wehrey 2019, 3).

Moreover, individual Mauritanians had been part of the movement of transnational Islamist armed actors; for example, groups such as AQIM have included Mauritanians in their ranks (Bøås 2019). The combination of traditional religious austerity and economic underdevelopment may have contributed to many Mauritanians feeling called to travel abroad to take up jihad against foreign powers, starting with the campaign in Afghanistan. According to Boukhars (2016, 1), "no other country in the Sahel and Sahara region produces as many jihadist ideologues and high-ranking terrorist operatives as Mauritania does," as seen in relation to their population size. This means that Mauritania was an ideological environment not entirely alien to the message of militant Islamists. Additionally, there were individuals and organizational networks that could be used to broaden the battlefield for armed Islamist groups. Therefore, it is no surprise that "Mauritania was long considered a natural candidate for terrorist recruitment and destabilization" and that the country "seemed primed for destabilization by al-Qaeda in the Islamic Maghreb" (Boukhars 2016, 11). American military officials even warned that the "largely ungoverned swath of territory stretching from the Horn of Africa to the Western Sahara's Atlantic coast," which includes Mauritania, could be the "new Afghanistan, with well-financed bands of Islamic militants recruiting, training, and arming themselves" (Smith 2004).

When AQIM launched a front in Mauritania, the Mauritanian regime under the leadership of Ould Taya initially sought to establish intergovernmental collaboration as a way to fight the Islamist insurgency. This was seen as a strategic move, not only in relation to the threat emerging from the Islamist armed actors but also as a way to galvanize external Western support: "Ould Taya had leveraged the early War on Terror to improve relations with the United States in the early 2000s" (Thurston 2020, 286). The government, in collaboration with the US, used military measures in its response to the establishment of Islamist armed actors and joined the Pan-Sahel Initiative (PSI) (Jourde 2007). Like many other countries, the Ould Taya regime of Mauritania framed the arrests and clampdown on armed Islamists and Islamists more generally as part of a larger global battle not restricted to Mauritania. This was done to gain a favorable relationship with the US, despite Mauritania's lack of democracy (Jourde 2007). While Ould Taya, initially, during his regime, sought to co-opt radical Islamist groups, he later turned against them (Elischer 2019).

A Move toward Defense Containment

After a series of military coups and turbulence, Mohamed Ould Abdel Aziz seized power in 2009. The Aziz regime implemented a markedly different policy toward the threat of mobilization by armed Islamist actors. Following criticism from the opposition and religious authorities of how Mauritania facilitated the American War on Terror, the president's legitimacy was questioned, and he had an interest in trying to seek national reconciliation and improve his reputation among the religious community (Bouhlel 2013). This evolving Mauritanian strategy had several building blocks. While the Mauritanian government's approach included soft measures such as dialogue and reintegration, it also "implemented aggressive counterterrorism approaches" (Boukhars 2016, 11). From 2008 to 2018, the Mauritanian military's budget was also increased significantly – during this period, the budget quadrupled in size. It was also geared toward "structural reforms and the acquisition of equipment appropriate to their needs" (Boukhars 2020). Notably, the policy was predominantly domestically based and focused on counterterrorism campaigns. Mauritania did *not* join the regional operational Serval. As noted by Thurston (2020, 266), "in 2013, Mauritania was a notable exception among Sahelian countries when its government declined to send soldiers to Mali amid France's counter-jihadist Operation Serval". Instead, Mauritania fortified its borders and tightened border control (Wehrey 2019). While the Mauritanian government had previously targeted AQIM in neighboring Mali in 2010 and 2011, it came to pursue "a policy of defensive containment" by focusing on fortifying its border with Mali (Wehrey 2019, 11). As emphasized by Boukhars (2016, 13), the "Mauritanian government also reinforced its presence in the hinterlands by building its capacity to control border crossing routes and their interconnections, with help from the United States and the European Union." With Western support, measures to patrol the borderlands helped insulate Mauritania from the broader regional turmoil. This hindered the armed Islamist rebels' ability to receive transnational support. According to Thurston, the Mauritanian case shows how Sahelian states can reap benefits when they resist collaboration with external military forces (2018, 14).

Even more critical was that Mauritania never faced a military intervention on its soil. Foreign military troops were notably absent from Mauritanian territory. Even though the al-Qaeda network was seen as establishing a new front in the country, there was no direct external military intervention. The Mauritanian military did receive military support, but without foreign involvement on the ground. Thurston (2020, 315) concludes: "Where governments achieved anything approaching a resolution of their domestic jihadist challenges (Algeria and Mauritania), they did so without a heavy presence of foreign combat troops".

This threefold strategy of refraining from military interventions in neighboring countries, fortifying the borderlands to hinder transnational armed Islamist groups' mobilization attempts in Mauritania, and not inviting a foreign military intervention meant that the conflict with AQIM was contained. AQIM engaged in several failed attacks that triggered severe pushback from the Mauritanian government, and the Mauritanian movement faced another blow when regional leader Ould Sidi Aly was killed (UCDP 2024). The conflict with AQIM thus faded away relatively soon after its eruption: "Mauritania experienced significant jihadist attacks between 2005 and 2011 as well as some jihadist recruitment for actions at home and abroad. Yet since 2011, jihadist violence in Mauritania has almost completely fallen off" (Thurston 2020, 25). While AQIM has since been active in countries such as Mali and Algeria, the AQIM-related conflict in Mauritania has subsided.

The Mauritanian government's approach also came with other essential elements, such as dialogue and reintegration.[3] It legalized the Islamist party, allowing Islamists to legally pursue their political aspirations. The government provided some political space for unarmed Islamist actors and engaged in dialogue with imprisoned leaders and followers of the jihadist cause. Building on and empowering the mainstream religious establishment was a helpful governmental strategy in the case of Mauritania: "Promoting the arguments and perspectives of mainstream Sufism and Salafism, by contrast, has subsequently proven to be a highly effective strategy for isolating jihadists in Mauritania" (Ibrahim 2017, 13). Dialogue did play a role, albeit on the level of individual deradicalization rather than

[3] This strategy of largely abstaining from engaging in military attacks outside of its border, while also engaging in dialogue and providing amnesty to some elements, has also been pursued by Algeria (Boukhars 2020).

on a larger political level in terms of political settlements. The key to the government-sponsored dialogue in 2010 with Salafi prisoners was the inclusion of local scholars who had credibility among the armed Islamist actors (Ghettas 2014). This has been described as "the co-option of outspoken Salafi clerics with ties to the jihadists" (Wehrey 2019, 1). These dialogues were necessary to provide alternative pathways for individual fighters, serving as an inducement strategy against further recruitment: "Mauritania's prison dialogues allowed some hardliners back into society, with what seems to be a low rate of recidivism and a damper on overall recruitment" (Thurston 2020, 315). Thus, theological debates and active engagement with the armed Islamist actors also played a role in staving off the insurgency. It was a way of "dealing with this particular form of violence by 'endogenous' means" (Bouhlel 2013, 122). Moreover, the Mauritanian government has "created space for a number of outspoken clerics to continue speaking and preaching, provided they do not cross certain red lines of calling for violence against the government" (Wehrey and Boukhars 2019, 35). According to Wehrey and Boukhars (2019), this approach seems to have allowed for some discord, as long as it has been acceptable to the Mauritanian government.

This strategy of partial political openness, within the constraints of an overall authoritarian political structure, entailed accepting Islamist parties, engaging in dialogue, and allowing some freedom of speech, even to illiberal Islamist actors. The increasing political space allowed grievances to be aired against the possibility of Mauritania joining the Serval interregional operation.

It should be acknowledged that other factors may have also played a role in the termination of the Islamist civil war in Mauritania. The fact that Mauritania, since 2011, has only experienced low levels of Islamist conflicts can partly be explained by the fact that some Islamists (especially the most well-equipped and qualified) fled to neighboring countries' jihadist battlefields. The departure of the radicals to fight in other countries decreased pressure inside Mauritania (N'Diaye 2021). However, it is, from our perspective, not a convincing explanation for the lack of intractability in the Mauritanian civil war. Easing domestic pressure by exporting foreign fighters has backfired historically, as when regimes in MENA allowed volunteers to travel to Afghanistan to take up jihad and later received hardened returnees who took up arms against their regimes. In Mauritania, however, despite having trained and experienced fighters, which could be a pool for recruitment in a local Islamist insurgency, the Islamist civil war was terminated relatively quickly and has so far not recurred. Moreover, it is suggested that there was a tactical agreement between the government and the Islamist armed actors, including economic compensation for leaving Mauritania alone – a rumored secret deal between Mauritania and al-Qaeda (Kone 2019; Wehrey and Boukhars 2019, 34). The country's geographical location on the periphery and absence of previous insurgencies and rebel structures to tap into and build on (in contrast to the case of Mali) are also potential explanations for the termination of this civil war (Oxford Analytica 2023). Having said this, there is much to suggest that our argument has some bearing in this case. While the transnational Islamist dimension did feature in the Mauritanian civil war, several aspects contributed to preventing the conflict from being drawn into a global struggle. The absence of external interventions in Mauritania, a deliberate government decision to not join regional forces, and a border fortification strategy to prevent foreign fighters from entering Mauritania all played a role in insulating and terminating the conflict.

COMPARING VARIATIONS IN THE INTRACTABILITY OF ISLAMIST CIVIL WARS

While many factors differentiate Afghanistan and Mauritania, the cases exhibit some structural similarities that allow us to better understand the dynamics of intractability. We saw in the cases of Afghanistan and Mauritania that Islamist civil wars represent a blend of local grievances and transnational mobilization. In both cases, transnational networks tried to establish footholds, exploit tensions, and mobilize existing grievances. However, the trajectories of these conflicts are markedly different.

There are alternative explanations for the intractability of Islamist armed conflicts that rival the reason we propose here. However, these alternatives encounter difficulties in accounting for the trajectories of the civil wars in Afghanistan and Mauritania. In contrast to the essentialist perspective, which tends to emphasize the religious extremist nature of the insurgents as the key obstacle to conflict termination, we see that religious ideology plays a vital role in both cases. Still, Mauritania escaped the specter of almost endless civil war. Moreover, an essentialist explanation focusing on religious extremism cannot explain the variation over time.

The termination of the conflict was not brought about by decreasing the role of Islam and Islamism in Mauritania; quite the contrary, there was *increasing* room for religious actors. Similarly, in Afghanistan, when the war eventually ended, it was not due to a shift in the degree of religious radicalization of the Taliban but to a two-sided decoupling of external actors: a decoupling – or at least a weakening of the ties – of the Taliban movement from the transnational Islamist armed network, along with a decoupling of the main state sponsor, the US, from the Afghan government.

As we discussed earlier in the book, arguments focusing on foreign fighters on the rebel side (e.g., Toft and Zhukov 2015) have some bearing here – one of the reasons why Mauritania was able to end its civil war is that the government became better at policing its borders against the flow of regional fighters seeking to participate in Islamist civil wars – but this explanation does not give the complete picture: It misses out on the government side of the equation. As we have shown in this chapter, the government in Mauritania went to great lengths to contain the conflict and prevent it from becoming entangled with global battles.

The Afghan war is a brutal illustration of how external interventions can serve to enhance the intractability of Islamist civil wars. As shown in the case of Afghanistan, the external involvement and ties to external actors on both sides contributed to enhancing uncertainty about capabilities and resolve. In fact, there was uncertainty about the fighting spirit of the government forces until close to the termination of the war, when the Taliban came to power. Afghanistan is typical in the sense that it follows the general pathway of Islamist civil wars being more internationalized and intractable than other types of conflicts.

Mauritania shows an alternative route. We conclude that the key to the country's ability to terminate its Islamist civil war lies in its strategy of localization – its insulation from the transnational dimension – thereby helping to reduce uncertainty regarding capabilities and resolve. By deciding not to engage in regional military intervention and refusing military intervention on its soil, Mauritania's government ensured the domestic conflict was not drawn into a global or regional conflict. By increasing the protection of its borders, it furthermore decreased the chances for the networks of transnational Islamist armed actors to exploit local grievances and capitalize on tension in the country. Once the conflict was insulated, some conflict resolution methods proved effective in ending it: dialogue and (at least some degree of) political openness. It is not, however, a "success story" in every regard: As we will discuss in the concluding chapter, following the termination of war both Afghanistan and Mauritania have seen either a deterioration of gender rights or a continuance of an already difficult situation, with severe restrictions on women's rights and freedoms. Still, the case of Mauritania demonstrates that the typical pathway of Islamist civil wars – being transnationalized on both the government and rebel sides – is not necessarily the only way these conflicts can unfold. Mauritania is an exception to this general trend, as the conflict was largely contained locally and the civil war was able to come to an end. While this is no guarantee of future stability in Mauritania (Boukhars 2020; Wehrey and Boukhars 2019), the case does show that conflicts that are insulated from the regional or global struggle can follow a different trajectory.

5 Global Evidence of Conflict Resolution

Negotiations and Agreements

Islamist civil wars are generally less likely to end and more likely to recur than other conflicts, as shown in the earlier chapters of this book. Nonetheless, peace attempts also occur in Islamist civil wars. For example, on several occasions in Thailand's Patani conflict, the warring parties engaged in peace talks aimed at ending the intractable conflict. In February 2024, in Kuala Lumpur, Malaysia, representatives of the Islamist militant group Barisan Revolusi Nasional (BRN) sat down with representatives of the government of Thailand. The parties committed to an inclusive peace process aimed at ending the conflict (Reuters 2024). To what extent are conflict resolution efforts used in the context of Islamist armed conflicts? While the previous chapters focused on ending violence, including civil wars that ended through victory, we now turn to evaluate our hypotheses that focus on conflict resolution. Conflict resolution is the process of finding a solution to the issue at stake, de-escalating violent behavior, and reconciling belligerent attitudes through negotiation, often with the aim of resolving the conflict. Negotiation is one of the central steps during a conflict resolution process, which may or may not result in some form of peace agreement. In this chapter, we therefore explore the trajectories and outcomes of negotiations in Islamist armed conflicts. We examine the occurrence of negotiations and peace agreements in Islamist armed conflicts and compare them with other armed conflicts.

We rely on new data on negotiations in civil wars worldwide from 1989 to 2018 to explore the differences between Islamist civil wars and other civil wars. We also leverage peace agreement data from the UCDP to similarly examine if there are any differences between Islamist civil wars and other types of conflicts. Our argument leads us to expect a general trajectory of intractability, not only in terms of termination and recurrence, as we have demonstrated so far, but also in terms of negotiations and peace accords. As part of Chapter 2, we theorized that Islamist civil wars should be less likely to see negotiations, as well as peace accords (our fourth and fifth hypotheses), and that those fought over transnational Islamist claims should be particularly resistant to negotiations and peace accords (our sixth and seventh hypotheses).

We find support for our theoretical conjectures regarding negotiations, but not conclusive support concerning peace accords: Our findings show that Islamist civil wars tend to resist negotiations compared with other civil wars, but we do not find any robust evidence when studying peace accords. To further probe the testable implications of our argument, we use the RELAC data on Islamist claims to explore the transnational dimension in more depth. Not all Islamist civil wars are the same; they vary, for example, in terms of their degree of transnationalization. The Islamist group BRN in Thailand is locally anchored and oriented, and it has not relied on foreign fighters; the Thai state has been careful not to internationalize the conflict. For instance, it has resisted tying its military campaign to the larger global contestation between different governments and militant Islamist groups.

In this chapter, we not only compare Islamist civil wars with other conflicts but also focus on Islamist conflicts to explore whether there are any differences when comparing transnationalized Islamist civil wars with other types of Islamist civil wars. We argue that the intractability of Islamist civil wars is driven by their transnationalization. Therefore, those Islamist conflicts that appeal to a transnational global agenda are generally expected to be less open to negotiations and peace agreements. We study the extent to which conflict resolution efforts are more commonly used in Islamist civil wars that are insulated and decoupled from the global battle between transnational Islamist armed actors and interconnected governments. We also seek to assess whether our argument, focusing on the transnational element of Islamist conflicts, is better than rival explanations. In contrast to the instrumentalist perspective, we demonstrate that transnational Islamist conflicts exhibit a distinct empirical trajectory in terms of conflict resolution. Indeed, this category of conflicts does stand out in comparison with others. We further demonstrate that the propensity for negotiations and agreements can be best explained not by the terrorist character of rebel groups, religious identity differences, or religious aspirations more broadly, which an essentialist perspective would suggest, but by the transnational dimension.

NEGOTIATIONS AND AGREEMENTS

Let us begin by examining the patterns of negotiations regarding Islamist civil wars compared with other conflicts. Due to the strategic context in which Islamist conflicts are embedded, we expect governments and rebel groups in Islamist conflicts to be less receptive to negotiations than those in other conflicts. When exploring negotiations, we need a more detailed level of analysis to detect variations in the propensity to engage in talks. Therefore, we use NoWA data to study the patterns systematically and with a high degree of precision (Nilsson et al. 2024). Negotiations are conceptualized as talks about one or more central issues between representatives of the main warring parties. The meetings must be made public and occur in the same location. Thus, we do not include negotiations that remain secret or take the form of shuttle diplomacy in different locations. We focus on all intrastate armed conflicts that result in 25 battle-related deaths in a year between the government and one or more rebel groups, as defined by the UCDP (Harbom, Melander, and Wallensteen 2008; Pettersson, Högbladh, and Öberg 2019). In the NoWA dataset, each government–rebel dyad is included from its onset and is followed up to 24 months after violence has ceased. In this way, we also capture negotiations that occur after ceasefires. The NoWA dataset covers peacemaking efforts in intrastate armed conflicts between a government and rebel group on a monthly basis from 1989 to 2018, resulting in a sample of more than 23,000 government–rebel dyad months. The data collection is primarily based on news sources and follows procedures similar to those employed by the UCDP.[1]

[1] It should be noted that the time period is not the same here as in Chapter 3, due to data availability.

Regarding peace agreements, we draw on data from the UCDP peace agreement dataset (Högbladh 2020; Pettersson, Högbladh, and Öberg 2019). We focus on all peace agreements that address the incompatibility in some way, either partially or by providing a comprehensive settlement that fully addresses the incompatibility.

Our theoretical argument has implications for what we can expect regarding the conflict resolution process. Islamist civil wars are embedded in a particular strategic environment with extensive networks of support on both sides, which can serve to increase uncertainty about the warring parties' capabilities and resolve. Due to the high uncertainty in such a setting, it should be more difficult for the parties' expectations to converge, reducing the possibility that they will enter into negotiations with one another. We thus expect the chances of negotiations to be lower in Islamist armed conflicts compared with conflicts without claims over Islamist aspirations. In Figure 5.1, we display the occurrence of negotiations in Islamist civil wars compared with non-Islamist civil wars worldwide from 1989 to 2018. As theorized, negotiations are much less common in conflicts fought over Islamist claims. Of the 92 government–rebel dyads where the rebels had Islamist aspirations at

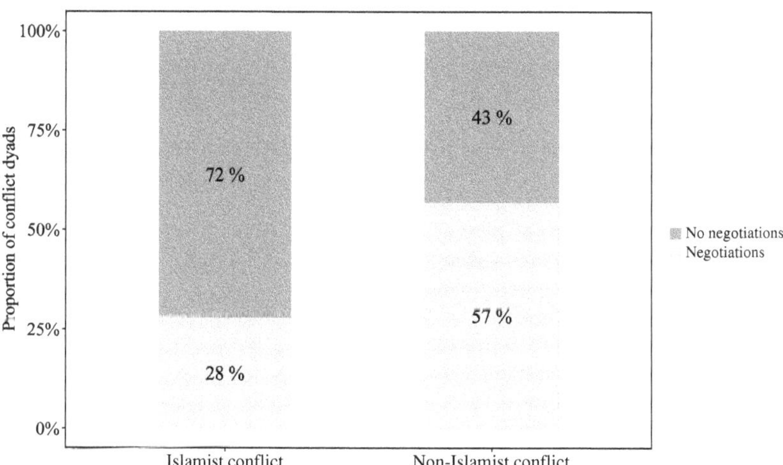

FIGURE 5.1 Proportion with negotiations, Islamist vs. non-Islamist conflicts.

the outset of the armed struggle, negotiations occurred in 28% of the cases (26 out of 92) at least once during this period. We can see that the corresponding figure for the non-Islamist conflicts was notably higher – 57% of these conflicts (158 out of 277) experienced negotiations between the primary warring parties during this period.

Since we have access to detailed data on monthly negotiations in these conflicts, it is also of interest to look more closely at the patterns. Some conflicts may see repeated negotiations within the same conflict, and the previous analysis would not capture such dynamics. For example, returning to the separatist conflict in southern Thailand, the meeting in February 2024 was not the first instance of a negotiation attempt: The government and the Patani insurgents have engaged in repeated negotiations over the years. If we focus on those conflicts fought over Islamist claims, negotiations occur in only 4% of dyad months, whereas in non-Islamist conflicts, this share is almost 10%. Hence, while the overall percentages are smaller, both analyses paint a similar picture. Negotiations are less frequent in the context of Islamist civil wars, which is consistent with our expectations. It should be noted, however, that even though they are less frequent, talks do take place also in this context.

We now move on to consider the signing of peace agreements in civil wars across the globe from 1989 to 2018. During this period, 77 of the 369 government–rebel dyads signed one or more peace agreements that addressed the incompatibility in some way – 43 signed one or more peace accords that addressed the incompatibility comprehensively, whereas 57 signed one or more peace accords that only partially addressed the conflict issues.

Just as the strategic context in which Islamist civil wars occur is likely to lead to increased uncertainty over capabilities and resolve and thereby reduce the chance of negotiations, such dynamics should also lower the possibility that the parties that do negotiate can reach peace settlements. In Figure 5.2, we show the signing of peace agreements in Islamist civil wars compared with non-Islamist civil wars worldwide from 1989 to 2018. As expected, whereas only 8% of the

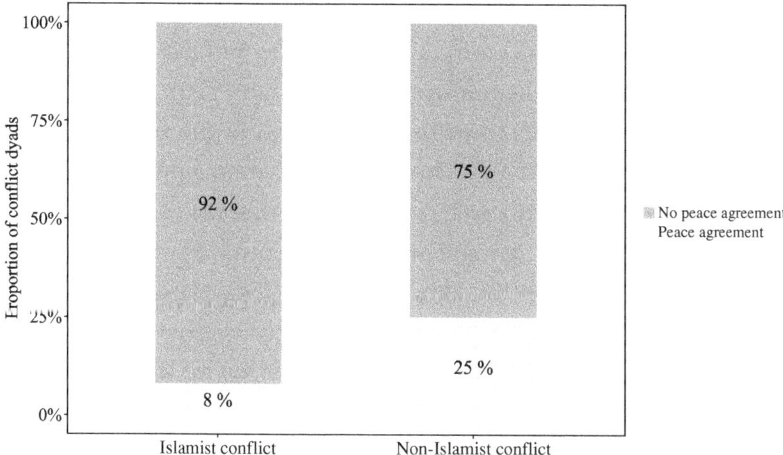

FIGURE 5.2 Proportion with peace accords, Islamist vs. non-Islamist conflicts.

government–rebel dyads in Islamist conflicts signed some form of peace accord, we see that peace accords were signed in 25% of those conflicts fought over non-Islamist claims.

Thus far, we have shown how Islamist and non-Islamist conflicts compare in descriptive patterns regarding negotiations and peace agreements. To ensure these differences are significant and robust to the inclusion of controls, we explore whether these results hold when relying on multivariate regressions. For summary statistics, see the Appendix, Table A17. In Figure 5.3 (see also the Appendix, Table A18), we present the results from a logit model, where our dependent variable, *Negotiations*, is coded 1 if the government and rebel group engage in negotiations in a given month and is otherwise coded 0. All figures presenting regression results display coefficient plots with 95% confidence intervals.[2] The variable *Islamist claim* takes on the value 1 if the rebel side at the outset of the armed struggle makes Islamist demands and is otherwise coded 0. In Model 1, we present the result for *Islamist claim*, accounting for temporal dependence, but without any additional

[2] The figures are created using the scheme plotplainblind (Bischof 2017) but adjusted to black and white.

controls. Next, we account for different conflict characteristics. In Model 2, we include a control for the *Number of rebel groups* in the conflict and whether the conflict was fought over *Territory* or not. We know from previous literature that the number of groups and the type of incompatibility can influence the negotiation prospects (Walter 2003, 2009). Previous research demonstrates that the costs of the conflict, in terms of intensity and duration, incentivize parties to engage in negotiations (Greig 2015; Mason and Fett 1996). Hence, in Model 3, we control for *Intensity*, measuring whether the conflict reached 1,000 battle-related deaths in one year.[3] We also control for the *Duration* of the conflict, measured as the number of years since the conflict dyad first reached 25 battle-related deaths for a given conflict episode. To account for temporal dependence in our data, in all models, we include a decay function of the time since the last negotiations, with a half-life parameter of four months. The results in Figure 5.3 show that Islamist

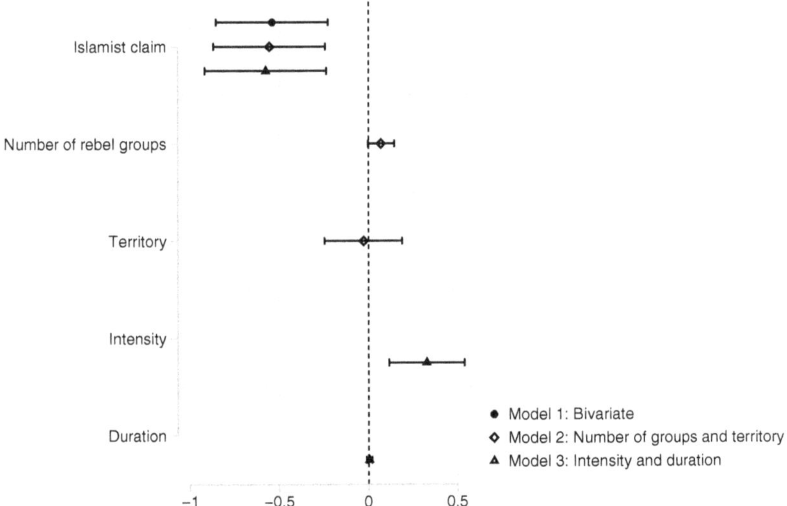

FIGURE 5.3 Logit models: Islamist conflicts and negotiations.
Note: In all models we account for temporal dependence.

[3] For inactive years, we rely on the last value, as previous intensity level is likely to affect conflict resolution efforts.

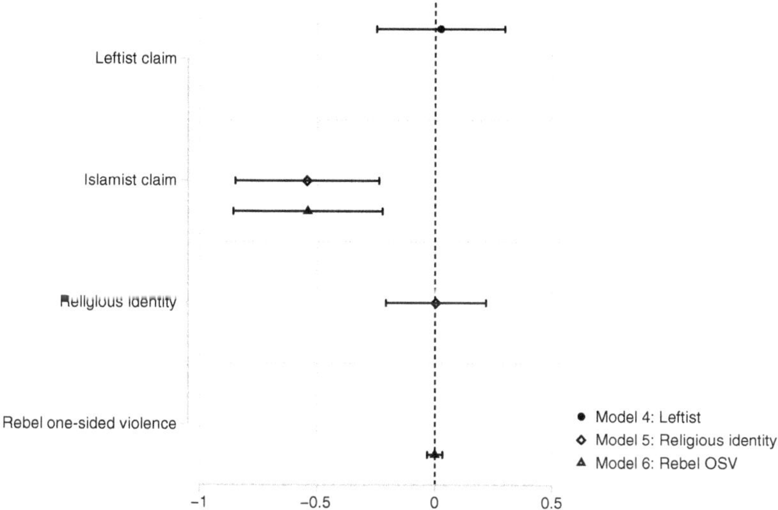

FIGURE 5.4 Logit models: Islamist conflicts and negotiations. Alternative explanations.
Note: In all models we account for temporal dependence.

armed conflicts are significantly less likely to experience negotiations even when controlling for these other factors.

Next, we account for a few alternative explanations (see Figure 5.4; see also the Appendix, Table A19). As we discussed in Chapter 1, there is an ongoing scholarly debate about whether Islamist armed conflicts are inherently different from other types of conflicts. An instrumentalist perspective emphasizes the structural similarities with revolutionary movements with leftist ideologies. Yet, as we saw in Chapter 3, Islamist armed conflicts do follow a distinct trajectory in terms of conflict termination. To explore the argument that the actors in these conflicts are the new revolutionaries, in Model 4, we explore whether leftist (or communist-leaning) rebel groups are also less likely to engage in negotiations. We created the variable *Leftist claim*, a dummy variable capturing whether the rebels make such claims. Here, we rely on data from the Rebels and Religion (R&R) dataset (Basedau, Deitch, and Zellman 2022). We find that leftist organizations are no more or less likely to be involved in negotiations with the government. Hence, the resistance to negotiations that we observe regarding Islamist civil wars is not identified in leftist movements. This would contradict the instrumentalist perspective, which emphasizes that Islamist civil wars are inherently similar to other conflicts, including revolutionary movements. Our findings here thus stand in contrast to the arguments that perceive Islamist armed actors as the new revolutionaries; rather, they suggest that these conflicts are distinct from other conflicts.

Next, we use data on religious identity to explore whether an essentialist perspective better accounts for the patterns we observe here. First, we rely on the RELAC dataset to create the measure *Religious identity*, which is coded 1 for cases where conflict parties are separated by different religious world traditions and is otherwise coded 0 (Svensson and Nilsson 2018). In Model 5, we thus probe whether our results are driven by religious identity cleavages, but we do not find any evidence to suggest this might be the case. We conclude that the actors' religious identity cannot explain the patterns we observe here.

Finally, we also explore whether our results are driven by whether the rebel groups engage in more extreme or radical behavior. To account for this dynamic, we rely on data from the UCDP to capture the number of civilians killed in one-sided violence by each rebel group (Eck and Hultman 2007). Since this measure is highly skewed, we created the variable *Rebel one-sided violence*, which takes the natural log of the number of civilians killed by the rebel group, lagged by one year. The results demonstrate that the extremist nature of the rebels, as manifested in the killing of civilians, is not significant and does not influence our key result that Islamist armed actors shy away from negotiations (see Model 6). We also rely on an alternative measure, which does not consider the number of attacks but merely whether rebel actors engaged in attacks against civilians, but the findings remain the same. In all models, the standard errors are clustered by conflict dyad. We also clustered on the whole conflict, but this does not change our findings. In addition, we control for liberal democracy and economic development, which do not change our results.[4] We consistently find that Islamist armed actors are less likely to be involved in negotiations. Hence, we find support for our fourth hypothesis, presented in this book, which suggests that Islamist civil wars are less likely to experience negotiations than other conflicts. This finding is also substantively meaningful: For non-Islamist civil wars, the predicted probability of negotiations is 8.7%, but this drops to 5.8% – a 33% relative decrease in the probability of negotiations – when the conflicts involve Islamist claims, holding all other variables constant.[5] Our findings thus highlight the significant barriers to negotiations in Islamist civil wars.

Based on our argument, we also propose that Islamist actors are typically less likely to reach peace agreements, which the descriptive data we present also indicate. We now turn to probe this relying on multivariate regression analysis. Our dependent variable in these analyses is *Peace agreement*, coded 1 if the government and rebel group reached either a full or partial peace accord in a given month, thus addressing in some way the incompatibility at stake. We rely on the same control variables as previously. Across all models, we account for temporal dependence by including a decay function for time since last peace accord, with a half-life parameter of four months. The results are presented in Figure 5.5 (see also the Appendix, Table A20). However, once we proceed to the multivariate analysis, account for temporal dependence in our data, and control for different factors, the variable Islamist claims is only significant at the 95% level in Model 3, and at the 90% level in Models 1 and 2. Hence, we do not find any conclusive support for our fifth hypothesis.

[4] The data on liberal democracy come from V-Dem (Coppedge et al. 2020), and the variable we use is an index (0 to 1) that focuses on the extent to which the ideal of liberal democracy is achieved, whereas the data on economic development come from the United Nations (2020), measured as GDP per capita logged. Both measures are lagged one year.

[5] This is based on Model 2, where we control for number of rebel groups and territory.

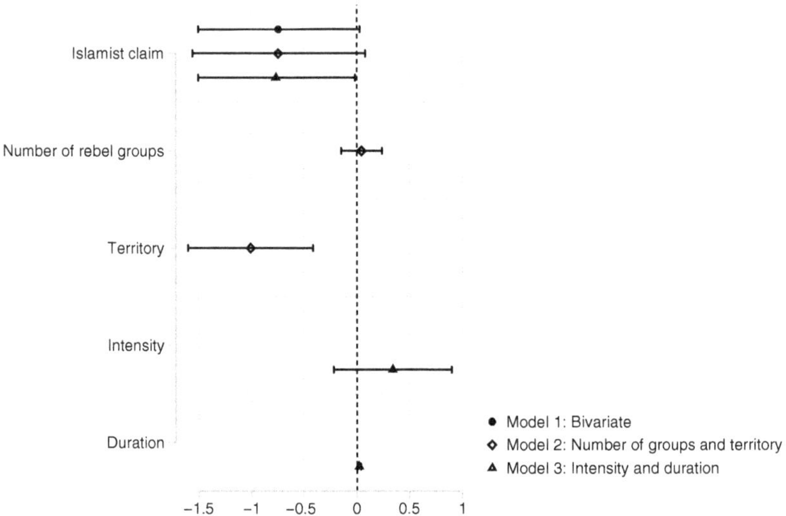

FIGURE 5.5 Logit models: Islamist conflicts and peace agreements.
Note: In all models we account for temporal dependence.

Regarding the alternative explanations, we find that none of these perform better. These results are shown in Figure 5.6 (see also the Appendix, Table A21). We find no evidence to suggest that armed actors in conflicts over leftist claims are more or less likely to reach peace agreements. Similarly, conflicts over religious identity are neither more nor less likely to see peace agreements. Our results regarding extremist actors, in terms of their propensity to target civilians, paint a similar picture. We can also note that in neither of these models are Islamist claims significant at the 95% level.[6] Although we find no conclusive evidence that Islamist conflicts are less likely to reach peace agreements, the other explanations do not perform any better.

In summary, the evidence presented here shows that Islamist civil wars systematically differ in terms of their lower frequency of negotiations. However, we find that they are not distinguishable from

[6] In Model 5, Islamist claims is not significant at the 90% level either, when clustering on conflict instead of dyad.

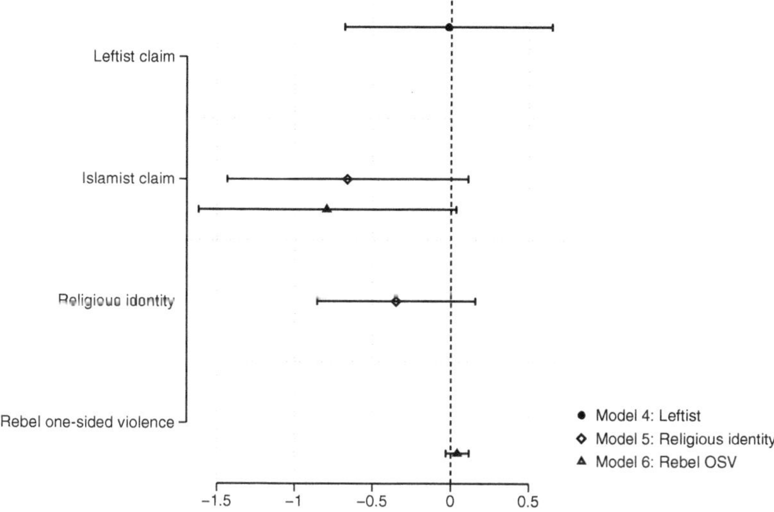

FIGURE 5.6 Logit models: Islamist conflicts and peace agreements. Alternative explanations.
Note: In all models we account for temporal dependence.

other types of conflicts in terms of the occurrence of peace agreements. Generally speaking, Islamist civil wars tend to be particularly complex cases to bring to negotiations, but as shown here and as we will discuss later, Islamist conflicts do not entirely escape possibilities for conflict resolution – negotiations and dialogue also occur in such contexts. As argued earlier in this book, we propose that the root of the intractability of Islamist armed conflicts lies in the transnational dimension. To further probe this aspect of our argument, we now explore some key differences within the category of Islamist conflicts.

DISAGGREGATING ISLAMIST CIVIL WARS

Negotiations do not occur uniformly across Islamist civil wars, and we have demonstrated elsewhere that there is considerable variation within the category of Islamist armed conflict when it comes to negotiations (Nilsson and Svensson 2020). Again, the key dimension here lies in the transnational character of Islamist civil wars. Here, we extend and develop the implications of our overall argument.

While all Islamist wars have the potential for external support and involvement due to the reasons laid out in Chapter 2, there are also important variations within Islamist conflicts. The degree of transnational dimensions and the associated strategic uncertainty will vary between Islamist conflicts and over time. Conflicts that have insulated themselves from the broader transnational battle between transnational Islamist networks, on the one hand, and intergovernmental alliances, on the other, have space that allows for conflict resolution processes. Such conflicts should not be significantly different from other types of disputes regarding openness to negotiations.

So far, we have dealt with Islamist armed conflicts on a structural level as one unified category of conflicts. We now focus on Islamist armed conflicts to explore variations within this broader category. The distinction here lies between those Islamist armed actors who have made claims that are transnational in scope and thus transcend the borders of nation-states, and other Islamist actors who have made claims that are confined to state borders, either concerning government power or relating to a specific piece of territory. Here, we rely on disaggregated data on Islamist claims from the RELAC dataset (Svensson and Nilsson 2018). Among the transnational Islamist conflicts, we find actors such as IS, AQIM, al-Shabaab, and al-Qaeda. Among Islamist civil wars with more localized claims about the governance of the state or a specific territory, we see groups such as MILF in the Philippines, the Islamic Supreme Council of Iraq (SCIRI) in Iraq, and the Patani insurgents in Thailand. Based on our argument, we expect conflicts where Islamist claims are insulated from the transnational struggle to be more likely to experience negotiations. When we distinguish between conflicts based on this dimension, we find that negotiations only occur in 7% (three of 44) of the transnational Islamist conflict dyads. In contrast, the share of negotiations in other Islamist civil wars is considerably higher: 48% of these conflicts engage in negotiations at some point during this time period (23 of 48; see Figure 5.7).

We now turn to our multivariate analysis to examine whether these results hold up when introducing our controls. We present these

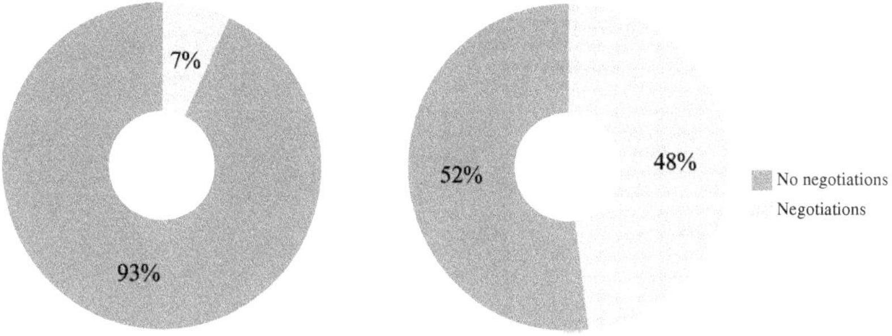

FIGURE 5.7 Proportion with negotiations, transnational vs. non-transnational Islamist conflicts.

results in Figure 5.8 (see also the Appendix, Table A22). As expected, Islamist conflicts fought over transnational claims resist negotiations in comparison with other types of conflicts. The pattern is similar for Islamist conflicts where the claims do not transcend state borders, and while this effect is also significant, it is not as large. This result remains robust when controlling for the conflict issue being fought over government or territory, the number of groups (see Model 2), and the intensity and duration of the conflict (see Model 3). In substantive terms, we find that the predicted probability of negotiations drops from 8.3% to just 0.9% – a relative decrease of 89% – when the conflict involves a transnational claim, holding all other variables constant. For conflicts over non-transnational Islamist claims, the probability of negotiations decreases more modestly from 8.5% to 6.3%.[7] Hence, while the likelihood of negotiations declines in both cases, the drop is far more pronounced in conflicts fought over a transnational claim.

Next, we account for alternative explanations. As shown in Figure 5.9, these do not fare well (see also the Appendix, Table A23). Leftist movements are no more or less likely to engage in negotiations (see Model 4). While we previously compared leftist movements with all other groups, including Islamists (see Figure 5.4),

[7] These estimates are based on Model 2.

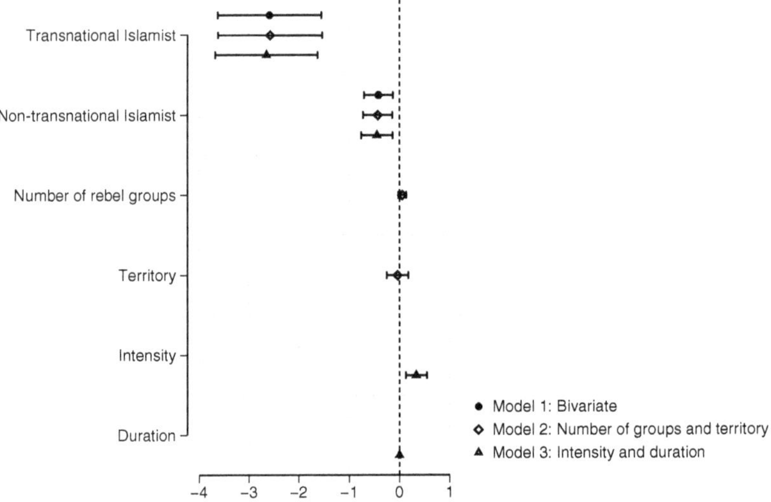

FIGURE 5.8 Logit models: different types of Islamist conflicts and negotiations.
Note: In all models we account for temporal dependence.

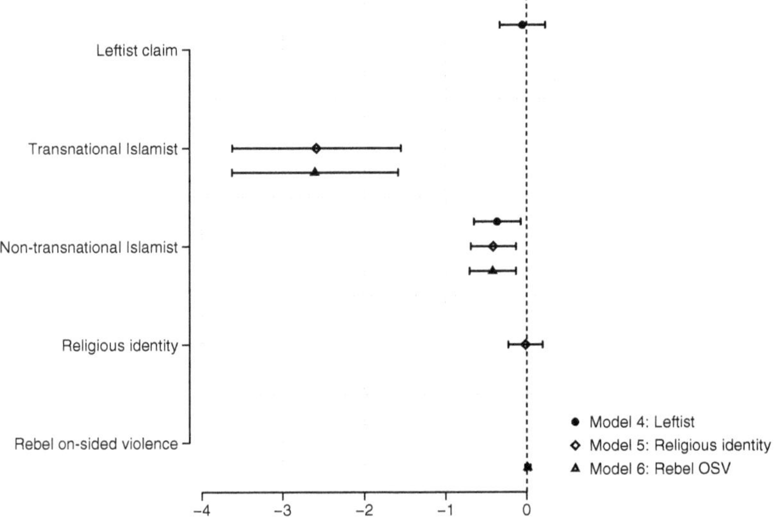

FIGURE 5.9 Logit models: different types of Islamist conflicts and negotiations. Alternative explanations.
Note: In all models we account for temporal dependence.

we now control for non-transnational Islamists. Yet, regardless of the point of comparison, we do not find any significant effect of leftist movements. Hence, the results suggest that Islamist conflicts – here focusing on those with transnational claims – stand out from other types of conflicts and that Islamists are not the new revolutionaries, at least regarding their propensity for negotiations. We further find that neither religious identity nor the extremist nature of the rebel side in terms of targeting civilians seems to influence the likelihood of negotiations, which thus goes against an essentialist perspective (see Models 5 and 6). To summarize, we find consistent support for our sixth hypothesis, suggesting that conflicts fought over transnational Islamist claims are less likely to see negotiations.[8]

So far, we have shown what the broader patterns look like, but how does this play out on the ground? Egypt is a case that illustrates how the transnational dimension of Islamist armed conflicts can affect conflict resolution efforts. The development of Islamist movements in Egypt has historically been formative for the larger Islamist movement globally. Government repression following the assassination of Anwar Sadat, perceived as a response to what was seen as un-Islamic governance, including the peace deal with Israel, further radicalized the Egyptian Islamist insurgency. Two of the main Islamist movements in Egypt followed distinctly different trajectories. Al-Gama'a al-Islamiyya (IG), although connected to the broader transnational armed Islamist movement, remained primarily focused on the domestic Egyptian context. It engaged in mediation efforts (aborted by the government side), initiated a process of fundamental ideological revision, and implemented a ceasefire (although one faction, closer to al-Qaeda, rejected the ceasefire and formed a splinter faction); key leaders transitioned into political power when participating in the brief post-Mubarak Egyptian democracy (Drevon

[8] As before, these findings remain robust when clustering on the whole conflict rather than conflict dyad, and when controlling for country-level factors such as liberal democracy and economic development.

2022b; Matesan 2020b). By contrast, Islamic Jihad (IJ) was transnationalized and later metamorphosed into al-Qaeda (its leader became the al-Qaeda leader after Osama bin Laden). This group consistently rejected peace efforts, just as the Egyptian government showed no sign of accommodating them. Thus, one of the defining distinctions between the two groups, which showed significantly different openings for conflict resolution, lies in their national versus transnational character.

While negotiations represent one important step in a conflict resolution process, we also aim to determine whether the warring parties successfully reach a settlement that addresses the core issues at stake. As shown previously, peace agreements in Islamist armed conflicts are rare but do happen. Next, we explore whether there are differences between those Islamist civil wars framed around a transnational global agenda and those conflicts where the issue at stake is more locally based. Figure 5.10 compares the share of peace accords in transnational Islamist conflict dyads with those not fought over a transnational claim. The differences are striking. No peace agreement has been reached in any transnational Islamist civil war (zero of 44). In the Islamist armed conflicts where Islamist claims are confined to state borders, either relating to government control or to a separate piece of territory within the state, we find that the warring actors reach

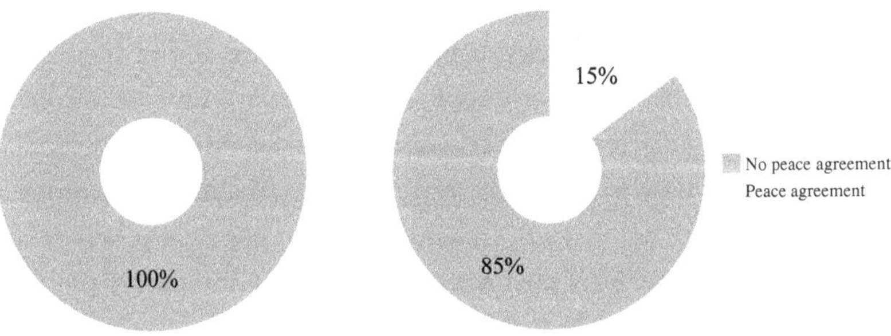

FIGURE 5.10 Proportion with peace agreements, transnational vs. non-transnational Islamist conflicts.

peace accords in 15% of cases (seven of 48). Therefore, solutions can be achieved when the issue at stake is centered around local issues, even if religiously framed. Since peace agreements are nonexistent in civil wars over transnational claims, we cannot further investigate this in multivariate analysis, as we have done previously. The results are noteworthy, as peace agreements occur in other types of Islamist armed conflicts but not in those Islamist conflicts fought over transnational claims. This lends support to our seventh hypothesis.

When peace agreements are signed in Islamist civil wars, they tend to occur in conflicts that have not been caught up in the broader transnational battle. This includes the conflict between the government of the Philippines and MILF, in which the parties reached a comprehensive settlement in 2014, ending the conflict. The southern region of Mindanao has long been an area of instability and contestation, rooted in a sense of marginalization among the Muslim minority population and fueled by political, religious, and economic grievances. The conflict traces its roots back to the independence of the Philippines and its state-formation project, but it became militarized in the 1970s with the rise of the Moro National Liberation Front (MNLF). This group mobilized primarily around an ethnic and leftist agenda, challenging the centrist state dominated by the political power in Manila and seeking independence. When it eventually settled for a regional autonomy solution, MILF continued to fight. However, MILF mobilized on an entirely different ideological ground: It was an explicit Islamist movement that sought the implementation of Sharia law in an independent Mindanao. The conflict between MILF and the government escalated over the years, finally ending through a comprehensive peace settlement in 2014, which had taken years to negotiate and included several other peace agreements. Although the implementation process faced challenges, the settlement seems to have held, and a fundamental transformation of what is now called the Bangsamoro region has been initiated. In the Philippines, the opportunity for negotiations toward a settlement arose from deliberate decisions by both the government and the rebel group to keep the struggle local and not transnationalize it. MILF had connections, ideological ties, as well as foreign fighters within the broader transnational armed Islamist network. It did not, however, mobilize based on a transnational agenda. Following the 9/11 attacks against the US, MILF in the Philippines made great efforts to distance itself from al-Qaeda and clarify that it was not part of the same type of movement. The leader of MILF even sent a letter to President Bush seeking to distance the group from al-Qaeda (Liow 2006, 21). The Philippine government largely resisted the temptation to draw the conflict into the Global War on Terror. Moreover, while there was some collaboration among different groups, foreign fighters in the Philippines were few to nonexistent throughout the conflict. Similarly, although the US provided extensive military support and training, there was no military intervention on the government's side. The absence of foreign intervention on either side arguably made it easier for the parties to overcome the information failure and converge in their expectations.

Other examples where Islamist armed actors have signed peace accords include Indonesia and Tajikistan. In Indonesia's region of Aceh, the rebel group Gerakan Aceh Merdeka (Free Aceh Movement, GAM) had taken up arms, at least initially framed through an Islamist agenda, but settled on a peace agreement in 2005, which gave Aceh considerable autonomy. Finally, in Tajikistan, the Islamic Renaissance Party of Tajikistan (IRP), an Islamist party, reached an agreement with the government in 1997. The religiously defined rebel group IRP shifted its emphasis from an Islamic agenda toward a more nationalistic agenda and concurrently also increasingly disengaged from the regional, international Islamist agenda and the Salafi-jihadist networks. In these cases, the conflicts were disconnected from the larger transnational armed Islamist networks.

Another empirical example that demonstrates the same underlying dynamic is the case of the Islamist civil war in Pakistan. The dialogue efforts and negotiations between the different groups belonging to the Pakistani Taliban and the Islamist insurgencies in the border areas of Pakistan, on the one hand, and the government of Pakistan, on the other, have resulted in numerous local peace agreements and ceasefire arrangements (Ali 2013; Sheikh 2020). These include offers of local autonomy under Sharia law to be practiced in Pakistan. While these arrangements have not resulted in the conflict being resolved, it is still significant that there have been efforts to settle the conflict, signifying that none of the parties (neither the rebels nor the government) rejected the possibility of finding solutions through negotiations. Nevertheless, not all actors engaged in the negotiation efforts, and in particular, "collaboration with transnational jihadi movements such as al-Qaeda and the Islamic State (by individuals or a few Taliban factions) has been an obvious obstacle to negotiations because of government policies (zero tolerance) toward these movements" (Sheikh 2020, 428). Thus, the government has demonstrated its interest and its capability to settle with local Pakistani armed Islamist groups as long as they do not collaborate with transnational Islamist networks, and these groups have also demonstrated their willingness to engage in negotiations at least in terms of local peace agreements and ceasefires. Again, the differences in transnational nature and orientation can help account for different conflict resolution opportunities within Islamist insurgencies.

WHAT DO WE KNOW ABOUT THE GLOBAL PATTERNS OF RESISTANCE TO RESOLUTION?

In line with our argument, we observe that Islamist conflicts are less likely to be negotiated, especially those with a transnational dimension. While we find no conclusive evidence that Islamist conflicts are less likely than non-Islamist conflicts to result in a peace settlement, the Islamist conflicts fought over transnational claims never result in peace settlements. As highlighted in Chapter 1, one prevalent explanation in previous discussions, which we labeled the *instrumentalist* perspective, perceives Islamist claims as epiphenomenal and expects that Islamist civil wars will not differ from other types of civil wars. This perspective has been pervasive in peace and conflict research with the implicit or explicit assumption that Islamist armed conflicts are not meaningfully differentiated from other types of conflicts. According to this perspective, Islamist claim-making will not affect the dynamics of armed conflict. Behind the veil of Islamist rhetoric and ideology lie the complex interests of power and money. The fact that some conflicts are framed in religious terms, such as Islamist claims, should not be expected to differentiate them from other conflicts. Yet the evidence presented in this chapter stands in contrast to the instrumentalist account of Islamist civil wars. We have seen that there are indeed systematic differences in the trajectories of conflicts once they are framed in Islamist terms.

In contrast to ideas commonly associated with the *essentialist* perspective, we also note that peace negotiations and peace agreements occur in Islamist conflicts. However, not all Islamist conflicts are the same. We have shown that the intractability of Islamist conflicts mainly stems from the sub-group of Islamist armed conflicts that are the most transnationally oriented. In contrast, those Islamist armed conflicts that are more locally oriented appear to be more open to negotiations and peace agreements. Thus, studying the empirical trajectories of Islamist civil wars tells us that the dim prospects for conflict resolution in Islamist civil wars are primarily driven by and associated with those conflicts most embedded in transnational networks.

In this chapter, we have presented evidence regarding broader negotiation patterns and peace accords. What is missing, however, is establishing the temporal order between de-transnationalization and openings for conflict resolution, and better understanding variation between different groups regarding the transnational dimension and how this shapes openings for conflict resolution. In the following chapter, we therefore delve deeper into our theoretical expectations by examining a few cases in greater detail, exploring variation both across cases and over time.

6 Conflict Resolution in Islamist Civil Wars

Mali and Syria

In this chapter, we focus on Islamist rebel groups in two of the countries in the world most affected by Islamist civil wars: Mali and Syria. Both countries have been brought to the brink of complete state failure due to the devastating impact of Islamist civil wars. Millions of civilians have been affected by the violence. In both countries, radical Islamist groups have taken up arms under the banner of jihad against secular-leaning governments. The Islamist civil wars in these countries have been tragically entrenched, seemingly defying any potential for conflict resolution. They represent some of the most arduous and challenging cases for conflict resolution. However, by closely examining these two cases, we can discern signs of openness to conflict resolution within the context of these Islamist civil wars. Can our argument, focusing on the transnational dimension, help us understand when and among which actors these openings for conflict resolution have occurred?

The cases are selected because they exhibit intriguing intracase variations that are valuable to explore for the purposes of this book. In Mali, the most significant variation to pay attention to is *between groups*. This chapter focuses on three groups – Ansar Dine, AQIM, and Katiba Macina. In the Malian civil war, several Islamist groups have taken up arms against the government, and there have been attempts at mediation and negotiations. It is interesting to note, however, that these attempts to settle the conflict have only involved some of the Malian Islamist groups and not others. Indeed, the Islamist groups Ansar Dine and Katiba Macina have shown more openness to engaging in dialogue than other groups. The government in Bamako has also signaled openness to dialogue with these Islamist groups, but not with others. Why do we see this variation across actors? Recognizing this variation is crucial for understanding the conditions for conflict resolution in Islamist civil wars.

In Syria, the group HTS, once one of the key Islamist armed groups in the Syrian civil war, has made a shift in the direction of openness for conflict resolution. This case thus offers an interesting example of variation *over time*. The group adhered to the Turkish–Russian decreed ceasefire for several years and has signaled openness to dialogue with other actors. In 2024, it took advantage of the weakness of the Assad regime and launched a military offensive, leading to the overthrow of the regime. Its leader, Ahmed al-Sharaa, shifted his focus from Islamist mobilization to Syrian unification. HTS is an Islamist rebel group that has undergone a remarkable transformation, although many questions remain regarding the depth and quality of the transformation. Studying such shifts over time is essential for understanding conflict resolution in Islamist civil wars.

One implication of our argument – that the transnational factor is the main reason behind the intractability of Islamist civil wars – is that when Islamist actors have decoupled or distanced themselves from the transnational dimension, there should be more space for conflict resolution. Thus, variations in the degree of transnationalization – across groups or within groups over time – should shape the underlying propensity for conflict resolution. Conflicts deeply embedded in transnational networks involving both governments and rebels are less likely to see attempts at dialogue or negotiation. However, as conflicts transition from transnational to local, actors' capacity and willingness to engage in negotiations tend to increase. We thus expect that once conflicts are disconnected from the global conflict narrative, more opportunities for conflict resolution attempts to settle these armed conflicts should arise. In this chapter, we first explore variations between Islamist groups in Mali and then variations over time in the case of the HTS conflict in Syria, studying how the decoupling from the transnational dimension can help explain their relative openness to conflict resolution.

TALKING TO THE JIHADISTS: ANSAR DINE, AQIM, AND KATIBA MACINA IN MALI

Mali presents a compelling case for exploration due to its diverse intra-insurgency dynamics: Several rebel groups have emerged, each with distinct positions along the local–global spectrum, challenging the government's authority. This section explores attempts to find a negotiated solution to the Malian civil war, focusing on intra-insurgency variations. Mali has seen the involvement of various Islamist armed groups, including Ansar Dine along with its breakaway faction the High Council for the Unity of Azawad (HCUA), AQIM, and Katiba Macina. While none of these attempts has succeeded in peacefully ending the conflict, they provide an intriguing lens through which to explore the framework developed in this book.

The Birth and Growth of the Islamist Insurgency in Mali

The civil war in Mali came about in the wake of the popular uprising and Western-backed military intervention against Muammar Gaddafi in Libya following the turbulent Arab Spring in 2011. When Gaddafi – who had enlisted members of the Malian nomadic minority group, the Tuareg, to support his revolutionary Islamist project – was ousted from power, it had a significant impact on the entire region. Mercenaries and weapons from Libya flooded into Mali, exacerbating longstanding grievances and enhancing the combat potential of the insurgents. The Tuareg population, primarily residing in the north of the country, has long felt marginalized and neglected by the central government based in Bamako. When the Tuareg and Islamist groups joined forces, they posed a serious challenge to the Malian state that was only overcome by a French-led military intervention.

The Islamist rebel group Ansar Dine was predominantly composed of Tuareg members. The group sought to establish Sharia law throughout Mali (Flood 2012, 2). Due to their shared Tuareg identity, they initially cooperated with fellow Tuareg group Mouvement National de Libération de l'Azawad (MNLA; later Coordination des

Mouvements de l'Azawad, CMA) at the onset in 2011. The collaboration was successful militarily, driving government forces out of northern Mali. But Ansar Dine gradually switched alliances from the Tuareg-separatist MNLA to fellow Islamist groups: AQIM, the local branch of al-Qaeda, and Mouvement pour le Tawhîd et du Jihad en Afrique de l'Ouest (MUJAO). Ansar Dine's leader, Iyad Ag Ghali, who had a long history of involvement in the struggle for the Tuareg people and experience serving in Libyan military foreign interventions, became increasingly radicalized religiously. While most previous insurgency groups in northern Mali had mobilized on an ethnic-nationalist agenda, Ag Ghali formed Ansar Dine in December 2011 with an explicit Islamist agenda. This group challenged Mali's secular constitution, which had been maintained since its independence from France. Islamism gradually gained traction in Mali, a country previously governed based on secular principles (Lebovich 2019).

Islamic organizations became more vocal and used the liberalization of the 1990s to increase their presence in Malian society, as well as in the political sphere (Gutelius 2007). Ansar Dine was part of this trajectory but took up arms to advance its goals of establishing an explicitly Islamic Mali. The group aimed for the strict implementation of Sharia law, which it was prepared to enact once it had established itself. After taking control of territory, Ansar Dine implemented Sharia law harshly in areas under their control, seeking to manifest their ideological project (Gaasholt 2012, 82). In sharp contrast to the traditional Malian culture of religious tolerance, Ansar Dine championed an agenda they described as a return to a more authentic Islamic basis for the state and society.

The rebel coalition was able to make significant gains on the ground. They established a jihadist proto-state in parts of northern Mali, where their interpretation of Sharia law was implemented with considerable brutality. Among the three armed Islamist organizations – Ansar Dine, AQIM, and MUJAO – in the rebel alliance operating in 2012–2013 in northern Mali, Ansar Dine "was the most Malian in character, given that its top leader, Iyad Ag Ghali, as well as his key advisors and lieutenants and the bulk of his fighters, were all Malians" (Thurston 2018, 11).

The Islamist rebel group AQIM was a very different organization in terms of its origins and aspirations. It grew out of the Algerian civil war, which started in 1991 when the military took power as the Islamist parties appeared to be on a path to winning the general election. While the Front Islamique du Salut (FIS) was the main Islamist actor in that conflict and focused primarily on the situation in Algeria, a more radical and internationally focused group, Groupe Islamique Armé (GIA), also emerged. GIA turned successively more extreme and eventually alienated the Algerian population and constituencies in Algeria that were fighting for a domestic agenda (Laub and Masters 2014). Together with successful attempts by the Algerian security apparatus to foment infighting and apply military pressure against GIA, the group was on the decline. Some in the group reconfigured themselves, first as Groupe Salafiste pour la Prédication et le Combat (GSPC) and later as AQIM, adopting a more internationalist agenda. Events in neighboring countries created new momentum for the group. AQIM was able to reverse its decline by capitalizing on the turmoil in Tunisia and the civil war in Libya following the Arab Spring in 2011 (Chivvis and Liepman 2013). AQIM in northern Mali tried to advance "the dream of a regional Islamic caliphate" (Chivvis and Liepman 2013, 8). When intervening in the Malian context, AQIM was often seen as "largely an Algerian organization focused on Algeria and North Africa" (Chivvis and Liepman 2013, 2). Both AQIM and MUJAO were transnational in character. MUJAO splintered from AQIM in 2011 and had broader aims than AQIM, wanting to spread jihad also in the wider West African region (BBC 2013). But the organizations have coexisted and continued to work together since the split (United Nations 2023).

Ansar Dine later merged with AQIM and some other Islamist groups in the rebel coalition Jamaat Nusrat al-Islam wal-Muslimin (JNIM), also known as the Group for Support of Islam and Muslims

(GSIM), which established itself as a branch of al-Qaeda, consisting of four different groups or so-called Katibas. One of the sub-groups of JNIM is Katiba Macina (Front de Libération du Macina, FLM), formed in 2015 and operating in central Mali under the leadership of Amadou Koufa. The group aspires to recreate the Macina Empire, a historical case in which the Fula ethnic group established a state formation anchored in Sharia law (1818–1862). Amadou Koufa is an Islamic preacher from the Fula ethnic group. Their recruitment was primarily indigenous (ICG 2019), and the group mobilized by exploiting local grievances in central Mali, mainly, but not exclusively, among the Fulani group. The Fulani people feared Tuareg hegemony. As an Islamist group, Katiba Macina rejected the secular Malian state.

Space for Conflict Resolution in the Islamist Civil War in Mali

During the 2012–2013 crisis, multiple attempts were made to engage with Ansar Dine and initiate negotiations. The initiative by the High Islamic Council of Mali under Mahmoud Dicko, a Muslim cleric with Salafist leanings, signaled an attempt to reach out to Ansar Dine from the government side through a civil society organization. It did not bear fruit, as Ag Ghali refused to meet with Dicko (Thurston 2018). Despite the unsuccessful outcome of this particular initiative, the High Islamic Council of Mali persisted in trying to establish a dialogue with Ag Ghali.

Burkina Faso, which had established networks from earlier initiatives for dialogue, also tried to reach out to Ansar Dine and Ag Ghali. In August 2012, news reports noted that "foreign minister, Djibril Bassolé, met in Kidal with a leading warlord, Iyad Ag Ghali, who directs the Islamist Ansar Dine movement" (Nossiter 2012). Burkina Faso's foreign minister met with Ag Ghali and clarified that "any negotiations were conditional on Ag Ghali rejecting AQIM" (Thurston 2018, 12). At the same time, Algeria was in talks with Ansar Dine to attempt to separate them from the transnational networks of armed Islamist actors. Hence, similar to Burkina Faso, Algeria "attempted to have Ansar Dine dissociate itself from AQIM and MUJAO" (Boutellis and Zahar 2017, 10). Later, in 2012, Burkina Faso initiated ceasefire talks on an Economic Community of West African States (ECOWAS) mandate between Ansar Dine, MNLA, and the Malian government. MNLA wanted an independent Tuareg state, Ansar Dine wanted Sharia law in northern Mali, and the government wanted to restore its control. As regards Ansar Dine's position on negotiations, "Ansar Dine had apparently stated its willingness to open peace talks – and by implication to loosen its ties with al-Qaeda" (Roetman, Migeon, and Dudouet 2019, 20). In May 2012, Ansar Dine joined the ECOWAS talks (Gaasholt 2012, 84), and in the following negotiations under ECOWAS and the United Nations (UN), Ansar Dine was represented, while AQIM was not, as the members were not "considered as credible partners for negotiations" (Gaasholt 2012, 86). This distinction cannot be accounted for by looking at the organizations' brutality or use of extremist violence: Ansar Dine had committed the same level of human rights abuses as AQIM in territories under their control (Gaasholt 2012, 86). The difference between the groups, observes Gaasholt (2012, 86), lies in their orientation: "In contrast to AQIM and the MUJAO, the MNLA and Ansar Dine were considered as Malian groups".

On January 1, 2013, Ansar Dine handed over a 17-page document to the mediator, Burkina Faso's president, calling for autonomy for northern Mali and the application of Sharia law. However, the aspirations went beyond focusing only on northern Mali: The group also demanded changes to the constitution, shifting Mali from a secular to an Islamic state. The government of Mali viewed these demands as unacceptable (Thurston 2018). After just two days, Ansar Dine's leader, Ag Ghali, stated in the media that he had decided to pursue a violent agenda with the group's allies instead. "According to one expert, Ansar Dine withdrew from the Ouagadougou negotiations because international actors closed the door on the idea of a dialogue around the issue of Islam" (Roetman, Migeon, and Dudouet 2019, 20). The group's advancements on the battlefield triggered the *Serval*, the French military intervention, in early 2013.

The three negotiation attempts of 2012–2013 by the High Islamic Council of Mali, Burkina Faso, and Algeria aimed to find a negotiated path forward. Despite Ansar Dine's clear affiliation with the Salafi-jihadist tradition, the group engaged in dialogue with third parties who sought to reach out to them, and the government appeared willing to engage in talks with them. The fact that Ansar Dine had been involved in jihad did not deter conflict resolution efforts. However, no negotiation efforts – by third parties, the government, or the insurgents themselves – took place involving the other two Islamist insurgency groups in the coalition, AQIM and MUJAO. Both of these were transnational Islamist groups. In the rebel coalition, the Malian-focused Ansar Dine emerged as the group most open to engaging in (albeit eventually unsuccessful) resolution attempts.

Third-party actors, especially Burkina Faso and Algeria, also sought to drive a wedge between Ansar Dine, which was more Malian-oriented in terms of constituency, leadership, outlook, and character, and the more transnationally oriented and based AQIM. The initiatives of 2013 were built on the premise that local actors could be separated from international actors (Lebovich 2013).

Failing to bring Ansar Dine into proper peace negotiations, the initiatives created a rift inside Ansar Dine between the moderates and Ag Ghali, who continued to pursue the fight. When Ansar Dine, under the leadership of Ag Ghali, withdrew from the negotiations, more moderate actors in the movement opted to remain committed to pursuing a negotiated path. Ansar Dine splintered. In May 2013, the breakaways from Ansar Dine formed a group called the HCUA (Sköns 2016, 169), a group with "a strongly Islamist agenda" (Boutellis and Zahar 2017, 10). The HCUA joined the Ouagadougou accord, an initial ceasefire between the Malian state and the secessionist armed groups in the north, as well as the Algerian-led peace negotiations leading up to the 2015 peace agreement in Mali. Thus, while Ansar Dine as an organization did not participate in the negotiations, segments of the movement and its leadership did. The HCUA used the negotiations as an attempt to advance their Islamist agenda, aiming to challenge the secular state of Mali: "[The] HCUA in particular attempted to remove the reference to secularism (*laïcité*)" (Boutellis and Zahar 2017, 13). While this aspiration was not met in the peace agreement, as it respected the secular status of the Malian state (Lorentzen 2022, 4), the group was still willing to lay down their arms and join the peace process. The HCUA joined an alliance of rebel groups known as the Coordination, which participated in the peace process and ultimately signed the peace agreement in 2015 (Boutellis and Zahar 2017, 20–21).

While the French intervention pushed back the Islamist groups, and the peace agreement of 2015 brought about a multilateral peacekeeping force, the United Nations Multidimensional Integrated Stabilization Mission in Mali (MINUSMA), the war was far from over. In 2017, the conflict escalated through the reorganization of the rebel alliance. Ansar Dine merged with AQIM and MUJAO's successor, al-Mourabitoun, as well as the Islamist group that had taken up arms in central Mali, Katiba Macina (FLM). JNIM established itself as a branch of al-Qaeda, and Ansar Dine's leader, Ag Ghali, who also became JNIM's leader, pledged allegiance to al-Qaeda (Roetman, Migeon, and Dudouet 2019). JNIM was not one unified organization but a rebel coalition of four independent and different groups, as mentioned earlier, so-called Katibas.

Both sides in the Malian armed conflict – the secular-based government in Bamako and the Islamist JNIM – expressed willingness to engage in dialogue with one another (ICG 2021b). The Conference of National Understanding in Bamako, March–April 2017, proposed a national dialogue process with Islamist groups to settle the conflict. However, preserving secularity was a prerequisite. Among the recommendations from the conference was that the government should "talk to Ag Ghali and the central Malian jihadist leader Amadou Koufa" (Thurston 2020, 144). However, the initiative was nipped in the bud, and it is interesting to see where the strongest resistance came from. It was not primarily from the Malian government, which had shown openness to negotiations. The resistance to negotiations came from the main external backer of the government. It was France that strongly objected to this initiative, with Foreign Minister Jean-Marc Ayrault stating: "How could one negotiate with the terrorists? It is a fight without ambiguity" (Roetman, Migeon, and Dudouet 2019, 33). This French resistance led to the Malian government opposing negotiations.

Yet, as the conflict dragged on, renewed efforts to establish dialogue with the Islamist groups were initiated. The first time the government side demonstrated its willingness to enter talks with the JNIM coalition was in February 2020, when then President Ibrahim Boubacar Keïta (2013–2020) expressed an openness to pursue dialogue with representatives of Islamist armed groups, such as JNIM leader Ag Ghali (RFI 2020a). JNIM reciprocated by signaling an openness to engage in negotiations with the government but made such talks conditional: The Islamist rebels responded that withdrawing all foreign forces (UN and French missions) was a prerequisite for negotiations (ARB 2020b; RFI 2020b). President Keïta faced increasing internal pressure due to the government's inability to end the conflict and the increasing anti-French sentiments expressed through public demonstrations. The government of Mali publicly acknowledged that it had been involved in talks with JNIM (also known as GSIM) and Katiba Macina, although the exact details remain uncertain. This was "the first time that President Keïta has confirmed that his government is in talks with Iyad Ag Ghali, leader of the main al-Qaeda affiliate in the Sahel, GSIM; and Amadou Koufa, a radical Fulani preacher who heads the Macina Liberation Front" (ARB 2020a).

However, the government was being challenged from within. The increasing instability in Bamako brought these efforts to a pause but not a complete stop. Following the *coup d'état* in Mali in August 2020, the new interim prime minister, Moctar Ouane, expressed a willingness to engage with Islamists, stating that local leaders had "very clearly indicated the need for an offer of dialogue with (jihadist) armed groups" (AFP 2020). But again, the leading external actor expressed strong reservations: The new French foreign minister rejected the idea (AFP 2020). According to the ICG, "Macron said he told transitional authorities that he would remove French troops from Mali if they engaged with jihadists" (ICG 2021b, 18).[1] This was a strong signal against pursuing negotiations. President Macron followed up on this warning. "In June 2021, shortly after the second coup, Paris suspended its cooperation with Bamako's security forces partly over concerns the junta might start talking with jihadists" (ICG 2021b, 18).[2] According to Thompson (2021), France was "opposed to negotiations with JNIM, and President Emmanuel Macron declared in November 2020 that, 'With terrorists, we do not discuss. We fight.' Because national-level negotiations would likely require a reduction in the pace of French counterterrorism operations in Mali, French opposition to negotiations constrains local political leaders and blocks potential avenues to a negotiated peace."

The fact that the rebels raised radical Islamist demands did not stop conflict resolution efforts from being pursued. "On 21 August 2017, Hamadoun [Amadou] Koufa, a JNIM leader, responded to a reported invitation to enter peace talks in Bamako by saying: 'What dialogue? What are we going to bargain for in this dialogue? Is God for bargaining? God cannot be bargained [about] … Either we prevail and establish the will of God, or we perish'" [Audio recording on file with the Crisis Group] (ICG 2021b, 1). This statement shows signs of religious intransigence and ideological absolutism. However, the group's behavior demonstrated, by contrast, that it was willing to consider a negotiated path. Efforts to take up dialogue continued:

> Ag Ghali and Koufa have reportedly engaged in negotiations with the Malian government and, at times, local authorities, showing at least the willingness to consider a cessation in fighting. Often,

[1] Original source: Le Journal de Dimanche (2021).

[2] Original source: Le Monde Afrique (2021).

> their demands are inconceivable, such as the full withdrawal of French troops from the region or the public enactment of an extreme interpretation of Sharia. Nevertheless, continuing this dialogue is valuable for exploring political avenues for resolving the conflict. (Eizenga and Williams 2020, 7)

The Transnational Dimension and Opportunities for Negotiations

The Malian case demonstrates how the transnational dimension, particularly the diverse interests and perspectives among different groups, is critical in shaping negotiations. Transnational support structures have undermined the conditions for peace talks and settlements, with efforts to encourage Islamist armed actors associated with al-Qaeda to sever their ties and participate in peace dialogue. Several governments in Mali have expressed willingness to engage in negotiations, but they have emphasized that such peace talks can only involve insurgents who identify as national Malians. As in Afghanistan, the Islamist insurgents have demanded the withdrawal of foreign intervention.

When we study the conditions for a negotiated settlement in civil wars, it is essential to examine not only full-fledged, comprehensive peace agreements but also gradual movements toward accommodation and openness to dialogue. Exploring the process can provide insight into the obstacles to achieving peace. The civil war in Mali is important to explore from the perspective of this book, as there have been several attempts at peace negotiations with the Islamist insurgents. The breakaway faction of Ansar Dine even agreed to a peace settlement. While these peace initiatives and attempts have not led to a comprehensive resolution to the conflict, they show that – among certain groups and under some conditions – there has been a degree of willingness to consider negotiations.

In the Malian case, the main fault line in this regard lies between those with a national outlook and perspective and those with a transnational orientation. Within the larger plethora of Islamist militant groups fighting in Mali over the last decade, it is possible to see a pattern: Groups with a national constituency, national or local prioritization of goals and aspirations, and a national-based leadership have, at some juncture, been ready to pursue or consider a negotiated path forward. While it is difficult to determine the exact mixture between the local and global dimensions in the Malian context (Lebovich 2013), it is clear that Ag Ghali and Koufa – both representing what have been seen as *local* Malian armed Islamist actors – have been the key interlocutors in these attempts to establish a dialogue. There seems to be broader public support for dialogue with Islamist armed actors who are Malian in outlook and background, with public perceptions of a distinction between Malian and international insurgents. There have also been plenty of local-level negotiations, including concerning questions about humanitarian access (Bøås, Iocchi, and Osland 2023).

Different governments in Mali have also signaled readiness to engage in dialogue with armed Islamist groups. While the global–local distinction is useful when openness to negotiations is discussed, it should be noted that, empirically, this is complicated: Local and international Islamist armed actors have dynamic relationships. Therefore, there is a high degree of uncertainty regarding whether a group is genuinely locally oriented or is pursuing transnational goals, thereby negatively affecting the chances for progression through peace talks.

Our quantitative analysis in Chapter 3 demonstrated that government-to-government military support may be one central factor behind the intractability of Islamist armed conflicts. As we have seen in the case of Mali, the leading external supporter of the government, France, has also been the main actor resisting negotiations (AFP 2020). France has consistently and repeatedly rejected initiatives for peace dialogue with jihadists, with statements indicating it wants to uphold a tough line against alleged terrorist actors. The primary way in which the Islamist insurgency has been managed – through French-led military intervention and UN-sanctioned peacekeeping – has largely failed to bring the conflict to an end. Instead, according to observers, military involvement in Mali has become a critical recruitment argument for Islamist insurgents: It has propped up incompetent and corrupt regimes in Bamako, and it has further contributed to polarization and escalation of the conflict. As summarized succinctly by Thurston (2020, 315), a scholarly authority on the Mali conflict, "Mali has sunk ever deeper into conflict despite – and I would argue because of – the lasting French combat presence there". Gutelius (2007, 59) reaches a similar conclusion: "The Malian state has actually become less stable ... not because of growing religious extremism per se but rather due to how the US and Malian governments have chosen to conduct and promote the war on terror".

In 2023, the remaining French troops left Mali together with other European militaries. The Russian military interventionist mercenary force known as the Wagner group replaced the French and other Westerners in Mali. We have observed how French involvement posed an obstacle to negotiations. Yet their withdrawal did not appear to suddenly open up new possibilities for conflict resolution between the government of Mali and (some of) the armed Islamist groups. This is possibly because the Malian conflict continued to receive external support, but the patterns of the international support structure were transformed. While the Russian mercenaries were able to pursue armed Islamist actors with fewer human rights considerations and did achieve some local successes in military terms, the conflict became more complex with this change of external supporters, and negotiations and dialogue seemed like a distant prospect.

BREAKING OUT OF GLOBAL JIHAD: HTS IN SYRIA

The Islamist group HTS in Syria was one of the fiercest armed Islamist groups fighting in the Syrian civil war. HTS was known for its jihadi credentials and for introducing suicide killings in the Syrian civil war. However, the group has honored a ceasefire, initiated humanitarian dialogue, and sought to mend fences with external actors. While no formal peace agreement was reached in the conflict, this nevertheless represents a considerable shift. How has this shift toward increased openness to conflict resolution been possible? It is important to look more closely at HTS as it "represents an interesting case of how a Jihadi group turns local in contrast to the well-established narrative of the internationalisation of Jihad" (Hamming 2023, 336). In this section, we explore changes over time that enabled this shift and, in particular, examine the extent to which the decoupling from transnational networks of armed Islamist actors made this shift possible.

The Birth and Growth of HTS

Understanding HTS requires situating it within the evolving and shifting dynamics of the Syrian civil war. The Syrian civil war was the bedrock for a cascade of various armed Islamist groups. It was in the Syrian civil war context that myriad Islamist armed groups of different orientations and leanings sprang up. Among them was the group HTS. In the early stages of the civil war, the group was known as Jabhat al-Nusra (or the al-Nusra Front) but would later switch its name to Jabhat Fatah al-Sham before the group reemerged (together with some other groupings) under the label HTS in January 2017.

In March 2011, the Syrian civil war started as a largely peaceful expression of popular dissent against the authoritarian leadership of Bashar al-Assad. In what became part of the Arab Spring, people took to the streets, demanding regime change. These protests occurred against the backdrop of popular grievances, including rising inequalities, corruption, drought, rapid urbanization, and continued dominance of the political sphere by the Alawite ethno-religious minority in Syria – a branch of the larger Shia tree – over a Sunni majority population, as well as a sense of political opportunity provided by years of slight openings of Syrian society under Bashar al-Assad, including inspiration from other popular revolutions. Fearing being overthrown by a people's revolution, as seen in the early stages of the Arab Spring in 2011 in countries such as Tunisia and Egypt, the regime put all its efforts into crushing the protests. As the uprising became increasingly violent, met by the brutality of the Syrian regime and its security forces, but also with more and more protesters arming themselves in self-defense, the uprising lost its transethnic appeal and became more polarized along sectarian lines. The uprising then appealed to and recruited primarily from the Sunni majority population, whereas the Alawite minority, fearing the dominance of the Sunnis, increasingly fell in line behind al-Assad.

The Syrian civil war was initially fueled by the more secular-oriented Free Syrian Army (FSA), dominated by Sunni Muslims but not founded on any Islamist ideological basis. But as the uprising continued, groups with a more explicit Islamist agenda mobilized against the Assad regime. The potential to attract foreign support from Gulf countries created the possibility for intra-insurgency outbidding, furthering the radicalization of the insurgency movement. Groups competed for influence and foreign backing, giving the more extreme groups an advantage vis-à-vis the others. This incentivized Syrian rebel groups to adopt a more hardened and ideologically pure stance to vie for influence and foreign support.

One of the first groups to adopt a radical stance was Jabhat al-Nusra (later known as HTS), formed formally in January 2012 by Abu Muhammad al-Jolani, a former commander of the Islamic State in Iraq (ISI, the group that later emerged as IS) (Haenni and Drevon 2025, 22). It was created by individuals with jihadist leanings. Championing the agenda of establishing Sharia law in Syria, the group grew out of and was intimately connected to transnational Islamist networks. Its core leadership, including its leader and founder al-Jolani, was steeped in the jihadist milieu and announced the group's formation through international jihadist news networks. While it had not made public any association with al-Qaeda, nor with ISI (which at that point had not splintered from al-Qaeda) – probably because it feared reprisals from external actors and communities in Syria – it still had close organizational, ideological, and personal ties to the wider al-Qaeda network. The Al-Nusra Front presented itself as a protection movement of the people, and while it focused on the situation in Syria – rather than on any lofty goals of a global Caliphate – the front's aspiration grew out of its ideology anchored in the transnational jihadist movement. The Al-Nusra Front aimed to create an Islamic state governed under Sharia law and sought to implement its vision whenever it got the chance to establish some governance structures in territories it gained through military campaigns. It welcomed foreign fighters and used suicide attacks as part of its repertoire of militant actions.

Al-Nusra gained traction through the civil war as an effective military force against the Assad regime. While the opposition and the general public were initially critical of the introduction of what was seen as an alien ideology and an extreme form of Islamism, Al-Nusra gradually increased in popularity. Having said this, widespread opposition by Syrian civilians against the group has occurred throughout the civil war (Svensson and Bamber 2022; Svensson et al. 2022). Nevertheless, the resolve and integrity of its fighters, known for their lack of corruption and piety, increased popular support as the Sunni population radicalized in response to the polarization of the war.

IS in Iraq, decimated by the American surge and tribal Awakening movement, established itself in Syria. The turbulence and chaos of the Syrian civil war provided an opportunity for IS to recreate itself there (Byman 2019, 167; Cockburn 2015, 73). With several jihadist groups having been established separately – and fighting side by side against the Assad regime – the question of authority over the movement became more acute.

Syria thus became one of the main focal points for the increasing intra-jihadist rivalry. The association between the Al-Nusra Front and al-Qaeda tightened, partly driven by rivalry with the emerging IS. As IS grew in size and standing, it started to aspire to hegemony over the jihadists in the Syrian and Iraqi contexts. The Al-Nusra Front had kept its connection to IS out of the public eye. However, seeing Al-Nusra's increasing success in Syria and fearing the group's burgeoning independence, IS leader Abu Bakr al-Baghdadi, who had been instrumental in the first formative stage of the Al-Nusra Front but also had a strained relationship with its leader al-Jolani, demanded that Al-Nusra make public its pledge of allegiance to IS in April 2013, as a way to create a unified front and one organization (Haenni and Drevon 2025; Lister 2016, 13). Thus, the initiative for a merger originated with IS, which unilaterally declared that Al-Nusra should merge with the group. Al-Nusra did not agree to this merger, and in response, Al-Nusra's leader al-Jolani instead turned to al-Qaeda, to which IS at that point was still associated, sidestepping al-Baghdadi, as a way to preserve the group's self-determination. Al-Nusra's leader chose to renew the group's allegiance to al-Qaeda to distance itself from IS and maintain cohesion within the group (Drevon and Haenni 2021, 2). By pledging allegiance to al-Qaeda, al-Jolani hoped al-Qaeda's leader, Ayman al-Zawahiri, would intervene between the groups. Al-Zawahiri did so and demanded that IS focus on Iraq and leave the Syrian context. But IS refused, thereby creating the definitive split between al-Qaeda and IS in the context of the Levant and marking the beginning of the fight of jihadists against jihadists (Byman 2019, 169; Filiu 2015, 204). IS turned its guns on al-Qaeda. The Al-Nusra Front, now an al-Qaeda associate, joined the war against IS in January 2014. Behind the intra-jihadi conflict were different strategic priorities, including divergent approaches to the recruitment of foreign fighters, as well as a leadership battle – who should be in the high seat of the jihadist movement – but the conflict can also be seen as a manifestation of a more fundamental ideological shift, as the movements of al-Qaeda and IS represent very different strategic visions (Haenni and Drevon 2025; Lister 2016).

Decoupling from the Transnational Movement

At this point, Al-Nusra did not distance itself from the transnational jihadist movement as such but rather deepened its ties with al-Qaeda as it broke off with IS. The ties to al-Qaeda, however, soon caused internal problems within the movement. Some factions feared they would be blacklisted because of the links to al-Qaeda or that it would legitimize al-Assad's rhetoric of a "war on terror" and cut off help from foreign parties. External powers' priorities shifted from supporting the opposition against al-Assad to worrying about the growth and expansion of the transnational armed Islamist movements in Iraq and Syria. The US and Russia began to plan for a military campaign against Al-Nusra (Al-Tamimi 2018; Lister 2016). Given the risk of internal fragmentation and increased external military intervention, Al-Nusra, in consultation with, and to some extent with the blessing of, the core al-Qaeda leadership, decided to distance itself from al-Qaeda. The reorientation of the movement also manifested in the group's change of name. Thus, on July 28, 2016, Al-Nusra changed its name to Jabhat Fatah al-Sham in an attempt to signal that they had severed ties with al-Qaeda. However, contacts, ties, and potentially also secret alliances were still in place behind the public rhetoric (Hamming 2023). Yet, "in 2016, Al-Nusra severed ties with al-Qaeda before transforming itself the following year into Hei'at Tahrir al-Sham (HTS), a group that claimed to be – and indeed thus far is – battling the Syrian regime rather than waging global jihad" (Drevon 2022a, 1). Hence, the group's merger in January 2017 with other more locally oriented and locally based Islamist groups to form HTS can be seen as the more definitive break with al-Qaeda. There was a "disconnection of HTS from the global jihad" (Drevon and Haenni 2021, 2; see also Carenzi 2020). This disconnection grew out of different strategic and theological analyses and interpretations of how to wage jihad, including differences over elite versus mass mobilization and whether collaboration with Türkiye was legitimate (Hamming 2023). HTS forswore transnational jihadist ambitions and instead focused only on governing locally. From then on, it allegedly pursued a more inclusive "Syrian Islamist agenda" rather than a transnational jihadist one (ICG 2020).

It was not only Al-Nusra that saw external involvement. On the government side, there was considerable involvement from foreign states. Iran and Russia sided with the Assad government from the beginning of the popular uprising but became increasingly involved as the insurgency gained traction and won territory. While this was driven by the rapid progress of IS, Iran's and Russia's ties to Syria preceded the civil war (Hamilton, Miller, and Stein 2020; Therme 2008). Iran supported Syria through its militias from the early years of the war, whereas Russia provided military equipment and, from 2015 onward, direct military air support. Militarily speaking, Iran was the more active supporter at the beginning of the civil war, but the war shifted decisively through Russia's involvement on the side of the government in 2015 (Lund 2019), and Iran simultaneously stepped up its land-based military operations (Lund 2016). The Iranian and Russian support on the side of the government arguably made it difficult for its opponents, including Al-Nusra, to get a proper sense of the resolve and power of the government. Russia's connections to Syria date back a long time, and its motivations for supporting the Syrian regime, despite international criticism, were related to issues such as concern over the spread of the color revolution, the risk of losing an allied partner, the need to stave off Western influence, and possibly (especially after the Libyan intervention) the desire to hinder a Western attempt at regime change through external force (Lund 2019). The more aggressive approach, perceiving the Syrian conflict through the prism of tension with the Western world, intensified notably after Putin resumed the presidency in 2012 (Lund 2019, 20). The Iranian-backed Hezbollah movement in Lebanon also supported the Assad regime, first through training and later through direct intervention in the conflict.

Space for Conflict Resolution

HTS has not been invited to participate in any peace talks, and there has not been any formal peace process between HTS and the Syrian government, but the group has signaled an openness to dialogue with internal and external actors (Drevon and Haenni 2022, 11; Tsurkov 2019). While HTS was once "as extreme as they come with roots in al-Qaeda," the group "has shown a growing willingness to compromise" (Tsurkov 2019). Its leadership has engaged in a public relations campaign, intending to "seek legitimacy by presenting a moderate face to the world, in order to be included in the political process and ensure its continued presence in Idlib" (The New Arab 2020).

The organization has shown an increased openness toward external actors; for example, HTS "has invited journalists and foreign researchers to visit Idlib under its protection," and the "group also allowed Turkey to establish observation posts in areas under its control, despite the opposition of hard liners in its ranks" (Tsurkov 2019). As part of the Astana negotiation process spearheaded by Russia, where Iran also played an active role, HTS allowed Turkish soldiers to enter Idlib to uphold a ceasefire agreement (Soliman 2021; Tsurkov 2019).[3] Thus, HTS largely respected the ceasefire decreed by Türkiye and Russia (Crisis Group 2020, 20). As the Syrian regime was able to establish control over most of Syria, with the exception of the Kurdish Rojava region and the Idlib territory neighboring Türkiye in the north, the prospect for a comprehensive political settlement looked ever bleaker. Still, it is evident that HTS has been seeking to play a constructive political role based on what it perceived to be its position as the protector of the people of Idlib. In fact, "Hei'at Tahrir al-Sham (HTS), the former al-Qaeda affiliate that is Idlib's dominant rebel group, has broken with transnational jihadist networks and now seeks entry into the realm of political engagement on Syria's future" (ICG 2021a, 2). For example, HTS has taken measures to protect religious minorities and their cultural heritage within its realms.

As HTS disengaged from global jihad, it reoriented its focus to the local context in northern Syria. HTS did not set up its own governance there but instead formed a civilian-technocratic governance structure in Idlib, its last stronghold. This measure can be seen as a move to appease the West. HTS also removed foreign fighters and arrested al-Qaeda-linked rebel leaders. The group engaged in military operations against IS and successfully rooted out IS cells from Idlib (al-Aswad 2020). Moreover, HTS also reluctantly concluded that it

[3] Hardliners opposing this broke off and formed Hurras al-Din.

must seek accommodation with Türkiye. While Türkiye has previously supported groups other than HTS in the civil war, the relationship between HTS and Türkiye has developed over time. From HTS's perspective, Türkiye became the only country able to act as a guarantor for the protection of Idlib province against the Syrian government and Russian air military attacks (Al Kanj 2018). External actors, including the International Crisis Group, have noted the change and reorientation of the group, and there have been increasing calls for engagement with the group to find solutions to the humanitarian situation in the region (ICG 2021a).

From De-transnationalization to Conflict Resolution

In the case of HTS in Syria, it is important to understand the dynamics of de-transnationalization and how this process forms the basic space for conflict resolution. HTS initially distanced itself from IS in 2013 and three years later broke ties with al-Qaeda, a disassociation driven in part by ideological differences but primarily by what was seen as a strategic adaptation given the context (Haenni and Drevon 2025). As HTS disassociated itself from global jihadist networks, it also signaled its willingness to engage in diplomatic encounters and dialogue with external actors. A few central observations about this case can be made.

The temporal order of events is crucial for making causal inferences. The case of HTS demonstrates how variation in the degree of transnationalization (the group's de-transnationalization) impacted the group's propensity for conflict resolution. Establishing the temporal order can help rule out alternative explanations. From a theoretical perspective, it is imperative that this case shows how ideological revisions came *after* the organizational break with the transnational networks. The organization broke with IS in 2013–2014 and with al-Qaeda in 2016–2017, while the group's less extreme, more tolerant ideological approach manifested after the severing of these transnational ties. This suggests that the transnational dimension is the key driver in terms of intractability rather than the ideological factor per se.

After all, even after the break with first IS and then al-Qaeda, the group sustained "Islamic State aspirations for creating a caliphate in Syria" and remained committed "to the jihadi vision of statehood" (Watts 2016, 4). As we saw earlier, HTS cut ties with IS and al-Qaeda primarily for strategic reasons and those relating to leadership issues rather than fundamental ideological differences.

Our argument suggests a causal chain from transnationalization (or de-transnationalization) to intractability (or conflict resolution). But the causal arrow may run in the opposite direction. It is theoretically possible that conflict resolution may be a way to encourage groups to disassociate themselves from transnational jihadist networks. From a theoretical perspective, it is therefore essential to notice that HTS's openness to conflict resolution – its willingness to accommodate – was demonstrated *after* the break with the transnational jihadist networks. Thus, conflict resolution did not lead HTS to break with its transnational partners, but rather the break with those partners created space for conflict resolution.

HTS – at that time named Al-Nusra – was formed with the aspiration of protecting the Syrian revolution from the government's attacks and repression, but also to introduce the ideas of a transnational jihadist movement into the revolution. The group's claims tapped into the worldview and imaginaries of the international jihadist movement, appealing to Muslim foreign fighters to come and join the fight. Once the conflict was framed in Islamist terms, any prospect of finding a solution with the government in Damascus became dim. What started as an internal Syrian conflict was hijacked by a partly foreign-influenced insurgency. This prompted the backers of the Syrian regime to increase their military support in response. The case thus demonstrates, in line with our argument presented earlier, how the formation of Islamist claims generates external support, which in turn can increase the intractability of the conflict. However, the case also adds nuance and further complexity to the analysis by demonstrating that external support was also conducive to the initial formation of the Islamist group. As the conflict polarized Syrian society and the insurgents radicalized, there was increased incentive for the rebels to seek external support. By appealing to the larger Muslim world and, in particular, an Islamist-leaning audience, HTS leader al-Jolani hoped to salvage support for the group and its aspirations. The framing was thus done in anticipation of external support.

HTS has significantly changed its organizational set-up and alliance patterns over time (Adraoui 2017). This demonstrates that Islamist groups can change. These shifts are strategic decisions in which the organization has struggled to survive and flourish in a dramatically shifting strategic environment, where the group has tried to achieve internal and external legitimization. Its transnationalization, with its close association with al-Qaeda, was a strategic move aimed at fending off IS. And so, too, was its de-transnationalization, as the group moved to cut ties with al-Qaeda (Jameel 2020). The organization adapted to the changing circumstances, fighting for its autonomy first against the Syrian regime and later against IS's hegemonic ambitions. The advantages outweighed the costs, and this calculation shifted over time (Drevon and Haenni 2022).

As long as HTS was associated with al-Qaeda, there was a high degree of uncertainty regarding HTS's resolve and capabilities, particularly the extent to which it could draw on foreign support from transnational Islamist networks and whether it was seeking to establish Islamist governance in Syria as just one step toward a broader transnational project. During this conflict phase, no negotiations or conflict resolution attempts occurred with the group. As HTS moved away from its connections with the transnational jihadist networks to become more localized in its approach, negotiations with the group became an option in a different manner than previously anticipated. Its limited but solid territorial control, along with its local goals of establishing Islamic governance for the Sunni Muslim population based in northern Syria, positioned it as a viable actor for negotiation. However, the classification of HTS as a terrorist group by the US, the UK, Russia, Türkiye, and within the UN has been perceived by the group as unwarranted and detrimental to its legitimacy. The designation of HTS's predecessor, the Al-Nusra Front, as a terrorist organization under UN Security Council Resolution 1267, was a consequence of its pledge of allegiance to al-Qaeda (as part of its separation from IS) (Haenni and Drevon 2025, 39). The proscription of and international sanctions against the group thus served as an obstacle to formal negotiations with HTS, as proscription of armed actors can make it harder for third-party actors to engage in resolution attempts (e.g., Haspeslagh 2021; Lundgren, Janson, and Lundqvist 2025).

While our primary focus has been on tracing the potential for negotiations with HTS, we here briefly touch upon the applicability of our argument for understanding the more recent events wherein HTS seized power. As we saw in the case of Afghanistan, described in Chapter 4, the civil war in Afghanistan was brought to an end once it was de-transnationalized. In the case of Syria, the external interveners were faced with dynamics beyond Syria, which led some actors on the government side to withdraw or substantially decrease their engagement. Hezbollah was weakened by the war with Israel in 2024 and needed to refocus on its home front in Lebanon. Iran was weakened by the damage suffered by its proxies Hamas and Hezbollah, as well as by Israeli actions against its air defense. Russia needed to prioritize its efforts in the war with Ukraine. Thus, the Assad regime no longer had the full backing of Iran, Hezbollah, and Russia. The rebels, spearheaded by HTS, used the opportunity to advance toward Damascus, and military support for the regime imploded. As pointed out by Drevon and Haenni, the victory of 2024 would not have been possible absent the transformation of the HTS, which enabled it to forge new connections – locally as well as internationally (2025, 2). As we have shown in this chapter, the rebel group HTS had previously de-transnationalized by breaking away from its international network of jihadists and instead focused on the local Syrian context. The conflict ended through military victory for the rebel side in late 2024. Thus, the conflict's termination (through rebel victory) was preceded and enabled by the withdrawal of external actors from Syria.

The victory of the rebels spearheaded by HTS led to another transformation. After HTS's leader al-Jolani, now under the name of Ahmed al-Shaara, led his troops in a successful overthrow of the regime in late 2024, the group and its leadership shifted their tone, rhetoric, and policies, now as leaders of the Syrian state, trying to mend fences with external actors (including Russia and the US) and build trust with local minorities. Communal violence, in which the Alawite and the Druze minorities were targeted, casts doubts about how thorough the transformation of HTS and al-Shaara into respectable statesmen really is. Still, the fact that the attacks against religious minorities were curtailed points to a possibility of a more profound transformation of Syria, beyond both sectarianism and authoritarianism. Whether such a development will occur is far from certain. Whether Syria can cultivate the fruits of its revolution and newly won freedom from the Assad regime remains an open question.

DECOUPLING FROM THE TRANSNATIONAL DIMENSIONS IN THE ISLAMIST CIVIL WARS IN MALI AND SYRIA

The Islamist civil wars in Mali and Syria have exhibited different dynamics and outcomes, but as shown here, studying Islamist armed actors in these cases is essential if we seek to understand the possibilities for conflict resolution in Islamist civil wars.

In both cases, we observe how the transnational element created obstacles to conflict resolution. Foreign fighters on the rebel side have been prevalent in Mali and Syria. The uncertainty created around the potential linkages between local Islamists and their international networks has affected the ability of the conflict actors to reach a resolution. The presence of foreign fighters on the rebel side is thus definitely part of the picture, but only one part. Internationalization on the side of the government also played an important role, if not a larger role, in making the Islamist civil wars more challenging to resolve. The Assad regime in Syria, backed by Russia and Iran, has been the most intransigent, while the HTS jihadists have gradually shifted to display a readiness for transformation and openness. In Mali, one of the main obstacles to conflict resolution with the local jihadists has been the French government, which has warned against the risk of negotiating with terrorists. As we have shown, the tension between the domestic and transnational elements of the Islamist movements has characterized the insurgency and shaped the contours of the attempts to negotiate peace.

In Syria, HTS has shown signs of moderation and change and signaled an opening for negotiations after it broke out of its trans-jihadist networks. The government of Syria never distanced itself from its regional external supporters and patrons (Russia and Iran) and showed little sign of any such transformation up to the point of its demise. In Mali, only one breakaway faction of the Islamist militant group agreed to a settlement, but two major Islamist rebel groups have demonstrated a willingness to pursue negotiations. Ansar Dine and Katiba Macina are two Islamist armed groups with Malian roots, orientations, and aspirations. As we have shown here, both Ansar Dine and Katiba Macina were as religiously motivated and anchored as AQIM (to which they were also allied), but both groups were, at several junctures during the conflict, open to considering negotiations, and the government of Mali also repeatedly showed interest in holding talks with them. AQIM, in contrast, had transnational ambitions and origins and consistently ruled out the possibility of negotiations with the Malian state. The Malian state similarly rejected the idea of conflict resolution with this group. We have identified some of the most critical negotiation attempts, clarifying how the different groups have very different track records in terms of their openness to negotiating with the government, whereas the government of Mali has tried to engage with Islamist groups (even of the Salafi-jihadist type), provided they are perceived as Malian. This important distinction has not been lost on case experts, and we are thus not the first to make this observation (Ero and Mutiga 2021). Conflict resolution attempts are not obsolete in Islamist armed conflicts as long as they are framed along local and domestic issues.

It is important to recognize that de-transnationalization is rare. Regarding religion in civil wars, Toft (2021) has identified a "ratchet effect": Once religion becomes central to a dispute, it tends to stay that way. We can see a similar dynamic regarding the transnationalization of Islamist armed conflicts. There seems to be a ratchet effect in the escalation patterns: When conflicts become connected to transnational Islamist networks, it is difficult to put the genie back in the bottle. The cases we explore here – in Mali and Syria – are exceptions; they are examples of Islamist rebel groups that have had various types of connections and alliances with transnational Islamist networks but have disassociated themselves from them.

Rival explanatory approaches to the one we propose here would have difficulty substantiating the trajectories of the two cases. The cases are examples of Islamist civil wars that have included conflict resolution efforts by Islamist groups and actors. On the one hand, the essentialist perspective suggests that Islamist rebel groups are simply too radical and extreme to be negotiated with, and thus it struggles to explain the negotiations that have occurred in these cases. On the other hand, the fact that these actors continued to be anchored in Islamist ideology, thought, and practice demonstrates that the ideological factor continues to be important, which goes against an instrumentalist perspective in which religion is seen as simply epiphenomenal. Moreover, in the earlier debate, these two explanatory approaches – taking the religious factor too seriously or not seriously enough – would also have problems accounting for the dynamics over time. When there were openings for conflict resolution, the Islamists of Mali and Syria were as religiously motivated as previously in the conflict; what had changed were their transnational outlook and alliances. As this chapter has shown, the local–global dimension was central for conflict resolution to take place.

7 Conclusion

How to End Islamist Civil Wars

WHAT WE ARGUE

This book has examined how to end Islamist civil wars. In contrast to essentialist as well as instrumentalist perspectives, we argue that once conflicts are framed in Islamist terms, these conflicts become embedded in a strategic context that can enhance uncertainty about the capabilities and resolve of the actors, thereby making these conflicts more intractable and difficult to end. Hence, our explanation of strategic embeddedness focuses on the strategic interaction between Islamist insurgencies and governments and how Islamist ideology creates a potential for transnational connections beyond the borders of the state. Islamist conflicts are therefore vulnerable to a type of external involvement that enhances the complexity and strategic uncertainty regarding the true strength and commitment of the parties. It is this, we argue, that is the key reason behind the longevity of conflicts involving Islamist actors. The type of external support that Islamist conflicts experience – a non-state network on the Islamist side and government-to-government support on the other side – creates a particular type of strategic environment characterized by higher levels of uncertainty, primarily because the military support conceals the resolve and true capabilities of the parties. Thus, the reason why it is so challenging to silence the guns in Islamist conflicts lies not primarily in their intrinsic nature, but in how they are embedded in a larger web of transnational connections supporting the Islamist rebels or the governments fighting them.

WHAT WE FIND

Let us now take stock of what we have found, using a combination of quantitative and qualitative methods. First, studying all intrastate conflicts globally, we show that Islamist conflicts are less likely to terminate and more likely to recur (re-erupting in old or new conflict manifestations) than other types of conflicts. This holds even after accounting for potential spurious effects as well as mainstream explanatory factors for termination and sustainable peace. We find that the international character of Islamist conflicts – the potential for access to a network of foreign fighters on the rebel side and the potential for government-to-government military support on the other – sets these apart from other types of conflicts. Exploring the plausibility of our argument qualitatively, we rely on two case illustrations – Afghanistan and Mauritania – where the former got locked into decades of internationalized civil wars, while the latter followed a different trajectory and its conflict was relatively brief. Afghanistan is a dark example of an intractable civil war, largely driven by transnational dimensions. By contrast, the case of Mauritania demonstrates that Islamist conflicts can be brought to an end, and that the key lies in insulating the conflict from external actors and avoiding entanglement in regional or global battles. The end phase of the Afghanistan case also testifies to this: Only after the conflict was de-transnationalized was the civil war brought to an end in the form of a decisive rebel victory. At the same time, while the war did come to a halt, and as we discuss later, the subsequent period has also involved many challenges, for example, in terms of the Taliban's strict authoritarian rule and a deterioration of human rights.

Developing the analysis beyond conflict termination and recurrence, we show that the transnational element of Islamist conflicts is the key explanation for the challenges regarding conflict resolution. We analyze whether our explanation, which puts the explanatory heavy lifting on the transnational dimensions of Islamist conflicts, can account for variations in conflict resolution within the category of Islamist conflicts. We explore two central dimensions of conflict resolution: negotiations and peace agreements. Our quantitative cross-country analysis shows that Islamist conflicts that are transnational in their orientation and organizational set-up are less likely to see both negotiations and peace agreements compared with other types of conflicts. Our analysis thus demonstrates that there are important variations within the category of Islamist conflicts. Deepening this analysis, we also examine two cases of Islamist civil wars – Mali and Syria – that display variations that are important for this book. In Mali, we focus on variations between groups and find that the transnational dimension has been critical in explaining differences in the parties' openness to peace negotiations and settlements. In Syria, we examine variation over time, focusing on the case of HTS, and show how this group transformed from a branch of a transnational Islamist network into a domestically rooted Syrian armed actor. This transformation enabled the movement to engage in dialogue and efforts at accommodation (although not negotiations and peace agreements) and paved the way for it to become a leading force in the post-al-Assad Syrian government.

DISCUSSING OUR FINDINGS

This book has sought to identify the scope for ending and resolving Islamist armed conflicts. We demonstrated that the key empirical insights generated in this book – the intractability of Islamist armed conflicts, as well as their exceptional magnitude and form of transnational involvement – continue to present a challenge for peace and security. In this section, we discuss our argument and findings in light of recent developments, particularly the winding down of Western interventions, and the potential negative effects on gender equality and religious minorities that may be associated with the termination of Islamist conflicts.

Our argument leads us to expect that the problem of intractability in Islamist civil wars is particularly prominent in conflicts that are highly transnationalized and also offers a way to address it. Our explanation suggests an alternative analysis and approach to Islamist civil wars than what has dominated the international discourse and practice over the last decades. If the primary reasons for the intractability of Islamist conflicts lie in the religious fervor and sentiments of the religious radicals, which have often been the key narrative and underlying assumption in previous debate and practice, then offensive military actions would be part of the recipe for the termination of these conflicts. Weak governments should thus receive military support to combat Islamist rebels. However, if the reason for intractability lies in the external dimension, as we suggest here, military intervention is part of the problem, not the solution. The question becomes how to de-link Islamist conflicts from their transnational connections. Military actors still have an important role to play in helping protect borders and containing the spread of movements. Yet the key to sustainable solutions lies in disconnecting Islamist conflicts from the support structures associated with transnational battles.

A recent political development has been the decreased military engagement, particular through the withdrawal of Western troops, which – if our argument is correct – could pave the way for better chances to end Islamist civil wars, including by peaceful means. But, as the US and its Western allies, including France and the UK, have wound down their military engagement, why do we not see more openings for conflict resolution? Recent years have seen indications of shifts in the overall trend of internationalization of Islamist civil wars in terms of the type of state actors intervening with troops on the ground in Islamist armed conflicts. In some cases, Western withdrawal has not meant an end to external influence, but rather that the identity of the intervening states has shifted: When American and French troops on the ground have left, other countries have seemed keen to step in; for example, Russia has been increasing its involvement. Mali is a case in point. The decision by France to end its intervention, after the authoritarian Malian government turned against them, has led to Russian mercenaries, primarily through the Wagner Group, stepping in. As a result, Mali has sunk deeper into civil war. What we may be witnessing is thus a shifting empirical landscape in terms of diversification of the type of intervening countries; instead of being dominated by the US and France, other states are now more frequently intervening in other conflicts. Hence, to some extent, other states have stepped in to fill the void left by the US and France. This is thus *not* a case of localization, but a reconfiguration of the transnationalization of the Islamist civil war. The larger transformations of international power relationships that have been emerging in Africa and the Middle East – with an assertive Russia trying to spread its influence and presence, and with the clout of middle powers such as Türkiye and the United Arab Emirates rising – have complicated the processes of military disengagement. Hence, withdrawal by some countries may create vacuums that are filled by others with little interest in ending Islamist civil wars but who instead want to use such conflicts to advance their own interests.

The ending of Islamist civil wars may have negative consequences in other areas, such as a deterioration of gender equality. Policymakers in and outside countries facing Islamist insurgencies should recognize that while conflict termination may help alleviate humanitarian suffering that results from civil wars, such advancement can, at the same time, hinder the advancement of women's or minority rights. Hence, third parties should carefully consider how to effectively terminate conflicts without risking undermining developments in other areas. As we pointed out in the analysis of Afghanistan, the war ended once both sides de-transnationalized, but the way it ended empowered the hard core among the Taliban, which is one explanation for the authoritarian development of the country. The achievements of women in Afghanistan, in terms of education, political and cultural influence, and economic power, have been rolled back. Girls and women now suffer under an oppressive regime that allows them little space. While Afghanistan is not engulfed in a large-scale civil war, which, in some ways, is a respite for the civilian population, including women, the Taliban regime has, in direct contradiction of the commitment to international human rights obligations, implemented measures that severely restrict the opportunities for women and that violate their human rights (Qazi Zada and Qazi Zada 2024). Mauritania, which is an example of a country that has been able to end a civil war, has not witnessed any notable improvement in gender equality. Indeed, Mauritania is a conservative society, ranking 182nd out of 202 countries in 2023 in terms of gender equality in respect for civil liberties, according to data by V-Dem (Coppedge et al. 2025). Another case is Aceh in Indonesia, where an Islamist civil war ended through a peace agreement in 2005. The situation for women in Aceh following the peace agreement has taken a negative turn. Increased Islamization of Acehnese society affected women by limiting their room for maneuver, socially as well as politically. Afghanistan, Mauritania, and Indonesia are examples that illustrate a larger point: the gender dilemma involved in peacemaking, a subset of the more general tension between the normative goals of peace and justice. Bringing Islamist civil wars to an end has, in some cases, led to a deterioration of women's rights.

However, it is important to point out that this is not automatically the case; in Bangsamoro, in the Philippines, the 2014 peace agreement with the Islamist group MILF included gender provisions aimed at enhancing gender equality. The implementation of such provisions was accelerated by the combination of gender awareness among state actors and the active mobilization of women's civil society (Duque-Salazar, Forsberg, and Olsson 2022). The Bangsamoro peace agreement, a result of negotiations led (on the government side) by the chair of the government's Peace Panel, Miriam Coronel-Ferrer, the first woman to be a lead negotiator in a peace process, shows the potential of peace agreements, even in conflicts framed in Islamist terms, to be designed in a way that seeks to improve gender quality. Thus, the Philippines illustrates a path to avoid the trade-off between ending wars and safeguarding gender equality.

To engage with locally oriented Islamist actors does not mean, however, that mediators need to engage *only* with them. Bringing in larger sectors of society, not least representatives of women's organizations and religious minorities, can potentially help to alleviate some of the dangers that are associated with talking to such militants. Peacemaking efforts have often been too exclusive, on both ends of the spectrum. Peacemakers have usually refrained from engaging with violent Islamist actors, even those who are locally based and oriented. Concerning the broader population, mediators have often been too restrictive in including civil society actors through meaningful participation and various avenues. There is a need for more inclusive peacemaking on both ends. More inclusive approaches to peacemaking are therefore potentially important in addressing Islamist armed conflicts.[1] In the cases of Afghanistan and Mauritania, the outside world has more than just military means – including political, economic, and cultural tools – to push for greater protection of women's rights and to reduce potential negative effects on gender equality when bringing Islamist civil wars to an end. For external actors, it is important to stay engaged and work in collaboration with progressive actors and networks, including in the post-conflict phase. Openness to engagement with Islamist armed actors should not be interpreted as appeasement. Many of the Islamist armed actors that take up arms hold values that are diametrically opposed to those of a liberal democracy, including respect for women, religious minorities, and religious freedom. Governments facing Islamist insurgencies and external third parties should therefore be ready for critical engagement, not forsaking the values of democracy and pluralism. This means continuing, through political means, to press for democratic values while remaining open to dialogue and negotiations.

The ending of an Islamist civil war, if it empowers Islamists through political means, may also have negative repercussions for religious minorities. As the civil war in Syria ended through a decisive victory for the HTS rebels, which was preceded by HTS disconnecting from its earlier global jihadist networks as well as a decrease in international involvement by Iran and Hezbollah, the question

[1] On this point, see Göldner-Ebenthal and Dudouet (2019). For the wider literature on civil society inclusion in peacemaking, see, for example, Hellmüller (2024), Lanz (2011), Nilsson (2012), and Paffenholz (2014).

of how religious minorities will be impacted is an open question. The attacks in early 2025 on Alawites, the religious group that served as the backbone of the earlier Assad regime, demonstrates that even if the main conflict is terminated, minorities and other vulnerable groups may suffer in its wake. Hence, while the overthrow of al-Assad meant improved conditions for some groups and a clear improvement in terms of political freedom compared with the repressive regime that was ousted, the termination of the civil war did not translate into societal peace and harmony. After HTS took power, many members of religious minority groups in Syria feared a future dominated by the Sunni Muslim majority, particularly when led by a government consisting of former fighters from Islamist armed groups (e.g., Fefer 2025). The attacks against civilians that occurred in early 2025 showed that the al-Sharaa regime was not able to police its armed forces and created an acute sense of vulnerability among the Alawite minority. Still, international as well as domestic pressure incentivized the al-Sharaa regime to take measures to protect religious minorities in the country rather than simply replacing one repressive system with another. While long-term developments remain to be seen, the Syrian case illustrates the more general point that war termination in Islamist armed conflicts does not necessarily mean an end to violence, as violence may continue in new or other manifestations (Svensson, Nilsson, and Gåsste 2024).

CONTRIBUTIONS TO THE LITERATURE AND AVENUES FOR FUTURE RESEARCH

In this book, we have demonstrated that Islamist conflicts indeed are more intractable than other forms, and we have put forward an explanation that emphasizes the transnational dimension and the support structures that often embed these conflicts. One of the main contributions of this book is to bring the study of conflict resolution into the analysis of Islamist civil wars. For far too long, scholars interested in the termination and resolution of armed conflicts eschewed the study of Islamist civil wars and subsumed this category of conflict into other types. And for far too long, scholars studying Islamist civil wars did not engage with the civil war termination and resolution literature. This, however, has started to change. As we noted at the outset of the book, scholars have begun to uncover the prospects for conflict termination and resolution in Islamist civil wars (e.g., Krause 2025; Lundgren and Svensson 2020; Matesan 2020a; Nilsson and Svensson 2021; Sheikh 2020; Söderberg Kovacs 2020b; Thurston 2018; Toft 2007; Toros and Harley 2018) and in religiously framed conflicts more generally (e.g., Deitch 2022; Hassner 2009; Juergensmeyer 2022; Svensson 2007, 2012, 2021).

By understanding the specific features of Islamist conflicts, which become clear when studying Islamist civil wars in comparison with other types of conflicts, as we have done in this book, we are better positioned to understand the dynamics through which these conflicts can be brought to an end. By incorporating the study of conflict resolution into the analysis of Islamist armed conflicts, this book aims to help bridge scholarly fields that have been commonly isolated from each other, in particular strategic studies (including terrorism studies) and peace and conflict research.

Our book is situated within a broader debate on religious conflicts, where we find two contrasting perspectives on understanding religion in war. We have contributed to this debate by proposing a strategic explanation that takes issue with both instrumentalist and essentialist perspectives. In contrast to the instrumentalist perspective, our explanation suggests that Islamist conflicts do stand out from other conflicts; once framed in Islamist terms, they acquire a distinct dynamic that renders them more intractable. In contrast to the essentialist perspective, we argue that their intractability is not inherent in the ideology or their extremist nature but is due to the strategic environment in which they become embedded when the parties have adopted an Islamist rhetoric. In this book, we have provided evidence to support our explanation, demonstrating that Islamist conflicts follow a distinct path, which renders them more difficult to resolve once such rhetoric has been adopted. We also provide considerable evidence showing that their intractability does not lie in the ideology per se.

Our argument emphasizes that when armed actors frame their ideological struggle in Islamist terms, this comes with the potential of external support on the side of the rebel insurgents or the government. By shedding light on these dynamics and how they can shape the prospects for intractability and resolution of these conflicts, our book also contributes to a better understanding of the role of ideology in war. While this scholarly debate is both broad and deep, and we cannot fully engage with it here, we contribute with a better understanding of the *interaction* between ideological and material factors. These are commonly seen as polar opposites. Ideological claim-making, here in the form of the raising of explicit Islamist demands, however, comes with the potential for important material benefits (in terms of particular types of external engagement) that affect the strategic environment in which the conflicts are fought. We have shown that this affects Islamist conflicts in terms of a higher risk of intractability and makes the subcategory of transnational Islamist conflicts particularly unlikely to be resolved through negotiations and peace agreements. Making Islamist claims, particularly when appealing to transnational networks, increases the risk that foreign fighters will join and that other states will intervene militarily on the government side. This suggests a way to think about (religious) ideology in conflicts: It is an important explanatory factor, but it works through its material implications.

In this study, we have focused on the most manifest forms of external involvement – military interventions and foreign fighters. While the role of foreign fighters in enhancing intractability has been identified previously (Toft and Zhukov 2015), this is only one side of the coin, and our analysis contributes to this debate by showing how foreign intervention on the government side also limits the space for the termination and resolution of Islamist civil wars. Still, more research is needed on other forms of support to rebels and governments. This includes taking into account material forms of support below full-scale intervention. It also suggests taking into account the impact of immaterial support – of a political, cultural, and social nature – to study how such support influences the dynamics of conflicts.

Showing that the applicability of conflict resolution has limitations when it comes to transnationalized conflicts should not be misunderstood as an argument for defeatism. It does not render conflict resolution inapplicable, but it does suggest that certain conditions need to be in place first, and it thus speaks to the question of sequencing when trying to find ways to resolve armed conflicts. In this book, we have shown that conflicts can be transformed in a manner that opens space for conflict resolution in Islamist civil wars. Conflict resolution needs a certain degree of localization to be applicable, but it can also help to create greater distance from transnational actors and connections, thus furthering the localization process. The study of the localization processes whereby Islamist actors either refrain from connecting with transnational global networks or disengage from these is an important contribution of this study. However, more work remains to be done in understanding the conditions under which this process can unfold.

This book has taken a broad approach to studying how Islamist civil wars are related to a number of outcomes: termination, recurrence, negotiations, and peace agreements. We have shown that Islamist civil wars stand out in terms of termination and recurrence, and that the subcategory of transnational Islamist conflicts represents exceptionally difficult cases in terms of peace negotiations and agreements. Still, more research is needed in terms of studying the outcomes of Islamist conflicts, including the quality of peace that may follow after different forms of conflict endings. It also requires taking seriously the question of gender inclusion and how gender equality may be negatively impacted by peacemaking with Islamist groups. Another important area to understand more deeply is how the termination of Islamist civil wars may affect processes relating to democratization and autocratization, particularly if such terminations empower Islamist groups (as we have seen in the case of Afghanistan).

Future research should also investigate the implications for the de-transnationalization of Islamist conflicts in the emerging polarized global politics. The world is undergoing a turbulent period as US dominance in world politics is being challenged and an era of wider great power conflicts is emerging. The threat posed by al-Qaeda and IS brought all the great powers together, even if not in a unified front, with at least a common purpose and a joint enemy. Russia and China, as well as the European countries and the US, all had Islamist insurgencies and threats that unified them in their military approach. For example, in Syria, despite standing on different sides (government versus the opposition), Russia and the US were unified in their resistance against IS. This unity is now evaporating as the focus is shifting toward increasing tensions and rivalries between the great powers, which accelerated after the Russian full-scale invasion of Ukraine on February 24, 2022. This may open both possibilities and risks in terms of ending Islamist civil wars. The dominant approach in the post-9/11 period was to rely on external military intervention and intergovernmental collaboration in combating Islamist insurgents, but this has now changed. As we have demonstrated in this book, transnationalization is an approach that has characterized Islamist civil wars more than other conflicts and helps to explain why they have become so intractable. The shifting global politics may therefore mean that Western states are less interested in investing in external interventions in Islamist civil wars, which may create possibilities for local actors to seek locally adapted approaches and solutions. Yet the emerging, more polarized global order also creates risks in terms of decreased capabilities for collaboration on constructive measures to approach Islamist civil wars, such as diplomatic measures, policing, sanction regimes, and international efforts to limit foreign fighters. And there is a risk that certain actors – especially Russia – will exploit states weakened by Islamist civil wars, particularly in the

MENA region surrounding Europe, to establish a stronger foothold for larger strategic purposes.

This book has centered on Islamist civil wars, which are armed conflicts where Islamist thought and ideas have been used in mobilization efforts in support of violence. It is important to recognize that we have only focused on the negative and destructive aspects of religious mobilization (and more secular counter-mobilization). This is only one side of the coin. There is a duality to the role of religion in armed conflict, a "sacred ambivalence" (Appleby 2000): Religion can serve the purposes of war mobilization, but also of peace promotion (Kapshuk and Deitch 2022; Philpott 2007; Vüllers, Pfeiffer, and Basedau 2015).[2] Religious traditions have deep reservoirs of resources that are often necessary to bring about not only peace but also more profound reconciliation: commitments to truth, the ability to transform suffering, and ways to appeal to a sense of community that crosses boundaries and borders (Abu-Nimer 2013). Religious leaders can play – and indeed have played – key roles in bringing warring sides together, and they can appeal to justice and righteousness in a way that can address underlying causes of conflicts and wars (Bercovitch and Kadayifci-Orellana 2009; Johnstone and Svensson 2013; Vüllers 2019). Religious organizations and ideals can be essential for peacemaking to win broader legitimacy and acceptance (Powers 2010; Sampson 2007; Smock 2006). Hence, while our analysis has provided critical insights regarding how religion can be used for violent purposes, there is also a need to better understand the role of religious actors in resolving Islamic civil wars, in particular, how religious peacebuilders and other religious actors can contribute to disconnecting Islamist armed conflicts from their transnational ties.

Lastly, our study suggests avenues for further research on the implications of our findings for international mediation. Mediators, many of whom are steeped in secular perspectives, may have shied

[2] For a discussion on conflict resolution in territorial disputes from an Islamic law perspective, see Powell (2019).

away from engaging in processes aiming to bring Islamist civil wars to an end. How the changing landscape of mediators may affect the silencing of guns in Islamist civil wars remains to be understood. Can different types of mediators create different kinds of openings in the engagement with Islamist civil wars? We have, for example, seen much more assertive engagement from certain Gulf countries, not least Qatar, Oman, and Saudi Arabia, that are seeking to contribute to peacemaking (and thereby also increasing their international prestige). If the weight of international mediation engagement is shifting away from Western countries, including the Nordic countries (Svensson and Wallensteen 2025), in favor of countries such as Türkiye and the Gulf countries, then that may create new chances, but also more risks, when mediating these types of conflicts.

IMPLICATIONS OF OUR FINDINGS FOR POLICY

Ending Islamist civil wars is, by any account, a daunting challenge. Two decades of the Global War on Terror (a term that was used initially but was later phased out) following the 9/11 attacks were characterized by an unprecedented level of government military intervention and support to local governments fighting Islamist armed challengers. The increasing trend of internationalization of intrastate conflicts "has largely been driven by efforts by the United States and its European allies to combat transnational jihadist groups" (Davies, Pettersson, and Öberg 2022, 5). However, this type of internationalization has not proven to be a solution to Islamist civil wars; rather, it has been a contributing factor. Responding to the threat of Islamist wars through military intervention has thus often shown itself to be counterproductive. Backing up local government through direct military intervention against a potentially networked, transnational actor risks heightening the uncertainty and thereby enhancing the intractability of these wars.

We saw in the analysis of Afghanistan, in Chapter 4, that the American withdrawal, combined with the Taliban's cutting of ties with the al-Qaeda network, paved the way for the termination of the conflict. Afghanistan is a case of conflict termination, but not of successful conflict resolution: The American withdrawal provided an opportunity for the Taliban to oust the sitting government in Kabul and establish their long-sought-after Islamist state in Afghanistan. While our argument suggests that disengagement, rather than intervention, can open up space for conflict resolution, it is at the same time important to underline that disengagement can be accomplished in different ways. While further military interventions are often counterproductive, increasing uncertainty about the resolve of the parties in conflict and thus contributing to further intractability, there are more and less responsible ways of withdrawing from previous commitments. In the Afghanistan case, the US, under Donald Trump, negotiated directly with the Taliban over the head of the Afghan government, and the Doha agreements thereby disempowered the Kabul government. The main point of leverage that the Americans had – their presence – was given away without credible reassurances from the Taliban that they would earnestly seek accommodation with the American-supported government in Afghanistan. While a power-sharing deal with the government was part of the Doha agreement, little effort was made to ensure that the parties lived up to this commitment, and when the Taliban broke the deal and advanced toward Kabul, they faced few repercussions. As previously discussed, some terminations, such as the rebel victories in Afghanistan and Syria, can have negative consequences for gender and minority rights, which third-party actors should devise strategies to mitigate.

Our research here also speaks to a broader debate on how to manage internationalized conflicts. Given that intrastate conflicts increasingly tend to engage states and actors beyond the boundaries of the state, we need to know more about how these conflicts can become open for resolution. There is a debate on whether internationalized conflicts should be settled outside-in or inside-out, that is, what the sequence of the accommodation process between the internal and external elements of a conflict should be (Kane 2022).

Much of the thinking around this has been informed by how revolutionary conflicts were terminated at the end of the Cold War. In many of these civil wars that were resolved peacefully, in countries such as Mozambique, Guatemala, and Cambodia, it was the higher degree of involvement of secondary actors that made the peace settlements possible. Conflict resolution in internationalized conflicts often requires that patron states mend their fences first and thereafter pressure their protégées into making peace with each other. We have seen this in many leftist revolutionary conflicts, where structural shifts in the relationships between the external actors – the end of the Cold War – brought about accommodation on the external level first, which created the structural conditions also within the civil wars to incentivize the parties to resolve their conflicts. Peace then required a higher degree of internationalization, not less. Peace settlements were achieved through a second-order accommodation between external supporting actors on the sides of the local governments and rebel groups.

However, our book shows that this type of accommodation by external actors is not a requirement for all types of conflict resolution processes in internationalized conflicts. While increasing pressure from external actors may facilitate conflict resolution in some Islamist civil wars, the complexity of the strategic environment in which these conflicts are embedded can make such transformations more difficult. On the side of the Islamist rebels, there is often a plethora of networks and support structures. An external peace between the external actors backing different sides in Islamist civil wars is in many cases not feasible. Instead, the reverse dynamics may offer some hope. Actors in Islamist civil wars that insulate themselves from external influence and refocus on local grievances can, as we have shown here, find ways to resolve their differences. This yields a critical policy recommendation. Whenever possible, peacemaking actors should try to encourage disconnection: Groups that do disconnect (or show signs of a willingness to do so) should be encouraged. And importantly, breaking the connection between networks of transnational Islamist armed actors and local Islamist groups requires policymakers to be able to discern the difference between types of Islamist actors and adjust their policies accordingly.

A key overall policy implication that follows from this book is that priority should be given to localization, whereby efforts are made to either prevent conflicts from becoming transnational or disconnect Islamist civil war from the global battlefront. Local conflicts, even if framed in Islamist terms, can offer space for conflict resolution efforts to succeed. We have shown that Islamist civil wars are less likely to terminate and more likely to recur if they do end, compared with other types of civil wars. We have also demonstrated that this is largely driven by the support structures in Islamist civil wars: government support and foreign fighters. The presence of foreign fighters and government alliances, predominantly associated with Islamist civil wars, creates uncertainty around capabilities and resolve, which prolongs these conflicts and makes them intractable. Hence, it is the external, international dimensions that are the main obstacles to progress toward the peaceful settlement of Islamist civil wars. Our book points to some ways to enhance this type of disconnection. The entry of foreign fighters will complicate the dynamics of conflicts and decrease the chances of termination of these types of conflicts. Countries in conflict should therefore prioritize, for example, protecting their borders against the potential influx of foreign fighters, and effective border protection measures can be an area where the outside world can also provide support.

Importantly, we also demonstrate that, in contrast to the conventional wisdom, Islamist civil wars *can* be resolved. By disentangling conflicts from these support structures across borders, local conflicts can become the focus, paving the way for a peaceful resolution. Our research also shows that Islamist conflicts that are locally oriented and anchored, and that have not been drawn into broader transnational networks, seem more open to conflict resolution efforts compared with those with a transnational dimension. Hence, for conflict resolution efforts to be successful, there are considerable gains to be made if conflicts can be insulated from the broader transnational struggle. This insight has garnered increasing attention in policy circles. In the context of Islamist conflicts in Africa, the International Crisis Group observes that "the military response to jihadism has contributed to its spread. Local grievances have become more global, interconnected and therefore tougher to address," and it concludes that "options for stemming the tide should include opening lines of communication to those militants pursuing local goals" (Ero and Mutiga 2021, 3, 1). Drawing on a comprehensive analysis of both quantitative and qualitative evidence, we argue that these insights can be generalized to Islamist armed conflicts more broadly. They encapsulate this book's central conclusions about the conditions under which Islamist civil wars can be brought to an end.

Appendix

Table A1 *Summary statistics, termination dataset*

Variable	N	mean	sd	min	max
Termination	1,923	0.270	0.444	0	1
Islamist claim	1,923	0.207	0.405	0	1
Territory	1,923	0.432	0.496	0	1
Strong rebels	1,830	0.072	0.259	0	1
Oil_{log}	1,853	10.84	9.993	0	25.31
Youth bulge	1,755	32.54	4.038	15.65	39.49
Muslim majority	1,923	0.336	0.472	0	1
Foreign fighter	1,923	0.270	0.444	0	1
Government support	1,923	0.153	0.360	0	1
War	1,923	1.200	0.400	1	2
Duration	1,923	4.955	6.623	0	40
GDP per $\text{capita}_{\text{log}}$	1,561	6.585	1.318	4.265	10.62
Anocracy	1,731	0.356	0.479	0	1
$\text{Population}_{\text{log}}$	1,816	16.99	1.477	12.81	21.00
Leftist	1,912	0.285	0.451	0	–
Muslim identity	1,923	0.495	0.500	0	–
Non-Islamist religious claims	1,923	0.092	0.289	0	–
GDP per capita over time_{log}	1,887	6.669	1.362	4.256	10.72
Population over time_{log}	1,887	17.14	1.484	12.81	21.00
Anocracy over time	1,820	0.346	0.476	0	1
Number of groups	1,923	1.761	1.300	1	8
Government secondary support	1,787	0.085	0.278	0	1
Rebel support	1,731	0.169	0.375	0	1

Table A2 *Summary statistics, recurrence dataset*

Variable	N	mean	sd	min	max
Recurrence	6,927	0.025	0.156	0	1
Recurrence-new	6,927	0.012	0.107	0	1
Islamist claim	6,927	0.105	0.306	0	1
Territory	6,927	0.333	0.471	0	1
Strong rebels	6,735	0.139	0.346	0	1
Oil_{log}	6,720	8.510	9.840	0	25.31
Youth bulge	6,423	32.88	4.095	15.65	39.49
Muslim majority	6,927	0.365	0.481	0	1
Foreign fighter	6,927	0.169	0.375	0	1
Government support	6,927	0.121	0.326	0	1
War	6,927	1.120	0.325	1	2
Duration	6,927	2.786	5.288	0	40
Ceasefire	6,927	0.102	0.302	0	1
Low activity	6,927	0.460	0.498	0	1
Government victory	6,927	0.195	0.396	0	1
Rebel victory	6,927	0.105	0.307	0	1
Peacekeeping	6,927	0.256	0.436	0	1
GDP per $\text{capita}_{\text{log}}$	6,143	6.525	1.286	4.265	10.38
Anocracy	6,396	0.364	0.481	0	1
$\text{Population}_{\text{log}}$	6,619	16.39	1.408	12.81	21.00
Leftist	6,847	0.185	0.388	0	1
Non-Islamist religious claims	6,927	0.053	0.224	0	1
GDP per capita over time_{log}	6,800	6.531	1.320	4.256	10.38
Population over time_{log}	6,800	16.49	1.428	12.87	21.00
Anocracy over time	6,671	0.374	0.484	0	1
Number of groups	6,927	1.366	0.704	1	5
Government secondary support	6,536	0.056	0.230	0	1
Rebel support	6,346	0.076	0.266	0	1

Table A3 *Islamist armed conflicts and the risk of termination. Alternative survival models*

	Weibull (1)	Exponential (2)
Islamist claim	0.639	0.626
	(0.090)**	(0.090)**
Territory	0.859	0.831
	(0.116)	(0.117)
Strong rebels	1.191	1.209
	(0.261)	(0.295)
Oil_{log}	1.003	1.002
	(0.005)	(0.006)
Youth bulge/adult pop.	1.017	1.016
	(0.016)	(0.017)
Muslim majority	1.172	1.195
	(0.141)	(0.156)
/ ln_p	0.931	–
	(0.029)*	
N	1,657	1,657

Note: $^{+}p < 0.1$; $^{*}p < 0.05$; $^{**}p < 0.01$. Robust standard errors in parentheses clustered on dyad. Without stratification.

We do not have strong theoretical expectations of the failure rate over time, and in such a case a Cox proportional hazards model, which is more flexible, is preferable over a parametric model (Box-Steffensmeier and Jones 2004). Having said this, in Tables A3–A5, we rely on alternative duration models, a Weibull model and an exponential model, respectively, in order to examine whether our model choice affects the results. Our results remain the same across all models, showing a reduced risk of termination (Table A3), and an increased risk of recurrence involving the same actors (Table A4), as well as recurrence involving new actors (Table A5).[1]

[1] We present these alternative survival models without stratification since Model 1, Table A3, did not converge. All other models in Tables A3–A5 have been estimated also with stratification, and the results are very similar.

Table A4 *Islamist conflicts and the risk of recurrence. Alternative survival models*

	Weibull (1)	Exponential (2)
Islamist claim	2.329	2.536
	(0.655)**	(0.710)**
Territory	3.103	3.071
	(0.811)**	(0.807)**
Strong rebels	0.937	0.978
	(0.386)	(0.405)
Oil_{log}	1.034	1.037
	(0.013)**	(0.013)**
Youth bulge/adult pop.	1.057	1.056
	(0.027)*	(0.027)*
Muslim majority	0.775	0.749
	(0.215)	(0.209)
/ ln_p	0.749	–
	(0.037)**	
N	6,194	6,194

Note: $^{\dagger}p < 0.1$; $^{*}p < 0.05$; $^{**}p < 0.01$. Robust standard errors in parentheses clustered on dyad. Without stratification.

Table A5 *Islamist armed conflicts and the risk of recurrence involving new actors. Alternative survival models*

	Weibull (1)	Exponential (2)
Islamist claim	2.109	2.485
	(0.659)*	(0.647)**
Territory	0.659	0.661
	(0.216)	(0.168)
Strong rebels	1.080	1.149
	(0.371)	(0.335)
$\text{Oil}_{\log}$	0.987	0.993
	(0.013)	(0.012)
Youth bulge/adult pop.	0.985	0.988
	(0.035)	(0.031)
Muslim majority	0.939	0.929
	(0.256)	(0.226)
/ ln_p	0.369	–
	(0.043)**	
N	6,194	6,194

Note: $^{\dagger}p < 0.1$; $^{*}p < 0.05$; $^{**}p < 0.01$. Robust standard errors in parentheses clustered on dyad. Without stratification.

Table A6 *Islamist armed conflicts and the risk of termination and recurrence. Two years of inactivity instead of one year. Cox proportional hazards models*

	Termination (1)	Recurrence (2)	Recurrence-new (3)
Islamist claim	0.661	2.383	1.813
	(0.092)**	(0.687)**	(0.481)*
Territory	0.829	3.254	0.624
	(0.106)	(0.940)**	(0.161)†
Strong rebels	1.155	0.036	1.109
	(0.159)	(0.043)**	(0.312)
Oil_{log}	1.003	1.039	0.983
	(0.005)	(0.013)**	(0.011)
Youth bulge/adult pop.	1.000	1.388	0.986
	(0.013)	(0.109)**	(0.031)
Muslim majority	1.141	0.899	0.941
	(0.116)	(0.252)	(0.226)
Strong rebels × ln(time)	–	6.134	–
		(3.327)**	
Youth bulge/adult pop. × ln(time)	–	0.855	–
		(0.030)**	
N	1,725	6,056	6,056

Note: †$p < 0.1$; *$p < 0.05$; **$p < 0.01$. Robust standard errors in parentheses clustered on dyad.

In line with many other studies we rely on a one-year cessation in fighting activity to determine if a termination has occurred (e.g., Karlén 2017; Kreutz 2010). However, to ensure that our results are not driven by this decision, we estimate alternative models where we instead require the fighting to have terminated for at least two years. As shown in Table A6, our results are very similar.[2] Conflicts over

[2] In Model 2, the tests for proportional hazards indicated violations for the covariates *Strong rebels* and *Youth bulge/adult pop*. We follow the advice by Box-Steffensmeier and Jones (2004) and interact these variables with the log of time and re-estimate the model. After this, the Schoenfeld tests (global and covariates) do not shown any evidence of violations of the proportional hazards assumption.

Table A7a *Islamist armed conflicts and the risk of termination and recurrence. Conditional effects, foreign fighters. Cox proportional hazards models*

	Termination (1)	Recurrence (2)	Recurrence-new (3)
Islamist claim	0.831	1.427	1.200
	(0.128)	(0.383)	(0.413)
Islamist*foreign fighters	1.012	1.100	1.260
	(0.242)	(0.497)	(0.563)
Foreign fighters	0.744	1.772	1.755
	(0.092)*	(0.539)†	(0.511)†
Territory	0.850	2.576	0.681
	(0.098)	(0.569)**	(0.183)
Strong rebels	1.182	0.857	0.939
	(0.169)	(0.307)	(0.255)
$\text{Oil}_{\log}$	1.000	1.022	0.983
	(0.004)	(0.010)*	(0.011)
Youth bulge/adult pop.	1.015	1.048	0.976
	(0.012)	(0.020)*	(0.030)
Muslim majority	1.133	0.793	0.871
	(0.118)	(0.164)	(0.211)
Government support	0.662	0.801	1.893
	(0.100)**	(0.215)	(0.453)**
N	1,657	6,194	6,194

Note: $^{\dagger}p < 0.1$; $^{*}p < 0.05$; $^{**}p < 0.01$. Robust standard errors in parentheses clustered on dyad.

Islamist claims still see a reduced risk of termination (Model 1), an increased risk of recurrence involving the same actors (Model 2), and recurrence involving new actors (Model 3)

Our argument does not imply a conditional effect, as Islamist claims create an uncertainty about external support, even if such support is not always materializing or forthcoming. Still, for transparency, we report such an analysis here (see Table A7a). We find no evidence of an interaction effect between foreign fighters and Islamist claims. Using a likelihood ratio test, we explore whether the model with the interaction term is preferable to our main model. However, across the different outcomes the likelihood ratio test shows no evidence to support this (Model 1: p-value, 0.9666; Model 2; p-value, 0.8296; Model 3: p-value, 0.7032). Moreover, in line with Mize's (2019) advice to explore interaction effects, we also use a Wald test, but we find no significant differences across the contexts (when foreign fighters are absent and present) (Model 1: p-value, 0.9666; Model 2: p-value, 0.8298; Model 3: p-value, 0.7048).

Moreover, when including the interaction term, we can observe the effect of our main variable of interest when the other component term is 0 (e.g., Braumoeller 2004). Thus, from this analysis, we can note that the effect of Islamist claims is not significant when there is an *absence* of foreign fighters (when the foreign fighters variable is 0).

To facilitate interpretation, we also explore the effect of Islamist claims when there is a *presence* of foreign fighters. See Table A7b. In these models, we have rescaled the foreign fighters variable so that it instead captures the absence of foreign fighters. The results then show that Islamist claims is not significant in this subsample either. As shown in Table A7b, the effect of Islamist claims is not significant in the presence of foreign fighters (when the foreign fighters-absent variable is 0). In other words, we find no evidence suggesting that the effect of Islamist claims on termination or recurrence is conditional on the presence or absence of foreign fighters.

While our argument does not imply a conditional effect, we report models with an interaction term between Islamist claims and government support. Using a likelihood ratio test, we explore whether the model with the interaction term is preferable to our main model.[3] When comparing our main model with the model

[3] In Model 2, the tests for proportional hazards indicated violations for the variable *Strong rebels*. In line with the recommendation by Box-Steffensmeier and Jones (2004) we interact this variable with time and re-estimate the model. After this, the Schoenfeld tests (global and covariates) do not show any evidence of violations of the proportional hazards assumption.

Table A7b *Islamist armed conflicts and the risk of termination and recurrence. Conditional effects, foreign fighters-absent. Cox proportional hazards models*

	Termination (1)	Recurrence (2)	Recurrence-new (3)
Islamist claim	0.841	1.570	1.511
	(0.175)	(0.598)	(0.488)
Islamist*foreign fighters-absent	0.988	0.909	0.794
	(0.236)	(0.411)	(0.355)
Foreign fighters-absent	1.344	0.564	0.570
	(0.166)*	(0.172)†	(0.166)†
Territory	0.850	2.576	0.681
	(0.098)	(0.569)**	(0.183)
Strong rebels	1.182	0.857	0.939
	(0.169)	(0.307)	(0.255)
Oil_{log}	1.000	1.022	0.983
	(0.004)	(0.010)*	(0.011)
Youth bulge/adult pop.	1.015	1.048	0.976
	(0.012)	(0.020)*	(0.030)
Muslim majority	1.133	0.793	0.871
	(0.118)	(0.164)	(0.211)
Government support	0.662	0.801	1.893
	(0.100)**	(0.215)	(0.453)**
N	1,657	6,194	6,194

Note: $^{\dagger}p < 0.1$; $^{*}p < 0.05$; $^{**}p < 0.01$. Robust standard errors in parentheses clustered on dyad.

with the interaction term, however, we find no evidence that the model with the interactive term performs any better (Model 1: p-value, 0.2457; Model 2: p-value, 0.3207; Model 3, p-value: 0.7948). We also use a Wald test, but we find no significant differences across contexts (when government support is absent and present respectively) (Model 1: p-value, 0.2499; Model 2: p-value, 0.3225; Model 3: p-value, 0.7946).

Moreover, as mentioned, when including the interaction term, we can observe the effect of our main variable of interest when the

Table A7c *Islamist armed conflicts and the risk of termination and recurrence. Conditional effects, government support. Cox proportional hazards models*

	Termination (1)	Recurrence (2)	Recurrence-new (3)
Islamist claim	0.901	1.397	1.288
	(0.132)	(0.306)	(0.365)
Islamist*gov.support	0.667	2.050	1.186
	(0.214)	(1.162)	(0.575)
Government support	0.757	0.575	1.786
	(0.128)†	(0.247)	(0.556)†
Territory	0.845	2.573	0.686
	(0.098)	(0.574)**	(0.186)
Strong rebels	1.172	0.538	0.961
	(0.166)	(0.260)	(0.270)
$\text{Oil}_{\log}$	1.000	1.022	0.984
	(0.004)	(0.010)*	(0.011)
Youth bulge/adult pop.	1.014	1.048	0.977
	(0.012)	(0.020)*	(0.030)
Muslim majority	1.151	0.765	0.868
	(0.119)	(0.164)	(0.212)
Foreign fighters	0.746	1.838	1.862
	(0.085)**	(0.425)**	(0.442)**
Strong rebels*time	–	1.080	–
		(0.063)	
N	1,657	6,194	6,194

Note: $^{\dagger}p < 0.1$; $^{*}p < 0.05$; $^{**}p < 0.01$. Robust standard errors in parentheses clustered on dyad.

other component term is 0 (e.g., Braumoeller 2004). Table A7c shows that Islamist claims is not significant in the *absence* of government support (when the variable government support is 0) for either of these outcomes.

We also rescaled the variable government support to explore the effect of Islamist claims in the *presence* of government support (see Table A7d). We then find that Islamist claim has a significant

Table A7d *Islamist armed conflicts and the risk of termination and recurrence. Conditional effects-government support absent. Cox proportional hazards models*

	Termination (1)	Recurrence (2)	Recurrence-new (3)
Islamist claim	0.601	2.863	1.528
	(0.172)†	(1.769)†	(0.642)
Islamist*gov. support-absent	1.499	0.488	0.843
	(0.481)	(0.277)	(0.409)
Gov. support-absent	1.321	1.740	0.560
	(0.223)†	(0.748)	(0.174)†
Territory	0.845	2.573	0.686
	(0.098)	(0.574)**	(0.186)
Strong rebels	1.172	0.538	0.961
	(0.166)	(0.260)	(0.270)
Oil_{log}	1.000	1.022	0.984
	(0.004)	(0.010)*	(0.011)
Youth bulge/adult pop.	1.014	1.048	0.977
	(0.012)	(0.020)*	(0.030)
Muslim majority	1.151	0.765	0.868
	(0.119)	(0.164)	(0.212)
Foreign fighters	0.746	1.838	1.862
	(0.085)**	(0.425)**	(0.442)**
Strong rebels*time	–	1.080	–
		(0.063)	
N	1,657	6,194	6,194

Note: $^{\dagger}p < 0.1$; $^{*}p < 0.05$; $^{**}p < 0.01$. Robust standard errors in parentheses clustered on dyad.

effect at the 90% level on termination and recurrence when there is a presence of government support (when the variable government support-absent is 0). There is thus some evidence suggesting that Islamist claims depends on the presence of government support, but the effect is only statistically significant at the 90% level. We do not find such an effect concerning recurrence involving new groups.

Table A8 *Islamist armed conflicts and the risk of termination and recurrence. Alternative secondary support measures. Cox proportional hazards models*

	Termination (1)	Recurrence (2)	Recurrence-new (3)
Islamist claim	0.854	1.598	1.373
	(0.134)	(0.283)**	(0.397)
Territory	0.932	2.350	0.574
	(0.129)	(0.569)**	(0.164)†
Strong rebels	1.303	0.796	0.965
	(0.171)*	(0.280)	(0.274)
Oil_{log}	1.001	1.022	0.984
	(0.005)	(0.012)†	(0.012)
Youth bulge/adult pop.	1.014	1.058	0.999
	(0.015)	(0.022)**	(0.032)
Muslim majority	1.183	0.803	1.004
	(0.127)	(0.174)	(0.241)
Gov. secondary support	0.579	0.096	1.774
	(0.139)*	(0.083)**	(0.594)†
Rebel support	0.611	1.605	1.471
	(0.108)**	(0.379)*	(0.477)
Gov. sec. support × ln(time)	–	3.798	–
		(1.668)**	
N	1,479	5,593	5,593

Note: $^{\dagger}p < 0.1$; $^{*}p < 0.05$; $^{**}p < 0.01$. Robust standard errors in parentheses clustered on dyad.

The evidence is in line with our argument that transnational support in the form of government support as well as foreign fighters are two pathways through which Islamist conflicts become particularly intractable. In Table A8, we rely on two alternative measures of secondary support. The first alternative measure *Government secondary support* is taken from UCDP's secondary support data and measures different types of support short of troops on the ground, including military, economic, political, and logistical support (Högbladh, Pettersson, and Themnér 2011). The second alternative measure *Rebel support* is based on data from the Non-State Actor dataset and captures whether the rebel group is supported militarily by transnational non-state actors (Cunningham, Gleditsch, and Salehyan 2013). It should be noted that adding these variables is not done in order to identify spurious relationships but rather to shed light on the potential pathways. Our results are similar, but slightly weaker (concerning recurrence) than when relying on our original measures. There is, however, a lot of missing data when using these alternative measures. When including these two variables in the model of Termination (Model 1), the coefficient for *Islamist claims* is no longer significant, whereas *Government secondary support* and *Rebel support* both are below 1 and significant, indicating a lower chance of conflict termination. In terms of recurrence, while *Islamist claim* is still significant, the effect is reduced when including the secondary support measures (see Model 2).[4] When estimating the risk of recurrence by new actors (Model 3), government support serves as a potential pathway. *Government secondary support* is significant at the 90% level and in the expected direction (i.e., above 1), indicating an increased risk of conflict recurrence, whereas *Islamist claim* is no longer significant.

In addition to our main controls, we also control for other factors such as economic development measured as GDP per capita (logged), type of political regime using a dummy for anocracy, and size of the population (logged), and we find overall that the results are robust across different specifications (see Tables A9–A11).[5] Data on the type of political system come from Polity2 (Marshall, Jaggers, and Gurr 2015), for GDP we rely on data from

[4] In Model 2, the tests for proportional hazards indicated violations for the covariate *Government secondary support*. In line with the advice by Box-Steffensmeier and Jones (2004) we interact this variable with the log of time and add this to the model. After this, the Schoenfeld tests (global and covariates) do not show any evidence of violations of the proportional hazards assumption.

[5] *Anocracy* is coded 1 if the political system receives a score between –5 and +5 on the Polity2 scale (which ranges between –10 and +10), thereby capturing those political systems that fall in-between democracies and autocracies.

Table A9 *Islamist armed conflicts and the risk of termination. GDP per capita, population and anocracy. Cox proportional hazards models*

	Termination (1)	Termination (2)	Termination (3)	Termination (4)
Islamist claim	0.704	0.719	0.746	0.734
	(0.099)*	(0.111)*	(0.098)*	(0.105)*
Territory	0.969	0.967	1.045	0.959
	(0.115)	(0.110)	(0.117)	(0.111)
Strong rebels	1.014	1.096	1.053	1.049
	(0.142)	(0.146)	(0.139)	(0.144)
Oil_{log}	1.018	1.004	1.017	1.003
	(0.006)**	(0.004)	(0.005)**	(0.004)
Youth bulge/ adult pop.	1.004	1.013	1.018	1.013
	(0.013)	(0.012)	(0.013)	(0.012)
Muslim majority	0.924	1.079	1.012	1.094
	(0.102)	(0.108)	(0.101)	(0.110)
GDP per $capita_{log}$	0.922	–	–	–
	(0.041)†			
$Population_{log}$	0.848	–	–	–
	(0.032)**			
Anocracy	–	1.145	–	–
		(0.095)		
GDP pc over $time_{log}$	–	–	0.928	–
			(0.039)†	
Population over $time_{log}$	–	–	0.850	–
			(0.033)**	
Anocracy over time	–	–	–	1.170
				(0.107)†
N	1,403	1,543	1,657	1,573

Note: $^{\dagger}p < 0.1$; $^{*}p < 0.05$; $^{**}p < 0.01$. Robust standard errors in parentheses clustered on dyad.

the UN statistics division (United Nations 2015), and population is based on the World Bank World Development Indicators, taken from Ross and Mahdavi (2015). To avoid post-treatment bias, we use the values on GDP per capita, population, and anocracy prior to

Table A10 *Islamist armed conflicts and the risk of recurrence. GDP per capita, population, and anocracy. Cox proportional hazards models*

	Recurrence (1)	Recurrence (2)	Recurrence (3)	Recurrence (4)
Islamist claim	1.804	1.645	1.698	1.768
	(0.408)**	(0.339)*	(0.366)*	(0.362)**
Territory	2.557	2.426	2.193	2.311
	(0.629)**	(0.569)**	(0.537)**	(0.533)**
Strong rebels	1.013	0.653	0.941	0.860
	(0.372)	(0.232)	(0.342)	(0.306)
Oil_{log}	1.008	1.021	1.013	1.017
	(0.012)	(0.011)†	(0.012)	(0.010)†
Youth bulge/adult pop.	1.056	1.045	1.043	1.040
	(0.029)*	(0.019)*	(0.026)†	(0.019)*
Muslim majority	0.911	0.852	0.897	0.885
	(0.219)	(0.175)	(0.183)	(0.178)
GDP per $capita_{log}$	1.095	–	–	–
	(0.088)			
$Population_{log}$	1.069	–	–	–
	(0.075)			
Anocracy	–	1.112	–	–
		(0.221)		
GDP pc over $time_{log}$	–	–	1.035	–
			(0.080)	
Population over $time_{log}$	–	–	1.063	–
			(0.072)	
Anocracy over time	–	–	–	1.080
				(0.210)
N	5,757	5,905	6,194	6,023

Note: $^{\dagger}p < 0.1$; $^{*}p < 0.05$; $^{**}p < 0.01$. Robust standard errors in parentheses clustered on dyad.

when the conflict broke out (see Models 1 and 2, Tables A9–A11). Nevertheless, we have also estimated our models using yearly time-varying data on these variables lagged one year (see Models 3 and 4, Tables A9–A11). When analyzing termination as well as recurrence, our results remain the same (see Tables A9 and A10),

Table A11 *Islamist armed conflicts and the risk of recurrence involving new actors. GDP per capita, population, and anocracy. Cox proportional hazards models*

	Recurrence-new (1)	Recurrence-new (2)	Recurrence-new (3)	Recurrence-new (4)
Islamist claim	1.681	1.356	1.705	1.567
	(0.424)*	(0.403)	(0.416)*	(0.424)†
Territory	0.513	0.578	0.576	0.588
	(0.167)*	(0.154)*	(0.172)†	(0.156)*
Strong rebels	1.102	0.937	1.062	1.129
	(0.318)	(0.292)	(0.305)	(0.318)
Oil_{log}	0.974	0.986	0.978	0.984
	(0.016)†	(0.012)	(0.015)	(0.012)
Youth bulge/ adult pop.	0.999	0.977	0.985	0.980
	(0.033)	(0.029)	(0.029)	(0.030)
Muslim majority	1.014	0.909	0.997	0.919
	(0.249)	(0.218)	(0.233)	(0.221)
GDP per $\text{capita}_{\text{log}}$	1.102	–	–	–
	(0.135)			
$\text{Population}_{\text{log}}$	1.073	–	–	–
	(0.125)			
Anocracy	–	1.602	–	–
		(0.375)*		
GDP pc over time_{log}	–	–	1.067	–
			(0.119)	
Population over time_{log}	–	–	1.005	–
			(0.107)	
Anocracy over time	–	–	–	1.121
				(0.258)
N	5,757	5,905	6,194	6,023

Note: $^{\dagger}p < 0.1$; $^{*}p < 0.05$; $^{**}p < 0.01$. Robust standard errors in parentheses clustered on dyad.

but when focusing on the recurrence of new groups and controlling for anocracy, Islamist claims is no longer significant at the 95% level (see Models 2 and 4, Table A11). However, this result

Table A12 *Leftist ideology, Muslim identity, and non-Islamist claims, and the risk of termination and recurrence. Cox proportional hazards models*

	Termination			Recurrence		
	(1)	(2)	(3)	(4)	(5)	(6)
Leftist	0.649 (0.073)**	–	–	5.043 (2.178)**	–	–
Leftist × ln(time)	–	–	–	0.468 (0.103)**	–	–
Islamist claim	–	0.628 (0.082)**	–	–	1.827 (0.455)*	–
Territory	0.903 (0.103)	0.906 (0.106)	1.000 (0.114)	2.475 (0.521)**	2.343 (0.556)**	2.268 (0.475)**
Strong rebels	1.038 (0.156)	1.112 (0.148)	1.125 (0.163)	0.962 (0.347)	0.913 (0.328)	0.905 (0.329)
Oil_{log}	1.004 (0.004)	1.004 (0.004)	1.002 (0.004)	1.019 (0.010)†	1.019 (0.011)†	1.020 (0.010)*
Youth bulge/ adult pop.	1.017 (0.013)	1.018 (0.013)	1.018 (0.013)	1.051 (0.021)*	1.042 (0.020)*	1.044 (0.021)*
Muslim majority	0.914 (0.088)	0.871 (0.125)	0.981 (0.091)	1.007 (0.187)	0.933 (0.237)	0.959 (0.182)
Muslim identity	–	1.338 (0.176)*	–	–	0.899 (0.229)	–
Non-Islamist rel. claims	–	–	0.829 (0.140)	–	–	1.516 (0.461)
N	1,657	1,657	1,657	6,193	6,194	6,194

Note: †$p < 0.1$; *$p < 0.05$; **$p < 0.01$. Robust standard errors in parentheses clustered on dyad. In Models 1–3 the unit of analysis is dyad-year, and in Models 4–6 it is dyad-termination-year.

should be interpreted with caution as there is some missing data on anocracy. Thus, overall, we find strong support for our conjectures, but the evidence is less clear-cut when it comes to explaining the recurrence involving new groups.

As part of Chapter 3, we discuss the results regarding leftist ideology, Muslim identity, and non-Islamist religious claims and the

Table A13 *Leftist ideology, Muslim identity, and non-Islamist claims, and the risk of recurrence involving new groups. Cox proportional hazards models*

	Recurrence-new (1)	Recurrence-new (2)	Recurrence-new (3)
Leftist	1.583	–	–
	(0.430)†		
Islamist claim	–	1.385	–
		(0.375)	
Territory	0.625	0.478	0.565
	(0.165)†	(0.134)**	(0.146)*
Strong rebels	1.130	1.037	1.012
	(0.328)	(0.277)	(0.286)
Oil_{log}	0.982	0.982	0.983
	(0.011)†	(0.011)†	(0.011)
Youth bulge/ adult pop.	0.984	0.982	0.982
	(0.031)	(0.030)	(0.030)
Muslim majority	1.249	0.623	1.137
	(0.270)	(0.204)	(0.244)
Muslim identity	–	1.946	–
		(0.696)†	
Non-Islamist religious claims	–	–	0.816
			(0.438)
N	6,193	6,194	6,194

Note: †$p < 0.1$; *$p < 0.05$; **$p < 0.01$. Robust standard errors in parentheses clustered on dyad.

risk of termination and recurrence (see Table A12). In Table A13, we present the same results as in Table A12, but now with recurrence involving new actors as the dependent variable. Our results as regards recurrence involving new actors is very similar to those obtained when studying termination as well as recurrence with the same actors. *Leftist* shows an increased risk of recurrence with new actors, significant at the 90% level (Model 1). However, in Model 2, Islamist claim is no longer significant, while the coefficient for Muslim identity is above 1 and significant at the 90% level, indicating a higher risk of

Table A14 *Islamist armed conflicts and the risk of termination and recurrence. Fragmentation in the form of number of groups. Cox proportional hazards models*

	Termination (1)	Recurrence (2)	Recurrence-new (3)
Islamist claim	0.724	1.796	1.500
	(0.104)*	(0.363)**	(0.365)†
Territory	0.947	2.238	0.631
	(0.110)	(0.490)**	(0.167)†
Strong rebels	1.100	0.921	1.107
	(0.151)	(0.338)	(0.299)
Oil_{log}	1.003	1.018	0.989
	(0.004)	(0.010)†	(0.011)
Youth bulge/adult pop.	1.016	1.041	0.981
	(0.012)	(0.019)*	(0.031)
Muslim majority	1.084	0.857	0.977
	(0.109)	(0.174)	(0.232)
Number of Groups	0.966	0.785	1.734
	(0.038)	(0.114)†	(0.163)**
N	1,657	6,194	6,194

Note: $^{\dagger}p < 0.1$; $^{*}p < 0.05$; $^{**}p < 0.01$. Robust standard errors in parentheses clustered on dyad.

recurrence involving new actors. Yet the overall evidence (focusing on termination and recurrence involving the same actors) suggests that it is the Islamist claim-making, and not the Muslim identity dimension, that drives the increased risk of intractability. When it comes to non-Islamist religious claims, we again find no evidence that these are more intractable compared with other conflicts (Model 3).

We explore the effect of rebel fragmentation by adding the number of groups to the three main models (see Table A14). We find that our results concerning Islamist claims and termination as well as recurrence is robust. When examining recurrence for new groups, however, the result is no longer significant, and in already fragmented conflicts there is an increased risk of new groups emerging. This does

Table A15 *Islamist armed conflicts and the risk of termination and recurrence, exploring the mechanisms. Duration and Intensity. Cox proportional hazards models*

	Termination (1)	Recurrence (2)	Recurrence-new (3)
Islamist claim	0.717	1.740	1.738
	(0.098)*	(0.356)**	(0.439)*
Territory	0.988	2.287	0.579
	(0.114)	(0.530)**	(0.154)*
Strong rebels	1.147	0.585	1.027
	(0.153)	(0.272)	(0.286)
Oil_{log}	0.999	1.022	0.984
	(0.004)	(0.011)*	(0.011)
Youth bulge/adult pop.	1.016	1.043	0.974
	(0.012)	(0.020)*	(0.030)
Muslim majority	1.067	0.848	0.940
	(0.112)	(0.174)	(0.218)
Duration	0.954	1.009	0.990
	(0.018)*	(0.018)	(0.024)
War	0.611	1.428	1.988
	(0.097)**	(0.418)	(0.495)**
Strong rebels × (time)	–	1.070	–
		(0.063)	
N	1,657	6,194	6,194

Note: $^{\dagger}p < 0.1$; $^{*}p < 0.05$; $^{**}p < 0.01$. Robust standard errors in parentheses clustered on dyad.

not make the finding spurious but it says something about *why* we see an increased risk of new groups emerging in Islamist conflicts. Hence, when it comes to recurrence involving new groups, we find that in addition to the two pathways we theorized about (foreign fighters and government support), fragmentation can increase the risk that we see recurrence via new groups emerging. In an alternative model concerning recurrence involving new groups (not reported here), where we include all three measures (foreign fighters, government support, and number of groups), all three measures are significant supporting this conclusion.

In Table A15, we examine the potential pathways to why Islamist conflicts are so intractable, assessing if the way the conflicts are fought could matter. We focus on two main characteristics of war – the intensity and duration of the conflict – yet the main results for our variable of interest (*Islamist claim*) remain the same across all models (see Models 1–3, Table A15).[6]

A potential concern is that Islamist conflicts are more intractable due to their high-intensity nature, and that this feature is driving the result. However, a closer look at the data shows that Islamist conflicts are not systematically different when it comes to intensity level compared with non-Islamist conflicts (11% and 13% respectively). Moreover, as our findings in Table A15 show, when adding a control that distinguishes between conflicts with more than 1,000 battle-related deaths and low-intensity conflicts, our results remain robust. Hence, there is little to suggest that the high-intensity nature of these conflicts is driving our findings, at least when it comes to distinguishing between civil wars that result in more than 1,000 battle-related deaths and those that do not.

To further tease out possible mechanisms, when studying different types of termination, we distinguish between full (or comprehensive) accords and other types of peace agreements relying on UCDP Peace Agreement Data (Pettersson, Högbladh, and Öberg 2019). But as shown in Table A16, the results do not change. Please note that in these models the reference category is government victory.

[6] In Model 2, the tests for proportional hazards indicated violations for the covariate *Strong*. We follow the advice by Box-Steffensmeier and Jones (2004) and interact this variable with time (*Strong* × *(time)*) and re-estimate the model. The test no longer shows any evidence of violations.

Table A16 *Islamist conflicts and risk of recurrence. Distinguishing between different forms of peace agreements*

	Recurrence (1)	Recurrence-new (2)
Islamist claim	1.656	1.668
	(0.335)*	(0.407)*
Territory	2.060	0.471
	(0.462)**	(0.129)**
Strong rebels	1.206	1.152
	(0.483)	(0.362)
Oil_{log}	1.022	0.983
	(0.011)*	(0.011)
Youth bulge/adult pop.	1.035	0.987
	(0.020)†	(0.031)
Muslim majority	0.849	0.860
	(0.178)	(0.204)
Peacekeeping presence	0.736	1.618
	(0.117)†	(0.343)*
Ceasefire agreement	2.851	1.845
	(1.167)*	(1.174)
Peace agreement-not full	1.838	2.840
	(0.935)	(1.744)†
Peace agreement-full	1.917	1.229
	(1.053)	(0.896)
Rebel victory	0.951	2.820
	(0.679)	(1.757)†
Low activity	3.480	3.804
	(1.196)**	(1.945)**
N	6,144	6,144

Note: † $p < 0.1$; *$p < 0.05$; **$p < 0.01$. Robust standard errors in parentheses clustered on dyad. Government victory is the reference category when evaluating different types of termination.

Table A17 *Summary statistics, conflict resolution dataset*

Variables	N	mean	sd	min	max
Negotiations	23,616	0.081	0.273	0	1
Peace agreement	23,616	0.007	0.084	0	1
Islamist claim	23,616	0.292	0.455	0	1
Transnational Islamist	23,616	0.089	0.284	0	1
Non-transnational Islamist	23,616	0.204	0.403	0	1
Number of rebel groups	23,616	1.602	0.902	1	6
Territory	23,616	0.473	0.499	0	1
Duration	23,616	4.607	6.225	0	43
Intensity	23,616	1.121	0.326	1	2
Leftist claim	22,134	0.165	0.372	0	1
Religious identity	23,616	0.373	0.484	0	1
Rebel one-sided violence (OSV)	23,066	1.119	2.238	0	10.31
Rebel OSV dummy	23,066	0.218	0.413	0	1
Log of GDP per capita	20,007	6.901	1.342	4.381	11.00
Liberal democracy	20,917	0.281	0.207	0.006	0.856
Decay function negotiations	23,616	0.188	0.332	0	1
Decay function peace agreement	23,616	0.028	0.133	0	1

Table A18 *Logit models: Islamist claims and negotiations*

	Negotiations (1)	Negotiations (2)	Negotiations (3)
Islamist claim	–0.542**	–0.557**	–0.577**
	(0.160)	(0.160)	(0.174)
Number of rebel groups	–	0.071†	–
		(0.038)	
Territory	–	–0.028	–
		(0.111)	
Intensity	–	–	0.328**
			(0.108)
Duration	–	–	0.005
			(0.008)
Decay function negotiations	3.804**	3.793**	3.769**
	(0.124)	(0.123)	(0.123)
Constant	–3.862**	–3.959**	–4.243**
	(0.079)	(0.121)	(0.150)
Observations	23,616	23,616	23,616
Log pseudolikelihood	–4640	–4637	–4629

Note: †$p < 0.1$; *$p < 0.05$; **$p < 0.01$. Robust standard errors in parentheses.

Table A19 *Logit models: Islamist claims and negotiations. Alternative explanations*

	Negotiations (4)	Negotiations (5)	Negotiations (6)
Leftist claim	0.024	–	–
	(0.140)		
Islamist claim	–	–0.543**	–0.540**
		(0.155)	(0.161)
Religious identity	–	0.004	–
		(0.109)	
Rebel one-sided violence	–	–	0.0003
			(0.017)
Decay function negotiations	3.780**	3.804**	3.837**
	(0.129)	(0.124)	(0.126)
Constant	–3.967**	–3.863**	–3.880**
	(0.090)	(0.082)	(0.081)
Observations	22,134	23,616	23,066
Log pseudolikelihood	–4449	–4640	–4518

Note: $^{\dagger}p < 0.1$; $^{*}p < 0.05$; $^{**}p < 0.01$. Robust standard errors in parentheses.

Table A20 *Logit models: Islamist claims and peace agreements*

	Peace agreement (1)	Peace agreement (2)	Peace agreement (3)
Islamist claim	−0.739†	−0.739†	−0.761*
	(0.391)	(0.418)	(0.380)
Number of rebel groups	–	0.047	–
		(0.099)	
Territory	–	−1.006**	–
		(0.303)	
Intensity	–	–	0.342
			(0.286)
Duration	–	–	0.020*
			(0.008)
Decay function peace agreement	3.411**	3.152**	3.349**
	(0.267)	(0.283)	(0.271)
Constant	−5.134**	−4.847**	−5.622**
	(0.140)	(0.250)	(0.377)
Observations	23,616	23,616	23,616
Log pseudolikelihood	−903.7	−887.8	−900.2

Note: †$p < 0.1$, *$p < 0.05$, **$p < 0.01$. Robust standard errors in parentheses.

Table A21 *Logit models: Islamist claims and peace agreements. Alternative explanations*

	Peace agreement (4)	Peace agreement (5)	Peace agreement (6)
Leftist claim	–0.016	–	–
	(0.339)		
Islamist claim	–	$-0.662^{\dagger}$	$-0.794^{\dagger}$
		(0.394)	(0.422)
Religious identity	–	–0.349	–
		(0.258)	
Rebel one-sided violence	–	–	0.043
			(0.038)
Decay function peace agreement	3.491**	3.384**	3.340**
	(0.243)	(0.271)	(0.290)
Constant	–5.259**	–5.039**	–5.143**
	(0.126)	(0.151)	(0.142)
Observations	22,134	23,616	23,066
Log pseudolikelihood	–885.8	–901.8	–899.8

Note: $^{\dagger}p < 0.1$; $^{*}p < 0.05$; $^{**}p < 0.01$. Robust standard errors in parentheses.

Table A22 *Logit models: Different types of Islamist armed conflicts and negotiations*

	Negotiations (1)	Negotiations (2)	Negotiations (3)
Transnational Islamist	–2.586**	–2.572**	–2.648**
	(0.529)	(0.533)	(0.523)
Non-transnational Islamist	–0.412**	–0.428**	–0.445**
	(0.146)	(0.148)	(0.159)
Number of rebel groups	–	0.060	–
		(0.039)	
Territory	–	–0.035	–
		(0.110)	
Intensity	–	–	0.340**
			(0.107)
Duration	–	–	0.005
			(0.008)
Decay function negotiations	3.742**	3.734**	3.705**
	(0.126)	(0.125)	(0.125)
Constant	–3.823**	–3.899**	–4.215**
	(0.079)	(0.121)	(0.150)
Observations	23,616	23,616	23,616
Log pseudolikelihood	–4620	–4618	–4609

Note: $^{\dagger}p < 0.1$; $^{*}p < 0.05$; $^{**}p < 0.01$. Robust standard errors in parentheses.

Table A23 *Logit models: Different types of Islamist armed conflicts and negotiations. Alternative explanations*

	Negotiations (4)	Negotiations (5)	Negotiations (6)
Leftist claim	–0.049	–	–
	(0.142)		
Transnational Islamist	–	–2.585**	–2.606**
		(0.529)	(0.522)
Non-transnational Islamist	–0.361*	–0.409**	–0.416**
	(0.148)	(0.143)	(0.146)
Religious identity	–	–0.013	–
		(0.107)	
Rebel one-sided violence	–	–	0.011
			(0.017)
Decay function negotiations	3.757**	3.742**	3.771**
	(0.124)	(0.126)	(0.129)
Constant	–3.881**	–3.818**	–3.848**
	(0.089)	(0.082)	(0.082)
Observations	22,134	23,616	23,066
Log pseudolikelihood	–4438	–4620	–4499

Note: $^{\dagger}p < 0.1$, $^{*}p < 0.05$, $^{**}p < 0.01$. Robust standard errors in parentheses.

References

Abu-Nimer, Mohammed. 2003. *Nonviolence and Peacebuilding in Islam: Theory and Practice.* Gainesville: University Press of Florida.

Abu-Nimer, Mohammed. 2013. "Religion and Peacbuilding." In *Routledge Handbook of Peacebuilding,* edited by Roger Mac Ginty, 69–80. London: Routledge.

Adili, Ali Yawar. 2021. "Preparing for a Post-departure Afghanistan: Changing Political Dynamics in the Wake of the US Troop Withdrawal Announcement." Afghanistan Analysts Network. http://bit.ly/4qfhxnh.

Adraoui, Mohamed-Ali. 2017. "The Case of Jabhat Al-Nusra in the Syrian Conflict 2011–2016: Towards a Strategy of Nationalization?" *Mediterranean Politics* 24 (2):260–267.

AFP. 2020. "France, Mali at Odds over Whether to Talk to Jihadists in Sahel Conflict." 26 October. https://bit.ly/48N9A2Z.

AFP. 2022. "US Blames Russia's Wagner Group for Worsening Security in Mali." 27 October. https://bit.ly/48NZ9MD.

Ahmad, Aisha. 2015. "The Security Bazaar: Business Interests and Islamist Power in Civil War Somalia." *International Security* 39 (3):89–117.

al-Aswad, Harun. 2020. "Coups on Allies: HTS Rids Syria's Idlib of Opponents." *Middle East Eye*, 19 September.

Ali, Arshad. 2013. "Peace Talks with the Pakistani Taliban: Challenges and Prospects." *Counter Terrorist Trends and Analyses* 5 (4):11–13.

Al Kanj, Sultan. 2018. "The Muslim Brotherhood's Next Move in Syria." Chatham House. https://bit.ly/49I79iN.

Al-Tamimi, Aymen Jawad. 2018. "From Jabhat al-Nusra to Hay'at Tahrir al-Sham: Evolution, Approach and Future." Konrad-Adenauer Stiftung/Al-Nahrain Center for Strategic Studies.

Appleby, R. Scott. 2000. *The Ambivalence of the Sacred: Religion, Violence, and Reconciliation.* New York: Rowman & Littlefield Publishers, Inc.

ARB, Africa Research Bulletin. 2020a. "Mali: Dialogue with Jihadists." 57 (2, February 1–29):22627.

ARB, Africa Research Bulletin. 2020b. "Mali: Jihadist Talks." 4 (March 1–31): 22663.

Asal, Victor, and David Malet. 2024. "Nobody More Terrible than the Desperate: Conflict Conditions and Rebel Demand for Foreign Fighters." *Studies in Conflict & Terrorism* 47 (2):135–153.

Asal, Victor H., Hyun Hee Park, R. Karl Rethemeyer, and Gary Ackerman. 2015. "With Friends Like These ... Why Terrorist Organizations Ally." *International Public Management Journal* 19 (1):1–30.

Asal, Victor, Amy Pate, and Jonathan Wilkenfeld. 2008. "Minorities at Risk Organizational Behavior Data and Codebook Version 9/2008." https://bit.ly/3YRut7q.

Ashour, Omar. 2009. *The De-radicalisation of Jihadists: Transforming Armed Islamist Movements*. London: Routledge.

Aslan, Reza. 2013. "Cosmic War in Religious Traditions." In *The Oxford Handbook of Religion and Violence*, edited by Michael Jerryson, Mark Juergensmeyer, Margo Kitts, 260. New York: Oxford University Press.

Atran, Scott. 2010. "A Question of Honour: Why the Taliban Fight and What to Do about It." *Asian Journal of Social Science* 38 (3):343–363.

Aydin, Aysegul, and Patrick M. Regan. 2012. "Networks of Third-Party Interveners and Civil War Duration." *European Journal of International Relations* 18 (3):573–597.

Bacon, Tricia. 2015. "Hurdles to International Terrorist Alliances: Lessons from Al Qaeda's Experience." *Terrorism and Political Violence* 29 (1):79–101.

Bakke, Kristin M. 2014. "Help Wanted? The Mixed Record of Foreign Fighters in Domestic Insurgencies." *International Security* 38 (4):150–187.

Bamber-Zryd, Matthew. 2022. "Cyclical Jihadist Governance: The Islamic State Governance Cycle in Iraq and Syria." *Small Wars & Insurgencies* 33 (8): 1314–1344.

Bapat, Navin A. 2011. "Transnational Terrorism, US Military Aid, and the Incentive to Misrepresent." *Journal of Peace Research* 48 (3):303–318.

Bapat, Navin A., and Sean Zeigler. 2016. "Terrorism, Dynamic Commitment Problems, and Military Conflict." *American Journal of Political Science* 60 (2):337–351.

Basedau, Matthias, Mora Deitch, and Ariel Zellman. 2022. "Rebels with a Cause: Does Ideology Make Armed Conflicts Longer and Bloodier?" *Journal of Conflict Resolution* 66 (10):1826–1853.

Basedau, Matthias, Jonathan Fox, and Ariel Zellman. 2023. *Religious Minorities at Risk*. New York: Oxford University Press.

Basedau, Matthias, Birte Pfeiffer, and Johannes Vüllers. 2016. "Bad Religion? Religion, Collective Action, and the Onset of Armed Conflict in Developing Countries." *Journal of Conflict Resolution* 60 (2):226–255.

BBC. 2013. "Mali Crisis: Key Players." *BBC*, 12 March. www.bbc.com/news/world-africa-17582909.

BBC. 2021. "Afghanistan's Ghost Soldiers Undermined Fight against Taliban – Ex-Official." *BBC*, 10 November. www.bbc.com/news/world-asia-59230564.

Bensahel, Nora. 2006. "A Coalition of Coalitions: International Cooperation Against Terrorism." *Studies in Conflict & Terrorism* 29 (1):35–49.

Bercovitch, Jacob, Theodore J. Anagnoson, and Donnette L. Wille. 1991. "Some Conceptual Issues and Empirical Trends in the Study of Successful Mediation in International Relations." *Journal of Peace Research* 28 (1):7–17.

Bercovitch, Jacob, and Ayse S. Kadayifci-Orellana. 2009. "Religion and Mediation: The Role of Faith-Based Actors in International Conflict Resolution." *International Negotiation* 14:175–204.

Berman, Eli, and David D. Laitin. 2008. "Religion, Terrorism and Public Goods: Testing the Club Model." *Journal of Public Economics* 92 (10–11): 1942–1967.

Biden, Joe. 2021. "Remarks by President Biden on the Drawdown of U.S. Forces in Afghanistan." 8 July, in Washington, DC, Transcript, The White House, The United States Government. https://bit.ly/4u5WiHx.

Bischof, Daniel. 2017. "New Graphic Schemes for Stata: Plotplain and Plottig." *The Stata Journal* 17 (3):748–759.

Bloom, Mia. 2005. *Dying to Kill: The Allure of Suicide Terror*. New York: Columbia University Press.

Bøås, Morten. 2019. "The Sahel Crisis and the Need for International Support." In *Policy Dialogue, 15*. Uppsala: Nordic Africa Institute.

Bøås, Morten, Alessio Iocchi, and Kari Osland. 2023. "Negotiating with Jihadi Insurgents in the Sahel? Local Opinion and Regime Change in Mali." Unpublished paper.

Bock, Joseph G. 2001. *Sharpening Conflict Management: Religious Leadership and the Double-Edged Sword*. Westport, Connecticut: Praeger.

Bormann, Nils-Christian, Lars-Erik Cederman, and Manuel Vogt. 2017. "Language, Religion, and Ethnic Civil War." *Journal of Conflict Resolution* 61 (4):744–771.

Bouhlel, Ferdaous. 2013. At-Tawba, expérience mauritanienne de redéfinition de la violence « légitime » entre repentance, médiation et exercice fiqhi en matière de djihad [At-Tawba, the Mauritanian experience defining "legitimate" violence between repentance, mediation and fiqhi practice in jihad]. In *Sahel: éclairer le passé pour mieux dessiner l'avenir*, edited by Bérengère Rouppert and Laurence Aïda Ammour, 95–122, Bruxelles: GRIP.

Boukhars, Anouar. 2016. *Mauritania's Precarious Stability and Islamist Undercurrent*. Washington, DC: Carnegie Endowment for International Peace.

Boukhars, Anouar. 2020. "Keeping Terrorism at Bay in Mauritania." Africa Center for Strategic Studies, 16 June. https://bit.ly/4tZsxI4.

Boutellis, Arthur, and Marie-Joëlle Zahar. 2017. *A Process in Search of Peace: Lessons from the Inter-Malian Agreement.* New York: International Peace Institute.

Box-Steffensmeier, Janet M., and Bradford S. Jones. 2004. *Event History Modeling: A Guide for Social Scientists.* Cambridge: Cambridge University Press.

Braumoeller, Bear F. 2004. "Hypothesis Testing and Multiplicative Interaction Terms." *International Organization* 58 (4):807–820.

Brubaker, Rogers. 2015. "Religious Dimensions of Political Conflict and Violence." *Sociological Theory* 33 (1):1–19.

Bunzel, Cole. 2021. "Al Qaeda versus ISIS: The Jihadi Power Struggle in the Taliban's Afghanistan." *Foreign Affairs*, 14 September.

Byman, Daniel. 2005. "Passive Sponsors of Terrorism." *Survival* 47 (4):117–144.

Byman, Daniel. 2006. "Remaking Alliances for the War on Terrorism." *Journal of Strategic Studies* 29 (5):767–811.

Byman, Daniel. 2014. "Buddies or Burdens? Understanding the Al Qaeda Relationship with Its Affiliate Organizations." *Security Studies* 23 (3):431–470.

Byman, Daniel. 2018. "What Happens When ISIS Goes Underground?" *Brookings*, 18 January, accessed 22 January 2018. https://bit.ly/4rGLldV.

Byman, Daniel. 2019. *Road Warriors: Foreign Fighters in the Armies of Jihad.* New York: Oxford University Press.

Cantey, Seth. 2018. "Beyond the Pale? Exploring Prospects for Negotiations with Al Qaeda and the Islamic State."*Studies in Conflict & Terrorism* 41 (10):757–775.

Carenzi, Silvia. 2020. "A Downward Scale Shift? The Case of Hay'at Tahrir al-Sham." *Perspectives on Terrorism* 14 (6):91–105.

CBS News. 2020. "Transcript: Mike Pompeo on 'Face the Nation,' March 1, 2020." 1 March, www.cbsnews.com/news/transcript-mike-pompeo-on-face-the-nation-march-1-2020/.

Cederman, Lars-Erik, Luc Girardin, and Kristian Skrede Gleditsch. 2009. "Ethnonationalist Triads: Assessing the Influence of Kin Groups on Civil Wars." *World Politics* 61 (3):403–437.

Chivvis, C. S., and A. Liepman. 2013. "North Africa's Menace: AQIM's Evolution and the U.S. Policy Response." Research Reports, RAND Corporation Website. https://bit.ly/4r3ww49.

Choi, Hyeseung, Minyoung Choi, and Jae-Suk Yang. 2022. "Longevity of Partnering Terrorist Organization: An Empirical Study Using a Network Diffusion Model." *Terrorism and Political Violence* 36 (1):39–54.

Chu, Tiffany S., and Alex Braithwaite. 2017. "The Impact of Foreign Fighters on Civil Conflict Outcomes." *Research & Politics* 4 (3). https://doi.org/10.1177/2053168017722059.

Clausen, Maria-Louise. 2022. "Exploring the Agency of the Affiliates of Transnational Jihadist Organizations: The Case of al-Qaeda in the Arabian Peninsula." *Studies in Conflict & Terrorism* 48 (3):250–264.

Clayton, Govinda, and Han Dorussen. 2022. "The Effectiveness of Mediation and Peacekeeping for Ending Conflict." *Journal of Peace Research* 59 (2):150–165.

Cockburn, Patrick. 2015. *The Rise of Islamic State: ISIS and the New Sunni Revolution*. London: Verso Books.

Coppedge, Michael, John Gerring, Carl Henrik Knutsen et al. 2020. V-Dem Codebook v10. Varieties of Democracy (V-Dem) Project. https://doi.org/10.23696/vdemds20.

Coppedge, Michael, John Gerring, Carl Henrik Knutsen et al. 2025. V-Dem Dataset v15. Varieties of Democracy (V-Dem) Project. https://doi.org/10.23696/vdemds25.

Crawford, Neta C. 2019. *United States Budgetary Costs and Obligations of Post-9/11 Wars through FY 2020: 6.4 Trillion USD*. Rhode Island: Watson Institute for International and Public Affairs, Brown University.

Crenshaw, Martha. 1991. "How Terrorism Declines." *Terrorism and Political Violence* 3 (1):69–87.

Crenshaw, Martha. 2017. "Transnational Jihadism & Civil Wars." *Daedalus* 146 (4):59–70.

Crescenzi, Mark, J. C. 2007. "Reputation and Interstate Conflict." *American Journal of Political Science* 51 (2):382–396.

Cronin, Audrey Kurth. 2012. *Ending Terrorism: Lessons for Defeating al-Qaeda*. London: Routledge.

Cunningham, David, Kristian Skrede Gleditsch, and Idean Salehyan. 2009. "It Takes Two: A Dyadic Analysis of Civil War Duration and Outcome." *Journal of Conflict Resolution* 53 (4):570–597.

Cunningham, David, Kristian Skrede Gleditsch, and Idean Salehyan. 2013. "Non-State Actors in Civil Wars: A New Dataset." *Conflict Management and Peace Science* 30 (5):516–531.

Davies, Shawn, Garoun Engström, Therese Pettersson, and Magnus Öberg. 2024. "Organized Violence 1989–2023, and the Prevalence of Organized Crime Groups." *Journal of Peace Research* 61 (4): 673–693.

Davies, Shawn, Therése Pettersson, and Magnus Öberg. 2022. "Organized Violence 1989–2021 and Drone Warfare." *Journal of Peace Research* 59 (4): 593–610.

Davies, Shawn, Therése Pettersson, Margareta Sollenberg, and Magnus Öberg. 2025. "Organized Violence 1989–2024, and the Challenges of Identifying Civilian Victims." *Journal of Peace Research* 62 (4):1223–1240.

Davis, David R., and Will H. Moore. 1997. "Ethnicity Matters: Transnational Ethnic Alliances and Foreign Policy Behavior." *International Studies Quarterly* 41 (1):171–184.

Deitch, Mora. 2022. "Is Religion a Barrier to Peace? Religious Influence on Violent Intrastate Conflict Termination." *Terrorism and Political Violence* 34 (7):1454–1470 (published online 2020).

The Doha Agreement. 2020. "Agreement for Bringing Peace to Afghanistan between the Islamic Emirate of Afghanistan Which Is Not Recognized by the United States as a State and Is Known as the Taliban and the United States of America." https://bit.ly/4kVbT8q.

Drevon, Jerome. 2022a. "The Al-Qaeda Chief's Death and Its Implications." In *Q&A/Asia-Pacific*: ICG, International Crisis Group.

Drevon, Jerome. 2022b. *Institutionalising Violence: Strategies of Jihad in Egypt*. Oxford: Oxford University Press.

Drevon, Jerome. 2024. *From Jihad to Politics: How Syrian Jihadis Embraced Politics*. New York: Oxford University Press.

Drevon, Jerome, and Patrick Haenni. 2021. "How Global Jihad Relocalises and Where It Leads. The Case of HTS, the Former AQ Franchise in Syria." Robert Schuman Centre for Advanced Studies, EUI Working Paper RSC 2021/08.

Drevon, Jerome, and Patrick Haenni. 2025. "Redefining Global Jihad and Its Termination: The Subjugation of al-Qaeda by Its Former Franchise in Syria." *Studies in Conflict & Terrorism* 48 (3):284–299.

Dudouet, Véronique. 2014. *Civil Resistance and Conflict Transformation: Transitions from Armed to Nonviolent Struggle*. Abingdon, Oxon: Routledge.

Duque-Salazar, Juan Diego, Erika Forsberg, and Louise Olsson. 2022. "Implementing Gender Provisions: A Study of the Comprehensive Agreement on the Bangsamoro in the Philippines." *International Negotiation* 28 (2): 306–337.

Duursma, Allard, Corinne Bara, Nina Wilén et al. 2023. "UN Peacekeeping at 75: Achievements, Challenges, and Prospects." *International Peacekeeping* 30 (4):415–476.

Duyvesteyn, Isabelle, and Bram Peeters. 2015. *Fickle Foreign Fighters? A Cross Case Analysis of Seven Muslim Foreign Fighter Mobilisations (1980–2015)*. The Hague: International Centre for Counter-Terrorism.

Eck, Kristine, and Lisa Hultman. 2007. "One-Sided Violence against Civilians in War: Insights from New Fatality Data." *Journal of Peace Research* 44 (2): 233–246.

Eizenga, Daniel, and Wendy Williams. 2020. "The Puzzle of JNIM and Militant Islamist Groups in the Sahel." *Africa Security Brief* 38:1–8.

El-Bay, Driss. 2021. "Afghanistan: The Pledge Binding al-Qaeda to the Taliban." BBC Monitoring, 7 September. www.bbc.co.uk/news/world-asia-58473574.

El-Jaichi, Saer, and Mona Kanwal Sheikh. 2020. "Explaining the Rise of Global Jihad." *Journal of Religion and Violence* 8 (2):196–208.

Elias, Barbara. 2021. "Why Rebels Rely on Terrorists: The Persistence of the Taliban–al-Qaeda Battlefield Coalition in Afghanistan." *Journal of Strategic Studies* 45 (2):234–257.

Elischer, Sebastian. 2019. "Governing the Faithful: State Management of Salafi Activity in the Francophone Sahel." *Comparative Politics* 51 (2):199–218.

Engvall, Anders, and Isak Svensson. 2020. "Peace Talks and Valid Spokespersons: Explaining the Onset of Negotiations in Southern Thailand." *International Negotiation* 25 (3):495–518.

Ero, Comfort, and Murithi Mutiga. 2021. "Africa: Escaping 9/11's Long Shadow." In *Commentary/Africa*. ICG, International Crisis Group.

Farrell, Theo, and Michael Semple. 2015. "Making Peace with the Taliban." *Survival* 57 (6):79–110.

Fearon, James D. 1995. "Rationalist Explanations for War." *International Organization* 49 (3):379–414.

Fefer, Adam. 2025. *Regime Change and Minority Risks: Syrian Alawites After Assad*. Washington, DC: Carnegie Endowment for International Peace.

Filiu, Jean-Pierre. 2015. *From Deep State to Islamic State: The Arab Counter-Revolution and Its Jihadi Legacy*. New York: Oxford University Press.

Findley, Michael G., and Joseph K. Young. 2012. "Terrorism and Civil War: A Spatial and Temporal Approach to a Conceptual Problem." *Perspectives on Politics* 10 (2):285–305.

Fish, M. Steven, Francesca R. Jensenius, and Katherine E. Michel. 2010. "Islam and Large-Scale Political Violence: Is There a Connection?" *Comparative Political Studies* 43 (11):1327–1362.

Fjelde, Hanne, Lisa Hultman, and Margareta Sollenberg. 2016. "Violence against Civilians During Civil War." In *Peace and Conflict 2016*, edited by David A. Backer, Ravi Bhavnani, and Paul K. Huth, 42–49. New York: Routledge.

Fjelde, Hanne, and Desirée Nilsson. 2019. "The Rise of Rebel Contenders: Barriers to Entry and Fragmentation in Civil Wars." *Journal of Peace Research* 55 (5):551–565.

Flood, D. H. 2012. "Between Islamization and Secession: The Contest for Northern Mali." *CTC Sentinel* 5:1–6.

Forsberg, Erika, and Niklas Karlén. 2013. "Bombs to Brethren, Cannons to Comrades: Kinship Ties and External Rebel Support." *The International Studies Association Annual Convention*, San Francisco, 3–6, April.

Fortna, Virginia Page. 2004. "Does Peacekeeping Keep Peace? International Intervention and the Duration of Peace after Civil War." *International Studies Quarterly* 48 (2):269–292.

Fortna, Virginia Page. 2015. "Do Terrorists Win? Rebels' Use of Terrorism and Civil War Outcomes." *International Organization* 69 (3):519–556.

Fox, Jonathan. 2007. "The Rise of Religion and the Fall of the Civilization Paradigm as Explanations for Intra-State Conflict." *Cambridge Review of International Affairs* 20 (3):361–382.

Fox, Jonathan, Meirav Mishali-Ram, Ariel Zellman, and Matthias Basedau. 2024. "Mobilizing for Jihad: How Political Exclusion and Organized Protest Contribute to Foreign Fighter Outflows." *Terrorism and Political Violence* 36 (7):887–902.

Freeman, Patricia K., and David J. Houston. 2010. "Belonging, Believing, Behaving: The Religious Character of Public Servants." *Administration & Society* 42 (6):694–719.

Furlan, Marta. 2025. *Inside Salafi-Jihadist Governance: The Strategies and Characteristics of Islamist Insurgent Rule*. New York: Columbia University Press.

Gaasholt, Ole Martin. 2012. "Northern Mali 2012: The Short-Lived Triumph of Irredentism." *Strategic Review for Southern Africa* 35 (2):68–91.

Gade, Emily Kalah, Mohammed M. Hafez, and Michael Gabbay. 2019. "Fratricide in Rebel Movements: A Network Analysis of Syrian Militant Infighting." *Journal of Peace Research* 56 (3):321–335.

Gardner, David. 2009. "Getting Out of Afghanistan: Obama Talks of 'Exit Strategy' for the First Time ... as He Sends 17,000 More Troops There." *Daily Mail*, 23 March.

Gerges, Fawaz A. 2009. *The Far Enemy: Why Jihad Went Global*. Cambridge: Cambridge University Press.

Ghettas, Lakhdar. 2014. "Sahel Platform on Peace Promotion: 2014 Meeting." In *Cordoba Workshops Reports*: The Cordoba Foundation of Geneva.

Gilady, Lilach, and Bruce M. Russett. 2002. "Peacemaking and Conflict Resolution." In *Handbook of International Relations*, edited by Walter Carlsnaes, Thomas Risse, and Beth A. Simmons, 392–408. London: SAGE Publications.

Gleditsch, Nils Petter, and Ida Rudolfsen. 2016. "Are Muslim Countries More Prone to Violence?" *Research & Politics* 3 (2):1–9.

Göldner-Ebenthal, Karin, and Véronique Dudouet. 2019. *Dialogue with Salafi Jihadi Armed Groups: Challenges and Opportunities for Conflict De-escalation*. Berlin: Berghof Foundation.

Grauer, Ryan, and Dominic Tierney. 2017. "The Arsenal of Insurrection: Explaining Rising Support for Rebels." *Security Studies* 27 (2):263–295.

Greig, J. Michael. 2015. "Rebels at the Gates: Civil War Battle Locations, Movement, and Openings for Diplomacy." *International Studies Quarterly* 59:680–693.

Greig, J. Michael, and Paul F. Diehl. 2012. *International Mediation*. Cambridge: Polity.

Grzymala-Busse, Anna. 2012. "Why Comparative Politics Should Take Religion (More) Seriously." *Annual Review of Political Science* 15 (1):421–442.

The Guardian. 2021. "Bush Rejects Taliban Offer to Hand Bin Laden Over." 14 October, accessed 9 September 2025. www.theguardian.com/world/2001/oct/14/afghanistan.terrorism5.

Gunning, Jeroen, and Richard Jackson. 2011. "What's So 'Religious' about 'Religious Terrorism'?" *Critical Studies on Terrorism* 4 (3):369–388.

Gutelius, David. 2007. "Islam in Northern Mali and the War on Terror." *Journal of Contemporary African Studies* 25 (1):59–76.

Haenni, Patrick, and Jerome Drevon. 2025. *Transformed by the People: Hayat Tahrir al-Sham's Road to Power in Syria*. London: Hurst & Company.

Hafez, Mohammed M. 2003. *Why Muslims Rebel: Repression and Resistance in the Islamic World*. Boulder, Colorado: Lynne Rienner Publishers.

Hamid, Mustafa, and Leah Farrall. 2015. *The Arabs at War in Afghanistan*. New York: Oxford University Press.

Hamid, Shadi. 2016. *Islamic Exceptionalism: How the Struggle Over Islam Is Reshaping the World*. New York: St. Martin's Press.

Hamilton, Robert E., Chris Miller, and Aaron Stein. 2020. "Russia's War in Syria: Assessing Russian Military Capabilities and Lessons Learned." *Proceedings of the Foreign Policy Research Institute*, edited by Robert E. Hamilton, Chris Miller, and Aaron Stein. Philadelphia: Foreign Policy Research Institute.

Hamming, Tore. 2023. *Jihadi Politics: The Global Jihadi Civil War, 2014–2019*. London: Hurst & Company.

Harbom, Lotta, Erik Melander, and Peter Wallensteen. 2008. "Dyadic Dimensions of Armed Conflict, 1946–2007." *Journal of Peace Research* 45 (5):697–710.

Harpviken, Kristian Berg. 2012. "The Transnationalization of the Taliban." *International Area Studies Review* 15 (3):203–229.

Hartzell, Caroline A., and Matthew Hoddie. 2007. *Crafting Peace: Power-Sharing Institutions and the Negotiated Settlement of Civil Wars*. University Park: The Pennsylvania State University Press.

Haspeslagh, Sophie. 2021. *Proscribing Peace: How Listing Armed Groups as Terrorists Hurts Negotiations*. Manchester: Manchester University Press.

Hassner, Ron E. 2009. *War on Sacred Grounds*. Ithaca: Cornell University Press.

Hassner, Ron E. 2011. "Sacred Time and Conflict Initiation." *Security Studies* 20 (4):491–520.

Hegghammer, Thomas. 2010. "The Rise of Muslim Foreign Fighters: Islam and the Globalization of Jihad." *International Security* 35 (3):53–94.

Hegghammer, Thomas. 2014. "Jihadi Salafis or Revolutionaries? On Theology and Politics in the Study of Militant Islamism." In *Global Salafism: Islam's New Religious Movement*, edited by Roel Meijer, 245–266. London and New York: Hurst and Columbia University Press.

Hegghammer, Thomas. 2020. *The Caravan: Abdallah Azzam and the Rise of Global Jihad*. Cambridge: Cambridge University Press.

Hegre, Håvard, Lisa Hultman, and Håvard Mokleiv Nygård. 2019. "Evaluating the Conflict-Reducing Effect of UN Peacekeeping Operations." *Journal of Politics* 81 (1):215–232.

Hellmüller, Sara. 2024. "Broadening Perspectives on Inclusive Peacemaking: The Case of the UN Mediation in Syria." *Third World Quarterly* 45 (5):963–980.

Henne, Peter. 2017. *Islamic Politics, Muslim States, and Counterterrorism Tensions*. New York: Cambridge University Press.

Hoffman, Bruce. 2006. "From the War on Terror to Global Counterinsurgency." *Current History* 105 (695):423–429.

Högbladh, Stina. 2020. UCDP Peace Agreement Dataset Codebook, Version 19.1. Uppsala Conflict Data Program, Department of Peace and Conflict Research, Uppsala University.

Högbladh, Stina, Therése Pettersson, and Lotta Themnér. 2011. "External Support in Armed Conflict 1975–2009. Presenting New Data." *52nd Annual International Studies Association Convention*, Montreal, Canada, 16–19 March.

Horowitz, Michael C., and Philip B. K. Potter. 2014. "Allying to Kill: Terrorist Intergroup Cooperation and the Consequences for Lethality." *Journal of Conflict Resolution* 58 (2):199–225.

Hultman, Lisa, Jacob D. Kathman, and Megan Shannon. 2016. "United Nations Peacekeeping Dynamics and the Duration of Post-Civil Conflict Peace." *Conflict Management and Peace Science* 33 (3):231–249.

Hwang, Julie Chernov. 2018. *Why Terrorists Quit: The Disengagement of Indonesian Jihadists*. Ithaca: Cornell University Press.

Ibrahim, Ibrahim Yahaya. 2017. "The Wave of Jihadist Insurgency in West Africa: Global Ideology, Local Context, Individual Motivations." In *West African Papers, No. 7*. OECD Publishing, Paris. https://doi.org/10.1787/eb95c0a9-en.

Ibrahim, Ibrahim Yahaya. 2021. "Jihadist Insurgencies in the Sahel." In *The Oxford Handbook of the African Sahel*, edited by Leonardo A. Villalón, 568–586. Oxford: Oxford University Press.

ICG, International Crisis Group. 2019. "Speaking with the 'Bad Guys': Toward Dialogue with Central Mali's Jihadists." *Africa Report No.* 276, 28 May.

ICG, International Crisis Group. 2020. "The Jihadist Factor in Syria's Idlib: A Conversation with Abu Muhammad al-Jolani." *Commentary/Middle East & North Africa*, 20 February.

ICG, International Crisis Group. 2021a. "In Syria's Idlib, Washington's Chance to Reimagine Counter-Terrorism." *Commentary/Middle East & North Africa*, 3 February.

ICG, International Crisis Group. 2021b. "Mali: Enabling Dialogue with the Jihadist Coalition JNIM." *Africa Report No. 306*, 10 December.

Isaacs, Matthew. 2016. "Sacred Violence or Strategic Faith? Disentangling the Relationship between Religion and Violence in Armed Conflict." *Journal of Peace Research* 53 (2):211–225.

Jameel, Rami. 2020. "HTS Leader al-Julani's New Strategy in Northwestern Syria." *Terrorism Monitor* 18 (18).

Johnstone, Naomi, and Isak Svensson. 2013. "Belligerents and Believers: Exploring Faith-Based Mediation in Internal Armed Conflicts." *Politics, Religion & Ideology* 14 (4):557–579.

Jones, Peter. 2015. "Talking with al Qaeda: Is There a Role for Track Two?" *International Negotiation* 20 (2):177–198.

Jones, Seth G. 2008. "The Rise of Afghanistan's Insurgency." *International Security* 32 (4):7–40.

Jourde, Cédric. 2007. "The International Relations of Small Neoauthoritarian States: Islamism, Warlordism, and the Framing of Stability." *International Studies Quarterly* 51 (2):481–503.

Juergensmeyer, Mark. 2018. "How Cosmic War Ends." *Numen* 65 (2–3):125–140.

Juergensmeyer, Mark. 2022. *When God Stops Fighting: How Religious Violence Ends*. Oakland: University of California Press.

Kalyvas, Stathis N. 2018. "Jihadi Rebels in Civil War." *Daedalus* 147 (1):36–47.

Kalyvas, Stathis N., and Laia Balcells. 2010. "International System and Technologies of Rebellion: How the End of the Cold War Shaped Internal Conflict." *American Political Science Review* 104 (3):415–429.

Kalyvas, Stathis N., and Mikael Hiberg Naghizadeh. 2025. "Islamism and Armed Conflict." *Annual Review of Political Science* 28 (1):393–411.

Kane, Sean William. 2022. "Making Peace When the Whole World Has Come to Fight: The Mediation of Internationalized Civil Wars." *International Peacekeeping* 29 (2):177–203.

Kao, Kristen, and Mara R. Revkin. 2023. "Retribution or Reconciliation? Post-Conflict Attitudes toward Enemy Collaborators." *American Journal of Political Science* 67 (2):358–373.

Kapshuk, Yoav, and Mora Deitch. 2022. "Religion, Peace and Justice: The Effects of Transitional Justice on Religious Armed Conflict Resolution." *Peacebuilding* 11 (1):78–103.

Karakaya, Süveyda. 2015. "Religion and Conflict: Explaining the Puzzling Case of 'Islamic Violence'." *International Interactions* 41 (3):509–538.

Karlén, Niklas. 2016. "Historical Trends in External Support in Civil Wars." In *SIPRI Yearbook 2016: Armaments, Disarmament and International Security*, edited by John Batho, Andrew Mash, Kathryn Millett, and Annika Salisbury, 117–128. London: Oxford University Press.

Karlén, Niklas. 2017. "The Legacy of Foreign Patrons: External State Support and Conflict Recurrence." *Journal of Peace Research* 54 (4):499–512.

Keels, Eric, and Krista Wiegand. 2020. "Mutually Assured Distrust: Ideology and Commitment Problems in Civil Wars." *Journal of Conflict Resolution* 64 (10):2022–2048.

Kepel, Gilles. 2006. *Jihad: The Trail of Political Islam*. London: IB Tauris.

Kim, Wukki, Dong Li, and Todd Sandler. 2019. "Resident Terrorist Groups, Military Aid, and Moral Hazard: Further Empirical Analysis." *Defence and Peace Economics* 32 (1):1–17.

Klocek, Jason 2017. *Fighting the Faithful: State Response to Religious Insurgencies*. Dissertation Manuscript. Berkeley: University of California.

Klocek, Jason, and Ron E. Hassner. 2019. "War and Religion: An Overview." In *Oxford Research Encyclopedia of Politics*, edited by William R. Thompson. Oxford: Oxford University Press.

Kone, Hassane. 2019. "How Has Mauritania Managed to Stave Off Terror Attacks." *Institute for Security Studies* 6. https://bit.ly/49BkLfD.

Krause, Dino. 2022. "How Transnational Is 'Transnational'? Foreign Fighter Recruitment and Transnational Operations among Affiliates of al-Qaeda and the Islamic State." *Perspectives on Terrorism* 16 (1):23–37.

Krause, Dino. 2024. "Negotiating Peace with Islamists? Reviewing the Literature." *Terrorism and Political Violence* 37 (8):1077–1091.

Krause, Jana, Werner Krause, and Piia Bränfors. 2018. "Women's Participation in Peace Negotiations and the Durability of Peace." *International Interactions* 44 (6):985–1016.

Kreutz, Joakim. 2010. "How and When Armed Conflicts End: Introducing the UCDP Conflict Termination Dataset." *Journal of Peace Research* 47 (2):243–250.

Kriesberg, Louis. 1998. *Constructive Conflicts: From Escalation to Resolution*. Lanham: Rowman & Littlefield.

Kroeker, Evgenija, and Andrea Ruggeri. 2022. "13. Peacekeeping and Conflict Resolution." In *Handbook on Peacekeeping and International Relations*, edited by Han Dorussen, 182–195. Cheltenham: Edward Elgar.

Kydd, Andrew H. 2010. "Rationalist Approaches to Conflict Prevention and Resolution." *Annual Review of Political Science* 13 (1):101–121.

Lanz, David. 2011. "Who Gets a Seat at the Table? A Framework for Understanding the Dynamics of Inclusion and Exclusion in Peace Negotiations." *International Negotiation* 16 (2):275–295.

Laub, Zachary, and Jonathan Masters. 2014. "Al-Qaeda in the Islamic Maghreb (AQIM)." *Council of Foreign Relations* 27. www.cfr.org/backgrounders/al-qaeda-islamic-maghreb.

Le Journal de Dimanche. 2021. "Emmanuel Macron, Confidences en Afrique." 30 May.

Le Monde Afrique. 2021. "La France Suspend sa coopération militaire bilatérale avec le Mali." 3 June.

Lebovich, Andrew. 2013. "The Local Face of Jihadism in Northern Mali." *CTC Sentinel* 6 (6): 4–10.

Lebovich, Andrew. 2019. *Sacred Struggles: How Islam Shapes Politics in Mali.* London: European Council on Foreign Relations.

Lefèvre, Raphaël. 2021. *Jihad in the City: Militant Islam and Contentious Politics in Tripoli.* Cambridge: Cambridge University Press.

Lia, Brynjar. 2015. "Understanding Jihadi Proto-States." *Perspectives on Terrorism* 9 (4):31–41.

Lia, Brynjar. 2016. "Jihadism in the Arab World after 2011: Explaining Its Expansion." *Middle East Policy* 33 (4):74–91.

Licklider, Roy. 1995. "The Consequences of Negotiated Settlements in Civil Wars, 1945–1993." *American Political Science Review* 89 (3):681–690.

Liow, Joseph Chinyong. 2006. "Muslim Resistance in Southern Thailand and Southern Philippines: Religion, Ideology, and Politics." In *Policy Studies*, edited by Muthiah Alagappa. Washington, DC: East-West Center Washington.

Lister, Charles. 2016. *Profiling Jabhat al-Nusra.* Washington, DC: Brookings Institution.

Little, David. 1996. "Religious Militancy." In *Managing Global Chaos*, edited by Chester Crocker, Fen Osler Hampson, and Pamela Aall, 79–91. Washington, DC: United States Institute of Peace Press.

Lorentzen, Jenny. 2022. "Malian Women's Participation in the Algiers Negotiations." *FAIR* Case Brief, PRIO.

Lund, Aron. 2016. "Not Just Russia: The Iranian Surge in Syria." In *Diwan – Syria in Crisis.* Carnegie Endowment for International Peace. https://rb.gy/7blx7n.

Lund, Aron. 2019. *From Cold War to Civil War: 75 Years of Russian–Syrian Relations.* Stockholm: Swedish Institute of International Affairs.

Lundgren, Magnus. 2020. "Causal Mechanisms in Civil War Mediation: Evidence from Syria." *European Journal of International Relations* 26 (1): 209–235.

Lundgren, Magnus, Emma Janson, and Martin Lundqvist. 2024. "Introducing the Proscription of Armed Actors Dataset (PAAD)." *Journal of Peace Research* 62 (4): 1241–1251.

Lundgren, Magnus, and Isak Svensson. 2020. "The Surprising Decline of International Mediation in Armed Conflicts." *Research & Politics* 7 (2). https://doi.org/10.1177/2053168020917243.

Lynch, Marc, and Jillian Schwedler. 2020. "Introduction to the Special Issue on 'Islamist Politics after the Arab Uprisings'." *Middle East Law and Governance* 12 (1):3–13.

Maher, Shiraz. 2016. *Salafi-Jihadism: The History of an Idea*. New York: Oxford University Press.

Malet, David. 2013. *Foreign Fighters: Transnational Identity in Civil Conflicts*. New York: Oxford University Press.

Malet, David. 2015. "Foreign Fighter Mobilization and Persistence in a Global Context." *Terrorism and Political Violence* 27 (3):454–473.

Maley, William, and Ahmad Shuja Jamal. 2022. "Diplomacy of Disaster: The Afghanistan 'Peace Process' and the Taliban Occupation of Kabul." *The Hague Journal of Diplomacy* 17 (1):32–63.

Marshall, Douglas A. 2002. "Behavior, Belonging, and Belief: A Theory of Ritual Practice." *Sociological Theory* 20 (3):360–380.

Marshall, Monty G., Keith Jaggers, and Ted Robert Gurr. 2015. "Polity IV Project: Political Regime Characteristics and Transitions, 1800–2014." Accessed 28 August 2015. www.systemicpeace.org.

Mason, David T., and Patrick J. Fett. 1996. "How Civil Wars End: A Rational Choice Approach." *Journal of Conflict Resolution* 40 (4):546–568.

Matesan, Ioana Emy. 2020a. "Failed Negotiations and the Dark Side of Ripeness: Insights from Egypt." *International Negotiation* 25 (3):463–494.

Matesan, Ioana Emy. 2020b. *The Violence Pendulum: Tactical Change in Islamist Groups in Egypt and Indonesia*. New York: Oxford University Press.

Mattes, Michaela, and Burcu Savun. 2009. "Fostering Peace after Civil War: Commitment Problems and Agreement Design." *International Studies Quarterly* 53 (3):737–759.

Matthiesen, Toby. 2022. "The Arab Counter-Revolution: The Formation of a Regional Alliance to Undermine the Arab Spring." In *Struggles for Political Change in the Arab World: Regimes, Oppositions, and External Actors after the Spring*, edited by Lisa Blaydes, Amr Hamzawy, and Hesham Sallam, 392–407. Ann Arbor: University of Michigan Press.

Melander, Erik, Therése Pettersson, and Lotta Themnér. 2016. "Organized Violence 1989–2015." *Journal of Peace Research* 53 (5):727–742.

Mendelsohn, Barak. 2009. *Combating Jihadism: American Hegemony and Interstate Cooperation in the War on Terrorism*. Chicago: University of Chicago Press.

Mendelsohn, Barak. 2016. *The al-Qaeda Franchise: The Expansion of al-Qaeda and Its Consequences*. Oxford: Oxford University Press.

Mize, Trenton D. 2019. "Best Practices for Estimating, Interpreting, and Presenting Nonlinear Interaction Effects." *Sociological Science* 6:81–117.

Moghadam, Assaf. 2008. *The Globalization of Martyrdom: Al Qaeda, Salafi Jihad, and the Diffusion of Suicide Attacks*. Baltimore: Johns Hopkins University Press.

Mukherjee, Bumba. 2006. "Why Political Power-Sharing Agreements Lead to Enduring Peaceful Resolution of Some Civil Wars, but Not Others?" *International Studies Quarterly* 50 (2):479–504.

N'Diaye, Boubacar. 2021. "Mauritania." In *The Oxford Handbook of the African Sahel*, edited by Leonardo A. Villalón, 108–126. Oxford: Oxford University Press.

Naghizadeh, Mikael Hiberg. 2025. "Why Islamism? A Micro-Institutional Approach to Explaining Ideological Choice." *Civil Wars* 27 (2):359–387.

National Consortium for the Study of Terrorism and Responses to Terrorism. 2013. *Terrorist Organization Profiles Dataset*. www.start.umd.edu/tops/.

The New Arab. 2020. "Jihadist HTS, Former Al-Qaeda Affiliate, Seeks 'Moderate Rebrand' to Secure Seat in Syria's Political Process." 4 June. https://bit.ly/4tX6emx.

Nilsson, Desirée. 2008a. "Partial Peace: Rebel Groups Inside and Outside of Civil War Settlements." *Journal of Peace Research* 45 (4):479–495.

Nilsson, Desirée. 2008b. "Rebels on the Outside: Signatories Signaling Commitment to Durable Peace." In *Resources, Governance and Civil Conflict*, edited by Magnus Öberg and Kaare Strøm, 247–265. London and New York: Routledge.

Nilsson, Desirée. 2012. "Anchoring the Peace: Civil Society Actors in Peace Accords and Durable Peace." *International Interactions* 38 (2):243–266.

Nilsson, Desirée, and Isak Svensson. 2017. "Mapping Armed Conflicts over Islamist Claims: Exploring Regional Variations." In *SIPRI Yearbook 2017: Armaments, Disarmament and International Security*, edited by John Batho, Andrew Mash, Kathryn Millett, and Annika Salisbury, 58–65. London: Oxford University Press.

Nilsson, Desirée, and Isak Svensson. 2020. "Resisting Resolution: Islamist Claims and Negotiations in Intrastate Armed Conflicts." *International Negotiation* 25 (3):389–412.

Nilsson, Desirée, and Isak Svensson. 2021. "The Intractability of Islamist Insurgencies: Islamist Rebels and the Recurrence of Civil War." *International Studies Quarterly* 65 (3):620–632.

Nilsson, Desirée, Isak Svensson, Kajsa Tidblad-Lundholm et al. 2024. *Non-Warring Actors in Peacemaking (NoWA) Dataset.* Uppsala: Department of Peace and Conflict Research, Uppsala University.

Nossiter, Adam. 2012. "Burkina Faso Official Goes to Islamist-Held Northern Mali in Effort to Avert War." *New York Times*, 7 August.

Olson, Laura R., and Adam L. Warber. 2008. "Belonging, Behaving, and Believing: Assessing the Role of Religion on Presidential Approval." *Political Research Quarterly* 61 (2):192–204.

Oxford Analytica. 2023. "Mauritania's Anti-Jihadist Success Cannot Be Imitated." *Expert Briefings*, 23 February. https://doi.org/10.1108/OXAN-DB276259.

Paffenholz, Thania. 2014. "Civil Society and Peace Negotiations: Beyond the Inclusion–Exclusion Dichotomy." *Negotiation Journal* 30 (1):69–91.

Pearce, Susanna. 2005. "Religious Rage: A Quantitative Analysis of the Intensity of Armed Conflicts." *Terrorism and Political Violence* 17 (3):333–352.

Pettersson, Therése, Stina Högbladh, and Magnus Öberg. 2019. "Organized Violence, 1989–2018 and Peace Agreements." *Journal of Peace Research* 56 (4):589–603.

Pettersson, Therése, and Peter Wallensteen. 2015. "Armed Conflicts, 1946–2014." *Journal of Peace Research* 52 (4):536–550.

Pew. 2012. *The Global Religious Landscape: A Report on the Size and Distribution of the World's Major Religious Groups as of 2010.* Washington, DC: Pew Research Center. www.pewforum.org/files/2014/01/global-religion-full.pdf.

Phillips, Brian J. 2017. "Deadlier in the U.S.? On Lone Wolves, Terrorist Groups, and Attack Lethality." *Terrorism and Political Violence* 29 (3):533–549.

Philpott, Daniel. 2007. "Explaining the Political Ambivalence of Religion." *American Political Science Review* 101 (3):505–525.

Pischedda, Costantino, and Manuel Vogt. 2025. "When Do Religious Organizations Resort to Violence? How Local Conditions Shape the Effects of Transnational Ideology." *Ethnopolitics* 24 (1):1–26.

Poljarevic, Emin. 2021. "Theology of Violence-Oriented Takfirism as a Political Theory: The Case of the Islamic State in Iraq and Syria (ISIS)." In *Handbook of Islamic Sects and Movements*, edited by Muhammad Afzal Upal and Carole M. Cusack, 485–512. Leiden: Brill.

Polo, Sara M. T., and Kristian Skrede Gleditsch. 2016. "Twisting Arms and Sending Messages: Terrorist Tactics in Civil War." *Journal of Peace Research* 53 (6):815–829.

Powell, Emilia Justyna. 2019. *Islamic Law and International Law: Peaceful Resolution of Disputes*. New York: Oxford University Press.

Powers, Gerald F. 2010. "Religion and Peacebuilding." In *Strategies of Peace: Transforming Conflict in a Violent World*, edited by Gerald F. Powers and Daniel Philhott, 317–352. New York: Oxford University Press.

Qazi Zada, Sebghatullah, and Mohd Ziaolhaq Qazi Zada. 2024. "The Taliban and Women's Human Rights in Afghanistan: The Way Forward." *The International Journal of Human Rights* 28 (10):1687–1722.

Quinn, J. Michael, T. David Mason, and Mehmet Gurses. 2007. "Sustaining the Peace: Determinants of Civil War Recurrence." *International Interactions* 33 (2):167–193.

Radio Free Europe/Radio Liberty. 2001. "Afghanistan: Taliban Refuses to Hand Over Bin Laden." 21 September.

Rashid, Ahmed. 2012. *Descent into Chaos: How the War against Islamic Extremism Is Being Lost in Pakistan, Afghanistan and Central Asia*. London: Penguin.

Rashid, Ahmed. 2022. *Taliban: The Power of Militant Islam in Afghanistan and Beyond*. New Haven and London: Yale University Press.

Rasmussen, Sune Engel. 2016. "Afghanistan's 'Ghost Soldiers': Thousands Enlisted to Fight Taliban Don't Exist." *The Guardian*, 17 May. www.theguardian.com/world/2016/may/17/afghanistan-ghost-soldiers-taliban-babaji.

Regan, Patrick M. 2002. "Third-Party Interventions and the Duration of Intrastate Conflicts." *Journal of Conflict Resolution* 46 (1):55–73.

Reuters. 2024. "Thai Govt Holds First Peace Talks with Insurgents since Taking Office." 7 February, accessed 8 September 2025.

RFI. 2020a. "Mali Open to Dialogue with Jihadists." 11 February. www.rfi.fr/en/international/20200211-mali-talk-jihadists-all-inclusive-dialogue.

RFI. 2020b. "Mali's Jihadists Demand French Withdrawal as Condition for Talks." 12 March. https://bit.ly/4aOtY3u.

Rich, Ben, and Dara Conduit. 2015. "The Impact of Jihadist Foreign Fighters on Indigenous Secular-Nationalist Causes: Contrasting Chechnya and Syria." *Studies in Conflict & Terrorism* 38 (2):113–131.

Roetman, Tim Jan, Marie Migeon, and Véronique Dudouet. 2019. "Salafi Jihadi Armed Groups and Conflict (De-)Escalation: The Case of Ansar Dine in Mali." In *Case Study Report*. Berlin: Berghof Foundation.

Romaniuk, Peter. 2010. "Institutions as Swords and Shields: Multilateral Counter-Terrorism since 9/11." *Review of International Studies* 36 (3):591–613.

Ross, Michael, and Paasha Mahdavi. 2015. "Oil and Gas Data, 1932–2014." Harvard Dataverse 2. Accessed 23 October 2017. https://dataverse.harvard.edu/dataset.xhtml?persistentId=doi:10.7910/DVN/ZTPW0Y.

Roy, Olivier. 2017. *Jihad and Death: The Global Appeal of Islamic State*. London: Oxford University Press.

Ryan, Missy, and Karen DeYoung. 2021. "Biden Will Withdraw all U.S. Forces from Afghanistan by Sept. 11, 2021." *Washington Post*, 13 April. https://bit.ly/3MRtv8A.

Salehyan, Idean. 2007. "Transnational Rebels: Neighboring States as Sanctuary for Rebel Groups." *World Politics* 59 (2):217–242.

Sampson, Cynthia. 2007. "Religion and Peacebuilding." In *Peacemaking in International Conflict*, edited by I. William Zartman and Lewis J. Rasmussen, 273–316. Washington, DC: United States Institute of Peace Press.

Sanín, Francisco Gutiérrez, and Elisabeth Jean Wood. 2014. "Ideology in Civil War: Instrumental Adoption and Beyond." *Journal of Peace Research* 51 (2):213–226.

Sawyer, Katherine, Kathleen Gallagher Cunningham, and William Reed. 2017. "The Role of External Support in Civil War Termination." *Journal of Conflict Resolution* 61 (6):1174–1202.

Schwab, Regine. 2023. "Same Same but Different? Ideological Differentiation and Intra-Jihadist Competition in the Syrian Civil War." *Journal of Global Security Studies* 8 (1):1–20.

Semple, Michael, Robin L. Raphel, and Shams Rasikh. 2021. *An Independent Assessment of the Afghanistan Peace Process June 2018–May 2021*. Edinburgh: Political Settlements Research Programme.

Shane, Leo III. 2022. "Trump Ordered Rapid Withdrawal from Afghanistan after Election Loss." *Military Times*, 13 October. https://bit.ly/3P3H0Tk.

Sheikh, Mona, and Saer El-Jaichi. 2022. "Transnational Jihadi Movements." In *Oxford Research Encyclopedia of Religion*, edited by John Barton. Oxford: Oxford University Press.

Sheikh, Mona Kanwal. 2012. "How Does Religion Matter? Pathways to Religion in International Relations." *Review of International Studies* 38 (2):365–392.

Sheikh, Mona Kanwal. 2016. *Guardians of God: Inside the Religious Mind of the Pakistani Taliban*. New Delhi: Oxford University Press.

Sheikh, Mona Kanwal. 2017. *Expanding Jihad: How al-Qaeda and Islamic State Find New Battlefields*. Copenhagen: DIIS – Danish Institute for International Studies.

Sheikh, Mona Kanwal. 2020. "What Do Islamists Bring to the Negotiation Table? Religion and the Case of the Pakistani Taliban." *International Negotiation* 25 (3):413–434.

Sheikh, Mona Kanwal, and Amina Khan. 2019. "Prospects of a Settlement with the Afghan Taliban: Exit, Peace and Governance from the Taliban Perspective."

Copenhagen: Danish Institute for International Studies (DIIS), DIIS Report Vol. 19, No. 1.

Sheikh, Mona Kanwal, Morten Valbjørn, and Dino Krause. 2023. "What Is Exceptional about Religion? Major Debates in International Relations, Islamism Studies and Peace and Conflict Research." In *Routledge Handbook of Religion and Politics*, edited by Jeffrey Haynes, 209–224. Abingdon: Routledge.

Sheikh, Mona Kanwal, Jan Werner Mathiasen, Lars Erslev Andersen, Dino Krause, and Ole Wæver. 2026. *How the Taliban Regained Power in Afghanistan.* New York: Taylor & Francis.

SIGAR. 2022. "Collapse of the Afghan National Defense and Security Forces: An Assessment of the Factors that Led to Its Demise." SIGAR 22-22-IP Evaluation Report.

Sköns, Elisabeth. 2016. "II. Challenges to the Peace Process: Complexity, Fragmentation, Extremism and Crime." In *SIPRI Yearbook 2016: Armaments, Disarmament and International Security*, edited by John Batho, Andrew Mash, Kathryn Millett, and Annika Salisbury. London: Oxford University Press.

Smith, Craig S. 2004. "U.S. Training African Forces to Uproot Terrorists." *New York Times*, 11 May. https://bit.ly/4aE5ET1.

Smock, David R., ed. 2006. *Religious Contributions to Peacemaking: When Religion Brings Peace, Not War.* Washington, DC: United Sates Institute of Peace.

Söderberg Kovacs, Mimmi. 2008. "When Rebels Change Their Stripes: Armed Insurgents in Post-War Politics." In *From War to Democracy: Dilemmas of Peacebuilding*, edited by Anna Jarstad and Timothy Sisk, 134–156. Cambridge: Cambridge University Press.

Söderberg Kovacs, Mimmi. 2020a. "A Matter of Faith? Negotiations with Boko Haram in Nigeria", *International Negotiation* 25 (3):435-462.

Söderberg Kovacs, Mimmi. 2020b. "Negotiating Sacred Grounds? Resolving Islamist Armed Conflicts." *International Negotiation* 25 (3):375–388.

Soliman, Nagwan. 2021. *The New Jihadists and the Taliban Model.* Washington, DC: Carnegie Endowment for International Peace.

Stanton, Jessica A. 2013. "Terrorism in the Context of Civil War." *The Journal of Politics* 75 (4):1009–1022.

Stedman, Stephen John, Donald Rotchild, and Elizabeth M. Cousens., eds. 2002. *Ending Civil Wars: The Implementation of Peace Agreements.* Boulder, Colorado: Lynne Rienner Publishers.

Stenersen, Anne. 2017. *Al-Qaida in Afghanistan.* Cambridge: Cambridge University Press.

Stollenwerk, Eric, Thomas Dörfler, and Julian Schibberges. 2015. "Taking a New Perspective: Mapping the Al Qaeda Network through the Eyes of the UN Security Council." *Terrorism and Political Violence* 28 (5):950–970.

Suhrke, Astri, Kristian Berg Harpviken, and Arne Strand. 2002. "After Bonn: Conflictual Peace Building." *Third World Quarterly* 23 (5):875–891.

Svensson, Isak. 2007. "Fighting with Faith: Religion and Conflict Resolution in Civil Wars." *Journal of Conflict Resolution* 51 (6):930–949.

Svensson, Isak. 2012. *Ending Holy Wars: Religion and Conflict Resolution in Civil Wars*. Brisbane: University of Queensland Press.

Svensson, Isak. 2016. "Conceptualizing the Religious Dimensions of Armed Conflicts: A Response to 'Shrouded: Islam, War, and Holy War in Southeast Asia'." *Journal for the Scientific Study of Religion* 55 (1):185–189.

Svensson, Isak. 2019. "Religion and Civil War – An Overview." In *Oxford Research Encyclopedia of Politics & Religion*, edited by Paul A. Djupe, Mark J. Rozell, and Ted G. Jelen. Oxford: Oxford University Press.

Svensson, Isak. 2021. "Resolving Religious Conflicts through Peace Agreements." In *International Law and Peace-Settlements*, edited by Marc Weller, Mark Retter, and Andrea Varga, 374–397. Cambridge: Cambridge University Press.

Svensson, Isak, and Matthew Bamber. 2022. "Resisting Radical Rebels: Variations in Islamist Rebel Governance and the Occurrence of Civil Resistance." *Terrorism and Political Violence* 35 (4):1126–1146.

Svensson, Isak, Daniel Finnbogason, Dino Krause, Luís Martínez Lorenzo, and Nanar Hawach. 2022. *Confronting the Caliphate: Civil Resistance against Jihadist Proto-States*. New York: Oxford University Press.

Svensson, Isak, and Desirée Nilsson. 2018. "Disputes over the Divine: Introducing the Religion and Armed Conflict (RELAC) Data, 1975–2015." *Journal of Conflict Resolution* 62 (5):1127–1148.

Svensson, Isak, Desirée Nilsson, and Tim Gåsste. 2024. "No End in Sight? Trajectories of War Terminations in Islamist Armed Conflicts." *Studies in Conflict & Terrorism*:1–20. https://doi.org/10.1080/1057610X.2024.2398691

Svensson, Isak, and Peter Wallensteen. 2025. *The Peacemaking Mandate: Nordic Experiences in International Mediation*. Cambridge: Cambridge University Press.

Therme, Clément. 2008. "Syria and Iran. Diplomatic Alliance and Power Politics in the Middle East. London-New York, IB Tauris, 2006, 359 p." *Abstracta Iranica. Revue bibliographique pour le domaine irano-aryen* (Volume 29).

Thompson, Jared. 2021. "Examining Extremism: Jama'at Nasr al-Islam wal Muslimin." Center for Strategic and International Studies. https://bit.ly/46Pv65V.

Thurston, Alex. 2018. "Political Settlements with Jihadists in Algeria and the Sahel." In *West African Papers, No. 18*. OECD Publishing, Paris. https://doi.org/10.1787/0780622a-en.

Thurston, Alexander. 2020. *Jihadists of North Africa and the Sahel: Local Politics and Rebel Groups*. Cambridge: Cambridge University Press.

Thurston, Alexander. 2021. "Negotiating Secularism in the Sahel." In *The Oxford Handbook of the African Sahel*, edited by Leonardo A. Villalón, 604–622. Oxford: Oxford University Press.

Toft, Monica Duffy. 2006. "Issue Indivisibility and Time Horizons as Rationalist Explanations for War." *Security Studies* 15 (1):34–69.

Toft, Monica Duffy. 2007. "Getting Religion? The Puzzling Case of Islam and Civil War." *International Security* 31 (4):97–131.

Toft, Monica Duffy. 2010. *Securing the Peace: The Durable Settlement of Civil Wars*. Princeton and Oxford: Princeton University Press.

Toft, Monica Duffy. 2021. "Getting Religion Right in Civil Wars." *Journal of Conflict Resolution* 65 (9):1607–1634.

Toft, Monica Duffy, and Yuri M. Zhukov. 2015. "Islamists and Nationalists: Rebel Motivation and Counterinsurgency in Russia's North Caucasus." *American Political Science Review* 109 (2):222–238.

Toros, Harmonie, and Stephen Harley. 2018. "Negotiations with Al-Shabaab: Lessons Learned and Future Prospects." In *War and Peace in Somalia: National Grievances, Local Conflict and Al-Shabaab*, edited by Michael Keating and Matt Waldman, 437–448. New York: Hurst.

Tsurkov, Elizabeth. 2019. "Idlib Faces a Fearsome Future: Islamist Rule or Mass Murder." *Foreign Policy*, 19 September. https://bit.ly/4tZtj8a.

UCDP, Uppsala Conflict Data Program. 2015. "UCDP Conflict Encyclopedia." Uppsala University. http://ucdp.uu.se.

UCDP, Uppsala Conflict Data Program. 2024. "UCDP Conflict Encyclopedia." Uppsala University. https://ucdp.uu.se.

United Nations. 2015. "The National Accounts Main Aggregates Database." http://unstats.un.org/unsd/snaama/Introduction.asp.

United Nations. 2017. *World Population Prospects: The 2017 Revision*. New York: United Nations Population Division.

United Nations. 2020. "The National Accounts Main Aggregates Database." Accessed December 2020. https://unstats.un.org/unsd/snaama/Index.

United Nations. 2023. "Sanctions List Materials/Narrative Summaries of Reasons for Listing/Mouvement Pour l'unification et le Jihad en Afrique de l'ouest (Mujao) (QDe.134)." https://bit.ly/4tZBHUW.

United Nations Security Council. 2020. Letter dated 19 May 2020 from the Chair of the Security Council Committee established pursuant to

Resolution 1988 (2011) addressed to the President of the Security Council. United Nations.

Urdal, Henrik. 2006. "A Clash of Generations? Youth Bulges and Political Violence." *International Studies Quarterly* 50 (3):607–629.

Valbjørn, Morten, and Jeroen Gunning. 2020. "Bringing in the 'Other Islamists': Beyond Sunni-Centric Islamism Studies in a Sectarianized Middle East." *Mediterranean Politics* 26 (4):476–483.

Van Linschoten, Alex Strick, and Felix Kuehn. 2012. *An Enemy We Created: The Myth of the Taliban–al Qaeda Merger in Afghanistan*. New York: Oxford University Press.

Vüllers, Johannes. 2019. "Mobilization for Peace: Analyzing Religious Peace Activism." *Conflict Management and Peace Science* 38 (4):391–410.

Vüllers, Johannes, Birte Pfeiffer, and Matthias Basedau. 2015. "Measuring the Ambivalence of Religion: Introducing the Religion and Conflict in Developing Countries (RCDC) Dataset." *International Interactions* 41 (5): 857–881.

Wallensteen, Peter. 2015. *Understanding Conflict Resolution*. 4th ed. London: Sage Publications.

Wallensteen, Peter, and Isak Svensson. 2014. "Talking Peace: International Mediation in Armed Conflicts." *Journal of Peace Research* 51 (2):315–327.

Walter, Barbara F. 2002. *Committing to Peace: The Successful Settlement of Civil Wars*. Princeton and Oxford: Princeton University Press.

Walter, Barbara F. 2003. "Explaining the Intractability of Territorial Conflict." *International Studies Review* 5 (4):137–153.

Walter, Barbara F. 2009. *Reputation and Civil War: Why Separatist Conflicts Are So Violent*. New York: Cambridge University Press.

Walter, Barbara F. 2017. "The Extremist's Advantage in Civil Wars." *International Security* 42 (2):7–39.

Wanandi, Jusuf. 2002. "A Global Coalition against International Terrorism." *International Security* 26 (4):184–189.

Watts, Clint. 2016. "It's Not You, It's Me: Al-Qaeda Lost Jabhat Al-Nusra. Now What?" *War on the Rocks*, 29 July.

Wehrey, Frederic. 2019. "Control and Contain: Mauritania's Clerics and the Strategy against Violent Extremism." *Carnegie Endowment for International Peace*. Accessed 25 June 2024. www.jstor.org/stable/resrep20967.

Wehrey, Frederic, and Anouar Boukhars. 2019. *Salafism in the Maghreb: Politics, Piety, and Militancy*. New York: Oxford University Press.

The White House. 2023. "The U.S. Withdrawal from Afghanistan." 6 April. www.whitehouse.gov/wp-content/uploads/2023/04/US-Withdrawal-from-Afghanistan.pdf.

Wiktorowicz, Quintan. 2003. *Islamic Activism: A Social Movement Theory Approach*. Bloomington: Indiana University Press.

Wintour, Patrick. 2021. "A Tale of Two Armies: Why Afghan Forces Proved No Match for the Taliban." *The Guardian*, 15 August. https://bit.ly/4bdurgU.

Zartman, William. 1995. *Elusive Peace: Negotiating an End to Civil Wars*. Washington, DC: The Brooking Institution.

Zenn, Jacob, and Mary Jane Fox. 2020. "Negotiating with Boko Haram? Examining the Jihadist Exception." *African Conflict and Peacebuilding Review* 10 (2):158–183.

Index

For EU product safety concerns, contact us at Calle de José Abascal, 56–1°, 28003 Madrid, Spain or eugpsr@cambridge.org.

www.ingramcontent.com/pod-product-compliance
Ingram Content Group UK Ltd.
Pitfield, Milton Keynes, MK11 3LW, UK
UKHW021923220726
473566UK00010B/433

* 9 7 8 1 0 0 9 6 8 8 0 7 9 *